Praise for
Every Purchase Matters

"*Every Purchase Matters* is a powerful testament to the transformative potential of ethical consumerism. With gripping stories and actionable insights, this book shines a spotlight on the interconnected roles of farmers, companies, and consumers in driving social and environmental change. Paul Rice's work inspires us all to see the ripple effect of our choices and to embrace the profound impact we can make in building a more equitable world."

> —Dr. Marshall Goldsmith, Thinkers50 #1 executive coach and *New York Times*–bestselling author of *The Earned Life*, *Triggers*, and *What Got You Here Won't Get You There*

"Fair Trade has done more than any other movement to improve the lives of the people who make our favorite products. Rice has written the fascinating story behind Fair Trade and shows us why, indeed, *Every Purchase Matters*. Read this book!"

> —Dan Buettner, founder, Blue Zones, and producer of the Emmy Award–winning series *Live to 100*

"A phenomenal read with so many wonderful stories and lessons from the leader who built the Fair Trade movement. Rice reimagined a more sustainable approach to how products are sourced, making it easier for us all to care for farmers, communities, and the land. Whether you're a conscious capitalist or a concerned consumer, this book is a must-read."

> —John Mackey, cofounder and former CEO, Whole Foods; and *New York Times*–bestselling author of *Conscious Capitalism*

"A day will come when every farmer, shepherd, and worker in the world will be honored and compensated for their unstinting labor and bounty, and Fair Trade is one of the reasons why. Rice has led this movement to restore dignity, equity, and fairness to farmers and workers everywhere. *Every Purchase Matters* is both his moving story—as a leader with a heart of gold—and a cris de coeur that echoes powerfully in a world coming to realize that fairness and justice for farmers are the bedrock of a just and durable civilization."

—Paul Hawken, environmentalist, entrepreneur, and *New York Times*–bestselling author of *Drawdown*

"Rice has been working for decades to make supply chains fair and sustainable—now a more critical issue than ever before. He's got much to teach the world. *Every Purchase Matters* is full of insight and inspiration."

—Jacqueline Novogratz, founder and CEO, Acumen; and *New York Times*–bestselling author of *The Blue Sweater*

"At Madewell and J. Crew, we are committed to caring for our people, including those across our global supply chains and in the communities where we operate. Fair Trade gave us a chance to lean into this important work—because it proved that doing good is good for business. *Every Purchase Matters* will show other companies how they, too, can take that next step—and that they should take it as soon as possible."

—Libby Wadle, CEO, J. Crew Group

Every Purchase Matters

HOW FAIR TRADE FARMERS, COMPANIES, AND CONSUMERS ARE CHANGING THE WORLD

PAUL RICE

FOUNDER, FAIR TRADE USA

PUBLICAFFAIRS

New York

PublicAffairs
Hachette Book Group
1290 Avenue of the Americas, New York, NY 10104
www.publicaffairsbooks.com
@Public_Affairs

Printed in Canada

First Edition: April 2025

Published by PublicAffairs, an imprint of Hachette Book Group, Inc. The PublicAffairs name and logo is a registered trademark of the Hachette Book Group.

The Hachette Speakers Bureau provides a wide range of authors for speaking events. To find out more, go to www.hachettespeakersbureau.com or email HachetteSpeakers@hbgusa.com.

PublicAffairs books may be purchased in bulk for business, educational, or promotional use. For more information, please contact your local bookseller or the Hachette Book Group Special Markets Department at special.markets@hbgusa.com.

The publisher is not responsible for websites (or their content) that are not owned by the publisher.

Print book interior design by Amy Quinn

Library of Congress Cataloging-in-Publication Data

Names: Rice, Paul (Founder of FairTrade USA), author.
Title: Every purchase matters : how fair trade farmers, companies, and consumers are changing the world / Paul Rice.
Description: First edition. | New York City : PublicAffairs, 2025. | Includes bibliographical references and index.
Identifiers: LCCN 2024044206 | ISBN 9781541704039 (hardcover) | ISBN 9781541704053 (ebook)
Subjects: LCSH: Social responsibility of business. | Environmental responsibility. | Fair trade associations.
Classification: LCC HD60 .R523 2025 | DDC 658.4/08—dc23/eng/20250103
LC record available at https://lccn.loc.gov/2024044206

ISBNs: 9781541704039 (hardcover), 9781541704053 (ebook)

MRQ-T

1 2025

To my dear friend, mentor, and father figure, Michael Shimkin, who introduced me to the Fair Trade movement and served with vision and wisdom as our first chairman.

To Maya Spaull Johnsen, who served the cause for over seventeen years with brilliance and dedication until her tragic passing in 2022.

To the hundreds of amazing Fair Trade USA team members who have contributed so much passion, creativity, and hard work to making the world better.

To the millions of Fair Trade farmers and workers around the world whose inspiring vision, courage, and resilience give me hope for our future.

CONTENTS

INTRODUCTION

"**W**HERE'S YOUR GUT ON THIS ONE? WHICH WAY DO YOU think they're leaning, Pablo?" asked my chief operating officer, Steve Sellers, in a tone both anxious and hopeful.

"Honestly, brother, I have no idea. I feel like it could go either way at this point. But we still have a good shot."

I tapped the large boardroom table nervously and looked around the conference room at my team members. They were all armed with multicolored folders and binders packed with charts, reports, and other data for the pitch meeting. Excited anxiety filled the room as people chatted quietly.

"They're here," one of my team members observed, looking out the large glass windows enclosing our conference room on the fourth floor of a downtown Oakland office building.

I got out of my chair and walked over to where she was standing. From our vantage we observed our guests making their way through the front door of our brick building. Smack dab in the middle of the pack was the main target of our pitch: Howard Schultz, Mr. Starbucks himself.

IT WAS 2008—A DECADE SINCE I HAD LAUNCHED FAIR TRADE USA—and we were on the verge of landing a historic deal that would change our organization's trajectory and could potentially transform the entire coffee industry. We were in negotiations with Schultz and his team to certify Starbucks' entire coffee supply—all of the roughly 400 million pounds of beans they bought each year—as Fair Trade. That meant the roughly 150,000 farmers around the world who grew beans for Starbucks would receive the protections and premiums our certification provides. We estimated the financial impact to be roughly $50 million per year, funneled up the supply chain to the farming families who needed it most. These are among the most marginalized farmers on earth, often surviving on just dollars a day and consistently teetering on the edge of poverty. The Fair Trade premiums would help pay for things like infrastructure development, health care, and educational programs, which we've found help start to break the chains of generational poverty that characterize coffee-farming communities worldwide.

From the perspective of my organization, this deal alone would increase our coffee certification volume by 500 percent. And we believed it would create a domino effect in the coffee industry, bringing other brands along and setting a new bar for coffee sustainability. The potential impact was enormous. The fact that Starbucks was even considering this kind of investment in Fair Trade was unprecedented. Since first partnering with Fair Trade seven years earlier, they hadn't increased their business with us in any significant way; nor had they shown any indication they planned to. Like many of the companies we work with, Starbucks started small, certifying only 5 percent of their coffee. We hoped they would increase their investment over time, but they simply hadn't.

Some critics suggested their lack of growth proved that Starbucks' commitment to Fair Trade was really just a form of greenwashing. They had originally come to us in 1999 in the midst of a global coffee crisis. Due to a prolonged downturn in the price coffee beans were fetching in the global marketplace, hundreds of thousands of farmers around the world were being driven out of business and into severe poverty. Starbucks was trying to get ahead of the PR nightmare that resulted from the crisis, which was garnering significant media attention around the world. So the perception was that they certified just enough of their coffee to be able to use our label and satisfy their critics, keeping the activists at bay.

Regardless of their motives, we were grateful for our partnership with Starbucks. Getting them to certify even a small fraction of their supply chain was a big deal for us at the time. Not only did their modest investment significantly increase the overall volume of coffee we certified, but affiliating our fledgling Fair Trade Certified™ label with the power of the Starbucks brand helped to legitimize us in the eyes of consumers and companies alike at a very early stage in the movement. It helped us to bring in more coffee companies following Starbucks' lead. Most importantly, it generated millions of dollars for the thousands of farmers who grew their certified beans.

But I also shared the concerns of many critics and believed that Starbucks could and should do more. Starbucks was emerging as a cultural icon. They had changed the way the world thought about coffee, bringing the high-end café experience to the masses. Now they had the chance to help bring more attention to the farmer. They had the ability to affect millions of lives for the better by doubling down on their commitment to "ethical sourcing" and compensating their farmers fairly. I believed we could convince them to do so. We just needed an opportunity.

It took almost ten years, but another shift in the global market brought Starbucks to our boardroom that day in Oakland.

One of Starbucks' biggest global rivals at the time was McDonald's, and both giants were competing to expand within the European market. McDonald's had partnered with Rainforest Alliance, a certification focused primarily on the environment, to certify their coffee as ecologically sustainable. They wanted to appeal to the more socially and environmentally conscious European consumer. To that end, they ran a huge marketing campaign in London and throughout the United Kingdom touting theirs as "the most ethical coffee on High Street." McDonald's had, in essence, landed the first punch in the sustainable coffee fight, and Starbucks needed a strong counter.

That's where we came in. If Starbucks went all in on Fair Trade, they could retake the moral high ground from a key competitor. We had the potential to craft a perfectly symbiotic partnership. Starbucks would shore up the socially conscious element of their brand for the new markets they were trying to penetrate, and we could dramatically increase the size of our impact and generate unprecedented momentum in the coffee world. It was a win-win situation.

But there was a catch.

IT WAS QUITE AN EXPERIENCE TO HAVE SUCH A BIG-NAME, CELEBrity CEO like Howard Schultz in the building. We planned a half day of activities prior to the pitch to give Howard and his team the full technicolor Fair Trade experience. We took them on a tour of the office and introduced our staff. We stood at our "Wall of Fame" and admired the packaging of other Fair Trade brands like Ben & Jerry's, Green Mountain Coffee Roasters, Numi Organic Tea, and Avon Cosmetics—some of which Howard was surprised to see. We gave them a slideshow presentation on our impact model with farmer photos from around the world. We even did a coffee tasting with some of our best beans. Along the way, we discussed the McDonald's campaign and Starbucks' motives for working with us, and I was impressed with the Starbucks team's passion for improving the livelihoods of their suppliers. After a couple of hours, it was time for the big event, and we all settled into our conference room to discuss the potential future of Fair Trade Certified Starbucks coffee.

The meeting started off smoothly. I was so proud of my team as they laid out our carefully constructed plan to help Starbucks make the necessary changes to their supply chain. It would require some investment on both our parts to make it work. Starbucks would need to share all its sourcing information with us and commit to transparency and independent auditing. Both parties would need to invest in increased farmer training around quality, productivity, and compliance with the Fair Trade standards. We would need to commit to a sustained consumer-awareness campaign. It was a big job!

Then there was the issue of economics. The way our model works is twofold: Fair Trade Certified farms must all meet our rigorous standards for both working conditions and environmental sustainability and agree to regular audits to make sure they remain in compliance. But the real gem of the Fair Trade model is our impact premium, which is an additional contribution companies agree to pay that goes directly to the farmers and workers. Not only would Starbucks need to agree to pay the farmers our guaranteed minimum price (which at the time was $1.20 per pound), but they would also need to pay the impact premium of ten cents per pound (it later increased to twenty cents per pound in 2011). This money goes directly back to the farmers in the form of a community development fund. Every year, the farmers vote democratically about how to invest their premiums, choosing projects like clean water, scholarship funds, medical clinics, or agricultural infrastructure to improve the quality and efficiency of their operations. Fair Trade is the only certification model that guarantees farmers a premium, and no other model generates the transformative community economic development that we do. We were able to show the Starbucks team that for a price tag of only $50 million per year—a drop in the bucket compared to their annual profits—they could go 100 percent Fair Trade and have a huge impact on coffee-producing communities around the world. And they would get more credit in the eyes of consumers and their critics.

Right around that time, Starbucks had made a big, public splash by announcing that they were extending health-care benefits to all of their baristas and other staff, including part-timers. It was a bold move and a statement of principle, benefitting more than 150,000 employees, about the same number of farmers Starbucks was sourcing from at the time. Part of our pitch was to draw a comparison between these two key stakeholders in the Starbucks business model: their employees and their farmers. We argued that, from a brand and reputational perspective, a more holistic approach would serve and support both key groups.

As the pitch went on, I periodically stole a glance at Howard to get a read on his response to our presentation. Each time, he seemed engaged and interested, nodding along and asking the occasional question. All seemed to be going well. I was hopeful. Then, finally, the conversation shifted to the elephant in the room.

"This all looks great," one of their senior team members said. "And we're excited about expanding our partnership with you. It's clear that doing so could do a lot for both of our organizations and the farmers we support. But in order to make it work, you're going to need to make some changes to the Fair Trade standards."

"Okay," I said. "What are you thinking?"

"It has to do with your small farmer co-op stipulation," she said. "That just won't work for us."

I KNEW THIS WAS COMING. AT THE TIME, OUR FAIR TRADE standards required that all certified coffee be grown on small farms (less than ten acres). The requirement was an important tool for giving the small farmers a chance to compete in a global market that often left them behind. Our other requirement was that all Fair Trade coffee farmers needed to organize themselves into cooperatives. As in many agricultural industries, co-ops play a huge role in the global coffee world. Co-ops are essentially companies owned by the farmers themselves; they buy and process coffee from their members and then export it directly into the global market.

Starbucks' supply chain reflected the majority of the coffee industry in that roughly 80 percent of their beans were grown on farms that didn't meet these two criteria. Either their farmers were too large to fit our Fair Trade standards, or they were not affiliated with a co-op. Adapting this aspect of their business model to the limitations of our standards was a big ask for Starbucks. It would require a complete overhaul of their buying practices and historic farmer relationships.

The coffee industry is extremely far-reaching and complex. There are so many actors involved in growing, processing, shipping, and roasting the beans that ultimately end up in our lattes and Keurig machines. The roasters who create the blends we enjoy, like Peet's or Starbucks, source their coffee from all over the world. It's not rare to drink a cup of coffee with beans from Nicaragua, Kenya, and Brazil. Coffee companies are focused more on finding the right mix of coffee qualities than on the types of farms that produce them. For the roast master, it's all about creating unique flavor profiles that will delight the customer. And to replicate those flavors consistently, roasters tend to form long-term relationships with their suppliers.

It was one thing for Starbucks to pay our premiums and ensure their suppliers met our social and environmental standards. Starbucks seemed willing and able to make that happen. But agreeing to source exclusively from small-farmer cooperatives, which would force them to switch roughly 80 percent of their supply chain, was a bridge too far. I would have loved it if they were willing to change their practices in this way, but in my heart I knew it was unrealistic.

MY ENTIRE CAREER, I HAVE BEEN A PASSIONATE CHAMPION OF small farmers and co-ops. I got my start with Fair Trade in rural Nicaragua, where I witnessed firsthand how small coffee farmers were completely marginalized from the global marketplace. The majority were living below the poverty line and didn't have the economies of scale to survive the sharp fluctuations in the commodity prices for their beans. They didn't have direct access to global markets and often relied on predatory middlemen who would pay them far below market value for their harvests. They rarely had access to banks and credit, forcing them to borrow working capital from unscrupulous moneylenders who could charge as much as 200 percent annual interest. This locked many small farmers into a cycle of generational poverty that was nearly impossible to break. They were the Davids in a battle against the Goliaths of the coffee world: large plantation owners, moneylenders, middlemen, and international traders.

For eleven years, I lived and worked in the remote mountains of Nicaragua, organizing farmers into cooperatives. I was Pablo, the "gringo" who helped farmers come together, build community-owned businesses, and learn to navigate the global market. In my experience, by organizing cooperatives, family farmers could band together, go around the middlemen, and create the scale required to compete against the plantations and the transnational traders. They could gain access to credit, equipment, and training they couldn't get on their own. They could build their market power and go from being victims of globalization to empowered actors in the global economy.

I've seen firsthand how cooperative agriculture can empower farming families and improve their lives. That's not to say that all cooperatives are perfect, competitive, or democratic. Just as there are bad apples and performance failures in private business, co-ops certainly have their fair share of challenges and failures. But on the whole, I firmly believe that a one-acre farmer who stands alone will always end up a victim of larger market forces, whereas 1,000 small farmers standing together, organized and selling a value-added product directly to the global marketplace, will almost always be more successful.

So, for a long time I was comfortable with the exclusivity of the Fair Trade model for cooperatives. But over the years, my thinking began to evolve. The initial success of our first decade of building the Fair Trade movement in the United States convinced me that our impact could happen at a much larger scale. In order to do that, however, we would need to expand the types of operations we were willing to certify as Fair Trade. I started to have a more inclusive vision and recognized that by limiting our support to small-farmer co-ops, we were excluding the vast majority of the global market. In doing so, we were ignoring the millions of unorganized smallholders as well as the legions of impoverished farmworkers who were working on large plantations in exploitative conditions often for as little as $4 per day. If we could find a way to extend the same kinds of policies and protections—price premiums and social and environmental standards—for farmers and farmworkers outside the co-op movement, we could have a much bigger impact globally.

And we could be a relevant partner for Starbucks and all the companies considering converting their business to Fair Trade.

THE MEETING WITH STARBUCKS ENDED AS POSITIVELY AS IT BEGAN. Howard and his team were enthusiastic about our pitch and impressed with our attention to showing them how Fair Trade could add significant value to their business model. Our negotiations with Starbucks were like many others we've had with companies over the years. They required empathy, creativity, and a willingness to adapt our model to create a win-win outcome. In this case, Howard and his team were asking us to change one of the core criteria of the Fair Trade standards. And we, as an organization, were ready to move in that direction because we could see the enormous potential for impact at scale for everyone in the coffee-growing community, including the cooperatives.

But a decision like this wasn't just up to my organization alone. At the time, Fair Trade USA was a member of a larger global certifying body called Fairtrade Labeling Organizations (FLO), now called

Fairtrade International. We were legally and fiscally independent of FLO, which is a voluntary membership organization, but we were connected in many important ways: we shared resources and infrastructure, especially the farm-auditing function that encompassed the globe. We also shared the same standards, so their Fair Trade label on a product in Europe meant the same thing as our distinct label in the United States. Changing the rules to allow all types of coffee farms under the Fair Trade banner would require convincing our global partners at FLO.

So we parted ways with the Starbucks team that day with an agreement to engage our colleagues at FLO and explore changing our criteria. Given the size and historic nature of the Starbucks opportunity, I was cautiously optimistic that my fellow Fair Traders in Europe would be receptive.

Weeks later, I went to FLO headquarters in Bonn, Germany, and made my pitch to the board (of which I was also an elected member). I argued that we shouldn't see expanding our standards to accommodate large farms and unorganized smallholders as a concession to big companies like Starbucks; nor should we assume that opening up the model to all kinds of farms would hurt cooperatives. On the contrary, I argued, this was our chance to partner with the icon of the global coffee industry to greatly widen the scale of our social impact, benefiting all producers. On the other hand, by keeping our standards narrow and exclusive to co-ops, we literally couldn't protect the majority of the coffee labor force worldwide—a fundamental betrayal of our social justice values. By staying narrow, I argued, we were doomed to stay small.

I managed to sway a few of the other FLO board members. But in the end, a change like this would require convincing a majority of the FLO board to agree. Some board members were representatives of coffee co-ops who were skeptical of the move, and I couldn't blame them. Many had spent their lives battling the Goliaths I was asking them to let into our Fair Trade community. These leaders were afraid that if we allowed larger farms to be certified as Fair Trade, they would capture the market and push the smaller farmers out. They assumed a "fixed pie" mentality and couldn't imagine the win-win scenario of an expanding market where all producers could thrive together.

The decision came down to a vote, and I lost. The FLO board rejected our proposed changes to the standards. I flew home empty-handed. And so we lost the Starbucks deal. It was simply unfeasible for them to go all in with us if we couldn't certify the thousands of farmers they had built trusted sourcing relationships with over many years. Later, I pitched Howard and his team on the idea of phasing in our plan over several years, which might give me more time to work with FLO to evolve our standards, but to no avail. Starbucks wanted to move quickly.

Within a year, the window of opportunity had closed. McDonald's didn't turn out to be nearly as big a threat as Starbucks had anticipated, and so their incentive to expand their partnership with us fizzled. Over the years, they continued to certify a few of their product lines as Fair Trade, which represented a small percentage of their total coffee. But in 2022, they dropped even that line. Instead, Starbucks leaned into developing their own in-house code of conduct called C.A.F.E. Practices, which has many similarities to Fair Trade but doesn't guarantee an impact premium or include the rigor of a third-party certification program. Today, Starbucks says 100 percent of their coffee meets this C.A.F.E. Practices standard. Interestingly enough, in early 2024 the National Consumers League sued Starbucks for misrepresentation. The lawsuit alleges that the company's claim that 100 percent of their coffee and tea is "ethically sourced" is false and misleading. It appears that their self-enforced C.A.F.E. Practices standards haven't been able to root out the human rights violations and labor abuses in their supply chains (Kavilanz, 2024).

AN OPPORTUNITY TO EVOLVE

LOOKING BACK ON IT NOW, THE FAILURE TO EXPAND OUR PARTNER-ship with Starbucks in 2008 may be, to this day, the biggest regret of my career. There's no telling exactly what kind of momentum the deal would have sparked within the Fair Trade and broader ethical sourcing movements, but it would have been significant. Imagine what seeing a Fair Trade label on every Starbucks cup and package would have done to accelerate the conscious consumer movement as a whole. Think about how much social and economic impact this would have created for the twenty-five million farmers and farm-workers around the world who grow coffee.

Yet, as failures do, the Starbucks deal also presented me and my organization with a huge opportunity to learn from our mistakes. As I'll explore in the book, these lessons eventually led to a profound shift in our business model—one that set the stage for the dramatic growth of our impact over the past decade. It's helped us to grow the little green-and-black Fair Trade Certified label into the third most recognized sustainability seal in the United States (behind only organic and non-GMO (non–genetically modified organisms), one that now adorns the products of over 1,700 leading brands and retail-ers, from Patagonia to Walmart. In 2024, our cumulative financial impact for farmers and workers grew to over $1.2 billion.

Despite all this growth, I'm convinced that we are still only scratching the surface of the impact Fair Trade and other types of ethical sourcing can have in the global economy. For example, in a recent consumer study we found that two-thirds of Americans recog-nize our label and have an accurate sense of what it represents. Yet, as of 2023, less than 1 percent of total US shopping dollars were spent on Fair Trade products. While we've partnered with many main-stream companies like Starbucks, in most cases their commitment to Fair Trade has been relatively small. This gap between awareness and purchase is common in this early chapter of the ethical sourcing movement. Even organic, which has been around a lot longer and enjoys over 80 percent consumer awareness, only accounts for 6 percent of total US food sales (Organic Trade Association, 2023).

How do we close this gap between consumer awareness and purchasing behavior? This is one of the main questions that sustainability leaders everywhere are grappling with. How do responsible sourcing movements like Fair Trade and organic evolve from niche market segments into mainstream models that fundamentally change the way the world does business? What needs to happen for sustainable supply chains, living wages, and responsible shopping to become the norm rather than the exception? Can ethically sourced products ever reach mainstream market penetration if priced higher than their conventional counterparts?

I'm a firm believer that we are in the early stages of a new phase of capitalism in which the interests of companies are starting to align with those of the farmers and workers who produce their goods. Some call this conscious capitalism or stakeholder capitalism. Others call it sustainable business or triple-bottom-line thinking. When applied to supply chain practices, this phenomenon is referred to as ethical or responsible sourcing. Fundamentally, it's based on the idea that business can be a powerful tool for tackling many of the economic, social, and environmental challenges we face today. It does so by creating what Harvard business professor Michael Porter describes as "shared value" for all the stakeholders in any given economic system: companies, workers, society at large, and the natural environment. As Porter points out, "Businesses create shared value when they can make a profit—create economic value—while simultaneously meeting important social needs" (Driver, 2012).

I've seen this growing movement toward creating shared value within the business community firsthand. I've sat with Fortune 500 CEOs who aren't only committed to short-term returns for their investors but also care about the working families their business models support. I've seen the dedication that many business leaders have to making sure their supply chains are responsible, both socially and environmentally. Many of those leaders have bet on the unknown when partnering with us. They've banked on the hope that customers will reward them by buying more of their products if they carry a Fair Trade Certified label because their customers increasingly care about the impact of their personal shopping choices. In most cases, those bets have paid off, often in unexpected ways. In other cases, not so much. But on the whole, our movement and impact have grown, and that gives me a tremendous sense of optimism for the long-term evolution of supply chain practices.

Most of the time, progress feels painfully slow. This is especially true for me because, over my forty years of world travels, I've come to know so many farmers and workers personally. I feel their pain and disappointment at not being able to provide the kind of life for their kids that they dream of because the market price for their harvests is so low. But if we zoom out and look at the evolution of supply chain practices and responsible sourcing over the last forty years, the progress is undeniable. If you talk to Fair Trade farmers and workers, their hope for the future is generally strong.

I'm convinced that this more enlightened future is coming, but I don't believe it will happen automatically. It certainly hasn't thus far. It will require continuous innovation and a willingness to evolve. As the Starbucks experience showed us, models of conscious business like Fair Trade must adapt in order to remain relevant. We must work with the business community to make sure that we are solving their problems and creating value for them. I've always believed that ethical sourcing won't work for farmers and workers if it doesn't work for industry and consumers as well. My organization has been built, brick by brick, through a series of negotiations, experiments, and partnerships with the companies we work with and the producers we support. It continues to be a dynamic dance between the different stakeholders involved in producing, selling, and consuming the products people buy every day. It's one that requires give-and-take and a willingness to learn, adapt, and evolve.

I've learned this evolutionary lesson the hard way over my twenty-six years at the helm of one of the world's most recognized and successful sustainability labels. I've experienced the direct consequences of failing to evolve in a timely way, like the Starbucks deal—"the one that got away." And I've experienced the shared value and social impact that can be unlocked when we've been willing to innovate. This book explores that evolution. I'll share stories of the visionary leaders who have risked their reputations and careers to make Fair Trade work. I'll reflect on the lessons learned in my efforts to turn business into a force for good and why I think they have implications for all of us who, in one way or another, participate in the global marketplace. Most importantly, I hope to share why I believe we should all feel hopeful and inspired about our future, despite there being so much bad news in the world today.

This book is the untold story of the Fair Trade movement, recounted by the protagonists and stakeholders who are building it. It's an encyclopedia of insights shared by the business leaders who are pioneering this new chapter in global capitalism. It's a how-to for practitioners of ethical sourcing in all its versions. It's a love story between hard-boiled corporate executives and the humble farming families in their supply chains. It's a road map for consumers who are curious about how they can make a difference. Ultimately, this is a book of hope.

1

TRADE NOT AID

BECOMING PABLO

ON THE SURFACE, HARNESSING THE POWER OF BUSINESS FOR GOOD may seem like a far-fetched idea. Our global economic system is shaped by multinational corporations that are driven by a seemingly never-ending hunger for short-term profits, often at the expense of people, communities, and the natural environment. So suggesting that business can be a positive force for making the world a more fair, equitable, and sustainable place could appear naive. Yet, twenty-six years into our Fair Trade experiment, I'm more confident than ever in the power of business—when done right—to help us tackle the biggest social and environmental challenges of our generation. You might say I'm a proud "conscious capitalist."

But it wasn't always that way.

In my early years, I was like many young idealists. I saw global power structures, including capitalism itself, as significant obstacles to my utopian vision of what the world could and should be. If you were to tell me during my undergraduate years at Yale that I would end up doing business with some of the world's largest corporations, I would have laughed in your face. This was the 1980s, after all—the Ronald Reagan years of trickle-down economics and neoliberalism. The US economic empire was expanding through the power of multinational corporations and free trade. In the wake of all this, there was a growing movement of people like me who were becoming aware of the negative consequences of globalization: the exploited people, communities, and nations who were getting poorer as the rich got richer. I wanted to do something about it. So I became a revolutionary.

For me, it started with a passion for helping marginalized farmers. During college I took a year off to study and work in China, where I learned about land reform and farming cooperatives. I spent some time doing volunteer work with farmers and began to feel connected to the daily struggles of farming folk. I became intrigued by the potential of rural cooperatives to enable more equitable, participatory, and grassroots economic development. I came to believe that historically disempowered people, through the formation of cooperatives, could gain more control over their individual and collective destinies—economically, socially, and politically. So after graduating from Yale with a degree in political science and economics in 1983, I decided to take a leap of faith and move to Nicaragua to work with farmers and cooperatives there. At the time, the country was in the midst of the Sandinista revolution, redistributing land to the poor and promoting cooperative organization as a way for farmers to develop their communities. I was fascinated. I had to go see it for myself and find out if I could help.

During my first seven years, I lived and worked in the mountainous Segovias region in the northern part of the country. This area, situated on the Honduran border, is characterized by high-altitude subtropical forests (above 4,000 feet) and rich, volcanic soil. The proud farmers of the Segovias are known for producing some of

the world's best coffee. My job was working on a variety of projects, funded by major international aid agencies, aimed at combat-
ing rural poverty and promoting agricultural development. We were
focused on building infrastructure and training farmers in "modern"
agricultural techniques to help alleviate poverty in the region. We
built irrigation systems. We introduced fertilizers and pesticides to
try to increase farm yields. We organized farmers into cooperatives
so they could start to benefit from the economies of scale that came
from pooling their resources. I was surrounded by smart, dedicated
professionals who shared my passion for sustainable development.
Every day was a real-time learning lab—a chance to test theories,
troubleshoot problems, and develop the skills to navigate the challenges of rural economic development. But for me, the attraction
was about much more than just the work.

This turned out to be the most formative period of my life. My
work took me deep into the communities we were trying to serve. I
lived in remote mountain villages and fell in love with the farmers I
met there. I rode horses to their homes. We worked together. We ate
together. I met their families, and I was welcomed into their lives.
They taught me how to identify the migratory birds who visited their
forests. I learned the ins and outs of small-scale coffee farming. I
developed a deep appreciation for a good meal filled with chicken,
corn tortillas, and beans grown on their own fincas for subsistence.
I grew a mustache and learned to dance salsa. I married a local gal
named Marisol, and we had two kids together. I tried to assimilate
and earn my stripes. I became Pablo.

My eleven years in Nicaragua also overlapped with Reagan's
Contra war, which was ravaging the country during the 1980s. The
US-backed Contras were fighting against the Sandinista "revolutionaries," and many of the farmers I knew and loved were victims
of the violence. It was a dangerous time to be working there, and I
never felt safe, especially after I was picked up by a band of heavily

armed Contras in 1985 and interrogated at gunpoint for six hours before being released. So many civilians around me, including many of my close friends, were not so lucky and died in Contra raids and ambushes. But that's a longer story, perhaps for another book. In Nicaragua, it was a time of idealistic, revolutionary fervor—a time when capitalism was viewed as the problem, not the solution. It shaped my worldview and made me who I am. If I close my eyes, it doesn't take much to be transported back to that turbulent, transformative time.

THE BIRTH OF AN IDEA

OVER TIME, SOMETHING BEGAN TO SHIFT FOR ME. I STARTED TO become skeptical about the long-term impact of big aid projects on the communities we were trying to help. The international agencies funding the work all had good intentions. But the millions of dollars we were investing had clearly failed to spark sustainable economic growth. For example, one of our big initiatives was to provide tractors and irrigation systems to the small farmers in a region called La Vigia. They used the infrastructure initially, but when the aid money ran out, the tractors and irrigation systems fell into disrepair. The farmers didn't know how to fix them; nor did they have the money to hire others to do it. So the equipment was abandoned, broken down, out in the fields—and later cannibalized for parts.

I began to realize that our aid wasn't empowering the farmers we were trying to help. Rather, we were inadvertently creating dependency on aid, and our anti-globalization mentality certainly wasn't helping farmers learn how to navigate the global market successfully. They didn't want handouts. They had too much pride and dignity for that. These proud farming families needed opportunity. They wanted access to capital and markets. They wanted the kind of support that would enable them to become self-reliant. They wanted to participate more directly in the global market that had, for the most part, marginalized them. But they needed a way to overcome the significant market barriers that kept them perpetually at a disadvantage.

The coffee industry is particularly difficult for the small farmers (less than ten acres) who grow more than half of the world's coffee beans. Coffee is a globally traded commodity, so the price that a pound of beans fetches tends to fluctuate dramatically. Larger operations can weather the ups and downs of the commodity market. But a significant drop in coffee prices can mean devastation for small farmers like those I worked with in Nicaragua. During these cyclical downturns, smallholders are forced to go into debt, often borrowing money from predatory lenders or selling their coffee beans to middlemen for pennies on the dollar. Most farmers don't have the education, scale, or business acumen to combat these dynamics and end up helplessly vulnerable to the whims of the global economy.

In early 1990, the Sandinista revolutionaries lost the presidential elections in Nicaragua and handed over power to the conservative Violeta Chamorro. Many rural development projects, which largely focused on marginalized, small family farmers, were shut down as the new government shifted the country's economic priorities to incentivize larger landowners. Soon, many of my colleagues and I found ourselves jobless. Rather than head back to the United States, I chose to stay in Nicaragua. The campesinos I had been working with for nearly a decade had become like family to me. I was afraid that many of them might get kicked off their land by the new government or large landowners, and I wanted to find a way to help them. During this time I received a letter that would forever change the course of my life.

The letter was from Michael Shimkin, my beloved friend and mentor. Michael, who passed away in 2019, was a publishing industry veteran. He served as the executive vice president of Simon & Schuster (a publishing company co-founded by his father, Leon) for years and had started several other book publishing ventures. But aside from books, Michael's other passion was social justice. He had financed several literacy programs throughout Latin America and, starting in 1986, became a trustee of the international development organization Oxfam America, which had inspired him to write to me.

While I no longer have the handwritten letter or remember its exact words, Michael essentially asked me if I'd ever heard of "this thing called Fair Trade." Through his work with Oxfam, he'd come into contact with some of the early Fair Trade organizations like Global Exchange, Oxfam America Trading, Pueblo to People, and Equal Exchange. Some of these companies were focused on buying and selling handicrafts on more equitable terms. Others were beginning to source coffee directly from small-farmer co-ops in Mexico and Costa Rica and selling it to conscious consumers who were willing to pay a premium for a more ethically sourced product. Because they were cutting middlemen out of the equation, these organizations could guarantee that a higher percentage of the price consumers paid for their coffee would end up in the hands of the farmers. "It's a 'trade not aid' approach," Michael wrote. I was intrigued.

Michael later introduced me to Jonathan Rosenthal, co-founder and executive director of Equal Exchange, one of the pioneers of Fair Trade coffee in the United States. It turned out that they were looking for a way to source directly from a small-farmer cooperative in Nicaragua. "We want to be in solidarity with the campesinos," Jonathan told me. He then made me an offer that blew my mind. If I could set up an export cooperative serving the smallholders of Nicaragua, Equal Exchange would be willing to pay us $1.40 per pound for our coffee. That may not sound like much, but in those days, most of the farmers I knew were selling their beans to middlemen for more like ten cents per pound.

I couldn't believe my ears. I knew nothing about the mechanics of setting up a coffee export business, but the promise of being able to offer my farming brothers and sisters a chance to increase their income tenfold was profoundly inspiring to me. An offer like that was the ultimate organizing tool, a chance to bring people together for almost immediate economic benefit. Something clicked for me. The farmers I knew had never been fans of charity or handouts. The opportunity to sell their coffee at such a high price to Equal Exchange would give them a chance to stay on the land and begin to build a better future for their kids. But first we needed to get organized and form an export co-op. So the idea for PRODECOOP (short for Cooperative Development Program) was born.

Now I just needed to convince the farmers to get organized, which was no easy task. Thanks to the strong relationships I had built in the community, I was able to get twenty-four families to take the risk and come on board that first year. This was a big leap of faith for them. Exporting their own coffee through the newly formed co-op meant that they would have to wait months before being paid, because as a new venture we weren't eligible for a line of credit. The beans had to be collected, milled, sorted, bagged, and then trans- ported by Maersk, a Danish ocean-shipping line, to Equal Exchange up in Boston, Massachusetts. All that took about five months. During that waiting period, the farmers had to go without any of the income from their hard work. I was essentially asking a group of people living below the poverty line to go without any money for an excruciatingly long period based on the promise of big profits in the future. When I look back on that experience, I'm amazed that they were willing to put so much faith in me, Pablito, trusting that I would make good on my promise. More amazing still was their courage and conviction that they could do something that had never been done before in Nicaragua: give birth to a farmer-owned coffee export business that took market power away from exploitative mid- dlemen and put it in the hands of the farmers themselves.

I remember how difficult that first shipment was. I was a green- horn in the coffee industry at the time and wasn't familiar with how things worked. Jonathan Rosenthal, our first buyer, was a huge help to me at the time, painstakingly walking me through the ins and outs of the coffee export process. I remember calling him weekly for a while to make sure things were on track. I was so nervous that something would happen to our precious shipment of coffee beans en route from Nicaragua to Boston and anxious about what that would mean for the twenty-four families who were depending on its safe arrival. At the end of our long wait, I was overjoyed to receive the phone call from Jonathan saying that the shipment had arrived at the Port of Boston. But my excitement quickly reverted to nervousness when he told me we were "only halfway there." The Equal Exchange quality-control guys still had to go down to the port and test our beans. They took random samples from the many bags of coffee in the container, brought them back to their facility, roasted them, and then taste-tested them, a process called "cupping." They had to make sure that the beans we had shipped matched the quality and flavor profile of the sample we had sent them months earlier.

A few days later, I got the phone call. "It's excellent," Jonathan told me. "We'll wire you the money today." That first shipment was worth around $50,000, and I wanted to share the good news with the farmers. I immediately called a meeting. They all came to the local schoolhouse in Santo Domingo that evening, bringing their families with them, anxious to hear the news. I decided to save the best for last. They all patiently listened as I walked them through the revenue and costs of the deal, and then I asked them each to come forward and receive their share of the earnings. I'll never forget the joy on their faces as each farmer received the roughly $2,000 in cash they were owed from that first shipment. It was more money than any of them had ever seen in their lives.

That night the families organized a celebration. There was home-cooked food, a bit of rum, and lots of laughter. A local trio played popular ranchero songs, and we danced for hours. A few of the farmers gave heartfelt speeches. It was an ecstatic experience. Besides the births of my children, it remains one of the greatest days of my life. These twenty-four farm families had put their faith in a crazy, untested notion, presented to them by this gringo from the United States, that they could be more than farmers, that they could take control of their harvests and sell directly to the global marketplace. They took a big risk, and the risk had paid off. We were, of course, celebrating the enormous windfall from the first shipment and all it could provide to these hardworking families. But our collective joy was coming from something much deeper than just money. We were celebrating the future. We were celebrating hope. We all felt that we were at the start of something big. This was the first in a series of Fair Trade exchanges that would change all of our lives forever.

THE FACE OF THE MOVEMENT

I'LL NEVER FORGET THE FIRST TIME I MET SANTIAGO RIVERA IN 1992, two years after starting PRODECOOP. It was midafternoon on a Saturday—my day to catch up on office work—and I was sitting at my old, wooden desk in the sunny co-op headquarters in Esteli, Nicaragua. As I reviewed revenue projections, trying to keep as much of my body as possible within range of the small electric fan blowing cool air in my direction, I heard a knock at the door.

In walked a man who might as well have been Juan Valdez, the fictional character who has—along with his mule—adorned cans of Colombian-grown coffee for decades. This Nicaraguan version wore a cotton working shirt, jeans, a well-worn cowboy hat, and a big smile. As he sat down in the chair in front of my desk, he took off his hat to reveal a full head of black hair, molded by sweat from the day's work. He was in his forties at the time and had a weathered face from a lifetime of hard work in the fields. He had a marked sense of both seriousness and good humor. He seemed humble and to the point.

"Don Pablo," he said after clearing his throat, "my name is Santiago Rivera and I've come to talk to you about joining PRO-DECOOP." These were the early days of the co-op, and inquiries like this were common. He proceeded to share his story with me. Santiago was a small coffee farmer from the neighboring Somoto region and also served as manager of his village's coffee co-op, which was essentially the financial engine of his community. Despite having only a second-grade education, Santiago was good with numbers, so his thirty fellow farmers elected him to manage the simple finances of their organization. Santiago had heard through the grapevine that there was a gringo in the area who had figured out a way to get a much higher price per pound for their coffee beans than the going rate paid by "coyotes," as the middlemen were known.

In the two years since PRODECOOP began, we'd continued to fetch the premium prices we'd received from Equal Exchange in that first shipment. We also developed a technical-assistance program to help our members improve their productivity and the overall quality of their coffee. We were even able to eventually certify most of our farmers as organic, allowing them to get even higher price premiums. Word of our success traveled quickly around the region, and by the time Santiago came to my office that day, we had grown from 24 to over 1,000 coffee-growing families. We were producing and exporting so much coffee that we'd outgrown Equal Exchange and were now selling to a variety of different buyers, almost exclusively in Europe, the epicenter of the global Fair Trade movement.

After our meeting, Santiago and his village co-op decided to join our program, and we welcomed them with open arms. They've been with the movement ever since. In fact, our initial meeting in my PRODECOOP office that day sparked a friendship that has lasted more than three decades. I have visited Santiago's small, two-acre finca many times and seen his children grow up. Along the way, I have witnessed the transformative impact of Fair Trade on Santiago's family and community over several generations.

A decade later, after starting Fair Trade USA in 1998, I would eventually bring Santiago to the United States "on tour." He and I went on a roadshow for many weeks, giving talks on campuses and in boardrooms across the country. It was his first time leaving Nicaragua; his first time eating pizza and using a flush toilet. In his inimitable way, cowboy hat always on, Santiago told his Fair Trade story to literally thousands of people on that tour. I introduced him to then Oakland mayor Jerry Brown and Congressman (now Senator) Sherrod Brown of Ohio. We publicly billed Santiago as "The Real Juan Valdez," until we received a letter from the National Coffee Federation of Colombia, which had created the original Juan Valdez character, demanding that we stop using the moniker. (We sheepishly complied and apologized to the federation, which since then has become a huge ally and supporter of our efforts.)

For reasons I'll explain shortly, Santiago has become an icon of the Fair Trade movement. He's a reminder that almost everything we eat is grown and harvested by hand by a real person, with a family, living in a community. He is the farmer at the bottom of every cup of coffee we drink. It's through personal relationships with salt-of-the-earth farmers like Santiago that I have gained so much confidence that ethical sourcing can make a huge impact in the lives of those who need it most.

MY CAPITALIST EPIPHANY

I HAD TO LEARN A LOT DURING MY FOUR YEARS AS GENERAL MANager of PRODECOOP in the early 1990s. This was different work than what I was accustomed to with the aid and government agencies I'd worked with before. This was a business. There were shipping deadlines to meet and coffee quality standards to adhere to. I had to learn about the dynamics of the coffee industry. I had to balance the needs of all our stakeholders: the farmers, the processors, and our customers, the buyers. I experienced the power of financial incentives to motivate the farmers who were part of the cooperative. I celebrated when our entrepreneurial drive and resourcefulness were rewarded with profits that went directly back to these farmers who had spent their lives surviving below the poverty line.

Our hard work was paying off. Within four years, we had grown to include over 2,500 coffee-producing families who co-owned Nicaragua's first coffee export cooperative. In our fourth year, we exported almost four million pounds of coffee at an average price of $1.20 per pound, generating close to $5 million in revenue. At the time, the average farmer in the region was only able to sell their beans for roughly $0.30 per pound to the local coyotes. So the price premiums we secured by selling directly to Fair Trade buyers represented over $3.5 million in extra income in a single year that our farmers wouldn't have received otherwise. Our success drew the attention of other farmers around Nicaragua and sparked a movement that eventually was emulated by almost 40,000 producers throughout the country. To this day, PRODECOOP remains a powerful example of success in the global Fair Trade producer movement.

My experience with PRODECOOP forced me to reconsider my previous anti-capitalist ideology. Over time, I began to embrace what I saw as an inevitable reality: globalization and capitalism were here to stay. The revolutionary idealism that inspired me to go to Nicaragua in the first place was maturing. I became convinced that trade, as opposed to aid, was a more promising tool to address rural poverty in agricultural communities like those I served in Nicaragua. The early success of PRODECOOP proved to me that it was possible to empower farmers to overcome their victimization by so many powerful economic actors. It was possible to organize poor farmers being left behind by globalization to reposition themselves in the global economy as competitive exporters of a higher-value product that could command a fair price. It was possible to help one-acre farmers pool their resources, create economies of scale, learn the tricks of capitalism, and harness the power of global markets. It was possible for them to embark on a journey out of poverty, through sustainable grassroots economic development, without depending on aid. It was possible for the poor and the powerless to become architects of their own futures.

BECOMING PAUL

THIS PROFOUND IDEOLOGICAL SHIFT LED ME TO AN INEVITABLE conclusion: the successful experience we had at PRODECOOP with direct market linkage and ethical sourcing could be a prototype for a much larger global movement. This would require tapping into the US market. At that time, by the mid-1990s, Fair Trade certification was well established and growing throughout Europe, where PRODECOOP sold most of its coffee. But Fair Trade was virtually unknown among US consumers, despite the tireless efforts of pioneers like Equal Exchange in coffee and Ten Thousand Villages in handicrafts. So I felt a calling. I felt compelled to leave my beloved Nicaragua and my "first baby," PRODECOOP, and return to the United States to see if I could replicate the European experience in my home country.

In 1994, I headed back to the United States inspired by the dream of building the Fair Trade movement here. But first I went to get an MBA from the Haas School of Business at the University of California, Berkeley. While I had learned a lot about the coffee business working for PRODECOOP, I knew that if we were going to launch the Fair Trade movement in the United States, I would need the deeper understanding of business that an MBA would provide. So I dove into my studies, which turned out to be quite a challenge. In fact, the MBA program really kicked my butt, not just because the coursework was hard but because I felt so socially disconnected. Here I was, a thirty-four-year-old in classes full of twentysomethings, just back from a decade in the mountains of war-torn Nicaragua. We had very little money, so I had to work while attending school. I lived with Marisol, my Nicaraguan wife, and our young son, Emiliano, in a two-bedroom, subsidized student apartment. I was juggling school, work, and family, all while trying to relearn English and reacquaint myself with US culture, which felt incredibly self-indulgent compared with the daily struggles of Nicaraguan farmers. For the first time, I really understood what culture shock was all about.

I was also experiencing a lot of self-doubt about my ability to bring Fair Trade to the US market. I often thought, "Who the hell am I to think I can pull this off?" But despite the inner critic, my amazing journey with PRODECOOP kept me going. I had seen for myself what Fair Trade made possible for the campesinos I lived with, and I felt profoundly inspired by their example. Truly, it felt like I had a duty to share that unique, transformative experience with the rest of the world and see if we could re-create that impact for millions of other farmers around the globe. So I persevered.

I wrote the original business plan for Fair Trade USA during my second year at Berkeley. It was based upon a simple premise: the coffee industry was ready to embrace sustainability, and the coffee consumer was ready to pay a little more for it. This was the beginning of the $3 latte era after all, and I believed that there was a growing audience for coffee that was not only high quality but also sustainably sourced. The concept was similar to what Fair Trade is today: coffee companies would agree to pay a minimum price to the farmer for their coffee in addition to an impact premium that farmers would reinvest directly in their communities. We would audit and verify the farmers' compliance with the Fair Trade standards, which would include rigorous social and environmental requirements. Companies buying coffee on Fair Trade terms would then be allowed to use our Fair Trade Certified label on their packaging, signaling to consumers that the product was grown and traded in a more ethical and sustainable way.

After graduating from Berkeley, I spent two years working as a consultant for international development organizations like Oxfam and Conservation International, which wanted to set up farmer-owned export cooperatives like PRODECOOP. I worked with farmers in many countries—Haiti, Peru, the Philippines, Honduras, Vietnam, Mexico, and Colombia. I learned about the common barriers faced by small farmers everywhere in their efforts to access global market opportunities, as well as some of the unique challenges posed by each product, culture, and market. This brief stint as a consultant and the breadth of farm-to-market initiatives I had a chance to learn from later proved invaluable in helping me develop Fair Trade USA's global model of ethical sourcing across so many diverse product categories and geographies.

I also spent those two years after business school talking about Fair Trade with anyone who would listen and exploring sources of start-up funding. I was soft-selling the concept to foundations and individuals who I thought might be interested in supporting a Fair Trade certification initiative. Meanwhile, Mark Ritchie, a kindred spirit and founder of the Institute for Agriculture and Trade Policy (IATP), decided to incorporate TransFair USA in 1997 as a nonprofit affiliate of the European Fair Trade certification network. Legally incorporated, but with no staff, funding, or operations, TransFair USA desperately needed a new home and entrepreneurial leadership. Soon after, in 1998, the Ford Foundation gave us our first $100,000 seed funding, IATP officially handed over a box of files, and I launched the organization as its founding CEO. The dream was becoming a reality!

I remember that first day: October 1, 1998. Staff size: two. My first hire, Philip Arca, and I picked up the keys from our landlord and opened the doors to our "headquarters" for the first time. For $500 per month, we rented a small office in a dusty, idle ball-bearing warehouse in gritty downtown Oakland, California. For the first few months, we worked on a shoestring budget. We found donated used furniture, convinced a law firm to give us pro bono services, and wrote grant proposals to raise more money. We developed our first contracts, registered our trademark, made sales calls, recruited coffee companies to our cause, interviewed prospective staff members . . . and made the coffee every morning, took out the trash, and swept the office every Friday. Then, after a few months, I hired two more people, and things began to feel more legit. I asked my dear friend and mentor Michael Shimkin, the guy who had introduced me to Fair Trade years earlier, to serve as our founding chairman, and he agreed. Slowly but surely, we recruited a board, a team, and a cohort of pioneering coffee companies inspired by the principles of Fair Trade. As in the PRODECOOP founding story, we succeeded in convincing folks to make the leap of faith and help create something that didn't yet exist in the United States: a movement dedicated to taking Fair Trade into the mainstream.

I started with what I knew: coffee. Our early allies were small, mission-driven companies like Equal Exchange, Peace Coffee, and Thanksgiving Coffee. These organizations were already founded on principles of social justice and environmental sustainability, and their brands had a small but loyal following among consumers who cared about farmer impact. In fact, at least initially, we probably benefited more from having our label on their package than they did. Our promise to consumers was then much what it is today. When people buy a product bearing our Fair Trade Certified label, they can have confidence that the people, community, and environment that produced it were treated well and got a better deal. There are, of course, a lot of complex mechanics behind that promise, which we'll explore more as we move through the book. But the general idea is simple: brands and consumers pay a little more for products with the Fair Trade Certified label on it, and those impact premiums are passed along the supply chain to farmers and workers who vote on how to invest the money in their communities. While our business model has evolved significantly since we started back in 1998, most of these fundamentals have remained the same.

SANTIAGO AND HIS MULE

ONE OF SANTIAGO'S PRIZED POSSESSIONS IS HIS MULE, BON BON. He named Bon Bon after the indulgent chocolate candy because the experience of having a farm animal carrying the heavy sacks of coffee beans down the steep slopes of his farm is so sweet for him. For a long time, he couldn't afford to buy a mule. So as the largest and strongest member of his family, he spent years doing all the heavy lifting around the farm by himself. He literally carried each 150-pound sack of coffee, one by one, down the path from the farm to the road at harvesttime each year. The backbreaking work was not just less efficient; it also took a toll on his health.

When I first met Santiago, life on the farm was particularly grueling. Not only did he have to play "mule" for his family, but he had to do it without proper boots—another luxury he couldn't afford. Their family of five lived in a small, two-bedroom farmhouse with no electricity or running water. At night, their only light came from kerosene lamps. They grew corn and beans and raised a few chickens for subsistence. He and his wife, Hermelinda, had only a few years of formal education and knew little more than the coffee-growing vocation passed down to them from their parents and grandparents. They had little prospect of improving their situation, and their children faced a similarly bleak future. In all this, their lives resembled those of the twenty-five million hardworking people around the world who grow and harvest coffee.

But all that began to change when Santiago convinced his village co-op to join PRODECOOP. As for so many other smallholders around the world, joining a Fair Trade co-op gave them a combination of access to markets and price stability, which helped begin to reverse the poverty cycle and build something sustainable—for their families and communities. In our approach, this stability starts with what we call the "minimum price guarantee." As discussed earlier in the chapter, one of the most difficult elements of smallholder coffee farming is extreme price fluctuations in the global market. We figured out a way to address this boom-and-bust dynamic by adding a price floor for all certified beans. Currently, our minimum price is $1.40 per pound. This means that any coffee company selling Fair Trade Certified coffee in their cafés or on grocery store shelves paid at least that price back to the cooperative for the unroasted, "green" beans that went into their unique roast or blend. Our minimum price is rooted in our research into the farmers' production costs and represents a rough global average.

At first glance, $1.40 per pound might not seem very high, especially considering the high price we pay for roasted coffee in the United States. But the key here is that this is a guaranteed minimum price regardless of how low the market may go. It's a buffer against the inevitable downswings in the market. For the smallholder farmers like Santiago who grow the majority of the world's coffee, this safety net can be the difference between survival and collapse. These smallholders aren't big or profitable enough to ride out the extreme dips in the global market for coffee, which are quite common. Having a price floor prevents them from having to go into debt with predatory lenders during bad years, which often forces farmers to sell their land and emigrate in search of work.

For the Riveras and their fellow farmers, the Fair Trade price floor has made all the difference. They have by no means gotten rich selling certified coffee beans. That's not what Fair Trade is designed to make happen. But the minimum price guarantee has given them something crucial: a stable foundation. They've been able to avoid going into debt during the down years and to save money in the high years. These savings have allowed them to improve their lives in so many ways, enabling them to afford a mule like Bon Bon to help out on the farm, boots to protect their feet from the rocky terrain, shoes for their children to attend school, and so on. Over time, they've also saved enough to invest in more advanced infrastructure on the farm, including better machinery to improve their quality and productivity.

But while the price floors may have given Santiago and thousands of other farmers around the world the income stability they need to build a more sustainable livelihood, our approach doesn't stop there. Another important element of our equation has had even more impact on producer communities around the world.

YOLANDA AND THE STREAM

When I first met Santiago's daughter, Yolanda, she was sixteen years old. In those days, she was the family's primary water carrier. Every morning at the crack of dawn, she would walk a quarter mile up the narrow path to the water well in the center of her village, a cluster of thirty or so homes. She used the hand-cranked pump to fill a large tin water can and carefully carried it back to the house, balanced on her head. Another trip or two to the well and back, and she had fetched enough water for all her family's needs for the day: drinking, cooking, cleaning, and bathing.

Hauling water was difficult work, but the Riveras were grateful for it. Prior to the installation of the village well, they got all their water from the small stream that ran through their farm. This was easier for them than hauling water, but the convenience came at a cost. Like many waterways in agricultural regions around the world, theirs ran through cattle ranches upstream of their house. Cattle ranches mean manure. Manure in the water stream breeds parasites like giardia and amoebas, causing dysentery in those who drink it.

During my years in Nicaragua, I was constantly afflicted with some form of dysentery. As a healthy adult, I was able to live with it. For the elderly, the sick, and especially young children, dysentery can be fatal. In fact, according to the World Health Organization, diarrhea from polluted water is the second-leading cause of death among children age five and younger in the world (World Health Organization, 2023). One could argue that the responsibility to ensure clean water for citizens should lie with local governments. But in many regions around the world—including some US communities like Jackson, Mississippi, and Flint, Michigan—local governments have limited resources and can't or won't provide the necessary water-treatment infrastructure, especially in rural areas. So many communities are on their own when it comes to sanitizing their water supply.

Santiago's village, Uniles, turned to their cooperative for a solution. They decided to use what is perhaps the most powerful Fair Trade tool—the community development or impact premium—to dig a well and bring clean drinking water to the village. The impact premium is essentially an added bonus that companies using the Fair Trade Certified label pay back to farmers and workers on top of the going market rate for any given product. For coffee, the current premium is an extra $0.20 for every pound of coffee beans. So when the market price climbs to $2.40 per pound, they pay $2.60. When it drops below the guaranteed minimum price of $1.40 per pound, they pay $1.60. These premiums might seem small, but they add up. In 2023, Fair Trade Certified coffee farmers received more than $40 million in impact premiums generated by our US industry partners.

The proceeds from the premium are deposited directly into the co-op's bank account. The co-op farmers then vote democratically on how to invest these funds within the community. This might take the form of a well, as in Santiago's case, or a scholarship fund for local children to go to high school or college. Premiums are often invested in the infrastructure of the co-op, like new processing equipment, or farmer training and technical assistance to boost productivity. They may even be disbursed as cash bonuses paid directly to the farmers for family needs, should the community vote to go that route.

I consider the impact premium to be, in many ways, the "secret sauce" of the Fair Trade model because it allows consumers and companies to invest directly in the communities that make the products we buy. That $0.20-per-pound extra they pay for their coffee empowers the farmers and farmworkers who grew it to target some of the unique issues they need to address in order to thrive as a community. The financial impact of those premiums on the coffee-producing communities with whom we work has been dramatic. Since we started in 1998, we have generated over $450 million in premiums for coffee-producing communities around the world. And the impact goes far beyond coffee. Companies pay premiums on all Fair Trade products, from blue jeans to blueberries. In 2024 we passed $1.2 billion in total impact premiums generated over the twenty-six years since we started.

In Santiago's case, his co-op's choice to invest in clean drinking water had a huge impact on the community. The instance of dysentery dropped dramatically, and the distended bellies that used to be common among children in the community all but disappeared. In making that improvement, they protected the health and well-being of the next generation. In even better news for Yolanda, the Rivera family was eventually able to save so much from their coffee sales that they installed their own well at the house. She hasn't had to take that long and tiresome trip with the water cans since.

SHOES MATTER

Education is one of the most important tools to combat global poverty. It is a fact that in many of the world's most poverty-stricken regions, not having shoes is one of the primary barriers to getting an education. That's right. Tens of thousands of kids worldwide can't go to school, because they can't afford shoes.

In 1996, the Recocarno co-op in northern Haiti used a portion of the impact premiums they earned selling coffee to Twin Trading, a Fair Trade buyer in the United Kingdom, to purchase hundreds of pairs of shoes so the kids in their community could go to school.

The photo I took on my trip to Recocarno that year still hangs on the wall of my office today and shows some of those kids wearing their "scholarship shoes." Their bright, smiling faces are a constant reminder to me of how a small investment in something that most of us take for granted can change the lives of an entire generation.

BREAKING THE CYCLE

When Santiago talks about Yolanda—which is often—his eyes sparkle, and a big, beaming smile comes over his face. His love for her is infectious. In fact, she is pretty much the pride and joy of his entire community. Yolanda is the first person in her family to not only graduate from high school but also to attend college. She is, in many ways, a poster child for the power of Fair Trade to break the cycle of poverty. But her future didn't always seem so bright.

Back in her water-carrying days, Yolanda was on track to do what so many "coffee kids" end up doing: forgoing their education to help out on the farm. Even though she was one of the smartest kids in her class, Yolanda had dropped out after the sixth grade. Not only was her labor needed at home, but her family couldn't afford to continue sending her to school. The school itself was free. But the Riveras didn't have the $200 per year for other things like shoes, uniforms, books, bus fare, and lunch money.

Yolanda's fate changed when their local co-op decided to do what so many Fair Trade communities around the world have chosen to do with at least a portion of their impact premiums: create a scholarship fund. Yolanda was part of the first generation in her village to take advantage of the $200-per-year scholarship to complete her high school education. But she didn't stop there. It turns out Yolanda was one heck of a student. She graduated top of her high school class, then won a Fair Trade–funded college scholarship from PRODECOOP (the larger co-op of which their local was an affiliate). She used it to attend the National University of Nicaragua, where she got a degree (with honors) in biology.

No one would have faulted Yolanda for using her college degree to start a new and better life in the city. But that's not who Yolanda is. She decided to return to her community and work in the laboratory of their local public health clinic. Years later, she reminisced with me about this decision. "I wanted to pay my community back for believing in me. I wanted to help my people because they helped me. And I wanted to show other girls in the community that they could dream beyond the farm, beyond the village."

This is the power of the impact premiums. They aren't just one-time cash infusions. More typically, they are investments that contribute to the long-term health and sustainability of communities. In many cases, the choices these communities make about how to use their premiums last for generations.

The long-term impact of this model is that it gives farmers and workers a voice and a vote in how to tackle community problems and make things better. As my dear friend Tristan Lecomte, founder of Paris-based Alter Eco, put it, "The biggest impact of Fair Trade is that it brings hope to small scale farmers. The premiums don't necessarily change their lives overnight, but because they are encouraged to work collectively, they get this tremendous sense of empowerment. They start to organize themselves with other peers and work for the sustainable development of their community. This gives them the sense that they are not alone, that they have a say in their future."

HOW DOES FAIR TRADE WORK?

So how exactly does our certification process work? It starts with a producer, which could be a factory, farm, fishery, or cooperative. These producers go through an in-depth annual audit to ensure that they are in compliance with our rigorous social and environmental standards. Once they've passed their audit, producers can sell their products—coffee, bananas, rugs, soccer balls—to our industry partners under Fair Trade terms and receive the established impact premium. In 2024, we had 1,700 industry partners, including brands like Dole and retailers like Whole Foods, who source from certified producers, pay the premiums, and put our Fair Trade Certified label on their packaging. The premiums are paid directly back to the producers, who vote democratically on how to invest the money in their communities.

> Consumers are the final link in the chain. These are shoppers like you and me who buy Fair Trade Certified products in the store and online, making a difference with every purchase.

TRADE *AND* AID

MY EARLY "CAPITALIST EPIPHANY" GREW OUT OF MY DISAPPOINTing experience with the limitations of the aid projects I worked on in Nicaragua and, in contrast, the powerful role I saw that business could play in addressing social and environmental problems. That said, I wouldn't dismiss the positive impact that philanthropy has had and continues to have in the world today. Fair Trade USA is a nonprofit organization, and we have benefited tremendously from donations, large and small, over the years. In fact, grants from a range of foundations—including Ford, Rockefeller, Packard, Walton Family, Moore, Skoll, and Stiller—and support from many generous individuals have funded much of our growth and innovation. Moreover, international development aid has become much smarter and more strategic over the years, embracing market-based solutions as a key approach for sustainable development. Public-private partnerships are increasingly seen as a model for amplifying the impact of aid and achieving more systemic change.

So for me, the "Trade Not Aid" mantra that I proudly championed in my PRODECOOP years has evolved into a more balanced "Trade *and* Aid" perspective. Clearly, philanthropy has an important role to play in both emergency relief and longer-term development efforts. In 2022, official development aid totaled more than $210 billion, much of it for health, education, infrastructure, and humanitarian assistance for the world's poorest countries. Aid programs, whether run by governments or nongovernmental organizations

(NGOs), often address problems that the market can't. Aid can also support innovation and help incubate new development solutions that the business community can then implement at scale—priming the pump, as it were, for market-based approaches to sustainability.

Some would argue that Fair Trade is a hybrid approach that combines aid and market-based solutions to poverty and development. Take Mark Muckerheide, for example, who is head of the Women's Economic Justice Program for CARE, a global nonprofit organization dedicated to fighting hunger and poverty around the world. As Mark says, "The thing that I love most about Fair Trade is how efficient it is at taking very little aid and turning that into lots of benefit for the communities it serves."

Efficiency is Mark's thing. After getting a business degree from the University of Minnesota, he worked his way up through the ranks at Target, with an emphasis on sales. Somewhere along the way he caught the sustainability bug, which is how I met him. In 2013, he became director of corporate social responsibility for Target, which is one of our major retail partners. When he eventually shifted from the for-profit to nonprofit worlds in 2017, he took his business acumen with him.

One of Mark's areas of interest at CARE is making sure all of the market-based projects the organization is involved in are using their aid dollars as efficiently as possible. In the world of philanthropy, the number of dollars of economic impact generated by each dollar of aid funding is one of the most important metrics for gauging success. Mark is a numbers guy, and he frames the global poverty issue in a compelling way. "The World Bank has estimated that low- and middle-income countries need $4 trillion more to achieve their sustainable development goals, and there is only $210 billion per year in international aid within the NGO community today," he told me in a recent conversation. "That means there's a twenty-to-one gap between money that needs to be in farmers' and factory workers' pockets and the amount of aid out there. Unfortunately, the current method of international development is woefully inadequate. Our research says that the average aid program is taking $1 and turning that into $2 in the pockets of community members. That's not a bad ratio, but if we keep doing two-to-one solutions, we will never fix a twenty-to-one problem."

Part of the reason Mark loves market-based solutions so much is that they've consistently shown the potential to have a higher return on investment for community members than average NGO economic programs. As he says, "I think one critical role nonprofits can play in development work is to address market failures. If they can combine their efforts with market partners, like Target, they can dramatically scale that impact. That, to me, is exactly what Fair Trade has done. It helps companies like Target to invest in communities through market mechanisms that amplify social impact." That's been our experience as well. We have found that with Fair Trade, for example, over the years we've been able to generate $4 in increased wealth for farmers and workers for every $1 that Fair Trade USA spends building the market and the movement. We study this return on investment carefully and always strive to increase the impact leverage of our model.

REGENERATIVE BUSINESS

IN THE SPRING OF 2023, WE HELD OUR ANNUAL FAIR TRADE USA board dinner for the first time in four years—the previous three had been canceled due to the Covid-19 pandemic. The event, held at the City Club of San Francisco on the tenth floor of a downtown building, presented us an opportunity to bring together our Fair Trade USA staff and friends of the organization to celebrate the accomplishments of the past year and reflect on lessons learned. The lively, festive gathering was attended by representatives from GAP, Williams-Sonoma, and other companies in our network as well as many of our philanthropic supporters. We ate grass-fed filet mignon, organic salad greens, and wild-caught salmon and drank Certified Organic pinot noir. It was a lovely night.

The evening's keynote speaker was my friend and longtime colleague Brian Durkee, who serves as CEO of Numi Organic Tea. Brian is an understated but compelling presenter. That night, in the company of fellow conscious capitalists and social entrepreneurs, he spoke from the heart. Sharing several stories from tea villages he had visited around the world, Brian talked about the important moment in history we find ourselves in today. Whereas in the past companies largely sought to "extract value" from the land and communities where they sourced their products, there has been a movement for several decades to shift toward "doing less harm" in those communities. This, Brian cited, would include things like providing higher wages for workers or paying for a local water-treatment project in a village, all of which are important developments.

But Brian wanted to push us further into what he sees as the next phase of business, which he calls "regenerative business." He defined this as using business as an engine to improve lives and communities. He talked about how Numi Organic Tea is transitioning from seeing itself as a tea company that also does good to one that does good through the vehicle of tea. In this new paradigm, the communities that businesses source their materials from become better—socially, environmentally, economically, and spiritually—as the result of the business being there. They breathe life into communities rather than leaving them destitute.

He told the story of the Da Zhang Shan Cooperative in the mountainous region of southwestern China, one of Numi's tea suppliers. During his initial visit to the community, he toured the farms, inspected the processing facilities, and walked around the community chatting with people through an interpreter. At the local elementary school, Brian met with schoolchildren and, at the end of their conversation, asked them what they wanted to be when they grew up. He heard a chorus of "doctor," "teacher," "engineer." Surprised, he asked if any of them wanted to work on tea estates like their parents, and they all vigorously shook their heads. Tea farm workers were among the poorest people in society, leading lives primarily of poverty and struggle. Why on earth would these children want to work plucking tea?

Brian returned to the village three years later. During that period, the community had generated a significant amount of money through the Fair Trade and organic premiums that Numi and other customers had paid for the tea they grew and harvested. They had chosen to invest their funds in the construction of a beautiful new school, not just for the children of tea workers but for the whole community. They had also begun to build new housing for many of the cooperative's families. When he went back to the same school he had visited during his first trip to the village, Brian asked the same question of the kids: "What do you want to be when you grow up?" While there were still plenty of aspiring doctors and teachers in the room, nearly half said they wanted to follow in the footsteps of their parents. In three short years, a business venture had breathed such new life into the community that its next generation began to see a future for themselves there.

This is the kind of progress and hope that inspired me to start Fair Trade USA in the first place. It's the kind of grassroots empowerment that converted me from a radical anti-capitalist in my youth into a passionate conscious capitalist today. I'm convinced that we can harness the power of markets and consumers to improve lives and protect the environment in communities around the world. We just have to get creative and collaborative in how we engineer win-win models of ethical sourcing. This realization was just beginning to unfold for me in the late 1990s when we launched Fair Trade USA. I had seen firsthand the power Fair Trade had to impact farming families and communities like Santiago's, and we had initial partnerships with some visionary companies that wanted to make a difference in the world.

But in order to grow beyond a market niche and scale our impact, we would clearly need to make the business case for Fair Trade. We would need to convince the Whole Foods and Targets of the world that partnering with us wouldn't just be the right thing to do; it would generate benefits for them as well.

2

MAKING THE BUSINESS CASE

THE INCOMPARABLE BOB STILLER

WHEN I FIRST APPROACHED BOB STILLER IN 2001 ABOUT PARTNER-ing with Green Mountain Coffee Roasters (GMCR), he was curious but somewhat skeptical. Stiller was already a pioneer in the fledgling corporate social responsibility movement. He took a meeting with me because he was sympathetic to the mission of Fair Trade, but he just wasn't sure how much value we could add to GMCR's already strong brand and sustainability programs.

In the two-plus decades since founding GMCR in 1981, Stiller had grown the company from a small, regional roaster into a leading specialty coffee brand. By their twenty-fifth anniversary in 2006, GMCR did $180 million in annual revenue and had over 7,000 wholesale accounts, including ExxonMobil and McDonald's (Neville, 2008). This success was one of the reasons that *Forbes* magazine named Stiller their 2001 Entrepreneur of the Year.

Yet it isn't just the market and financial success of GMCR that makes Stiller's story so compelling. It's that his business thrived alongside a dedication to both social and environmental sustainability. Stiller and GMCR, which has since merged with Keurig and Dr Pepper to become Keurig Dr Pepper (owned by JAB Holdings and the Reimann family), were early investors in organic coffee and built sustainability into the guiding ethos of their company. Bob—as I've come to call my dear friend and mentor in the years since—recently reflected, "We were always concerned with taking care of our farmers, and we had already done a lot of work towards that end. For us, it was really a question of helping our consumers take our efforts more seriously. We saw a third-party certification like Fair Trade as a possible way to do that."

But Bob still wasn't sure that it would be worth the investment GMCR would need to make to commit to our auditing practices and pay our premiums. Consumers already bought Green Mountain Coffee for its reputation for high-quality roasts, and in his eyes the company was already making efforts to compensate their suppliers more fairly. Why did they need Fair Trade? He was skeptical that a partnership would lead to business growth. He was the CEO of a large, publicly traded company, after all, and had a fiscal duty to his board and shareholders. He needed to have a business case for everything he did. He couldn't just make decisions because they were the right thing to do; they also had to be good for business.

The thing about Bob is that while he's a responsible executive, he's always been a risk-taker. He made his first fortune starting, growing, and eventually selling a cigarette rolling papers company called EZ Wider. He then got into coffee after tasting a particularly good cup at a specialty café in Sugar Bush, Vermont, where he was vacationing at his ski house. Like Howard Schultz, he saw a huge potential market for specialty roasts and decided to build a company to tap into it. He was always willing to jump into something new, as long as it had the potential to grow. So he made me an offer: Green Mountain would certify a line of their coffee as Fair Trade, and if sales improved, they would grow the program. "A little experiment," he called it.

And just like that, we made a deal.

BETTING ON ENLIGHTENED SELF-INTEREST

THESE WERE THE EARLY DAYS WHEN FAIR TRADE WAS QUITE SMALL and relatively unknown, so we were thrilled by the opportunity to partner with such a respected and successful company as GMCR. We quickly got down to business. We identified which of their coffee lines made the most sense to convert to Fair Trade. We settled on an organically certified roast sourced from small family farms in Mexico. The farmers and their cooperative already met our basic standards, which we verified through our auditing system. And we worked with GMCR to ensure the farmers received our guaranteed minimum price and the impact premiums that farmers invest in their communities.

I remember feeling a mix of anxiety and confidence about our experiment. Bringing on a strong brand like GMCR was a big deal for us at the time. I really wanted to get it right. If we could make our initial run with them a success, I believed they would expand their business and take our movement to a whole new level. But while I was confident Bob's bet would ultimately pay off, I couldn't be sure. His skepticism about the value of our Fair Trade label, which wasn't very well known at the time, could prove warranted.

We have made this bet hundreds of times over the years with our brand and retail partners. We often start small, certifying only a few of their products, because companies want to test the waters and see how consumers respond before committing significant resources. We're banking on the belief that these tests will be successful and will motivate the companies to expand their business with us in the future. We're betting that they will ultimately find that doing the right thing will also lead to more success. This "enlightened self-interest" is core to the promise of not only Fair Trade but the whole ethical sourcing movement. Simply put, it describes situations where the self-interest of an individual or company aligns with the interests of society as a whole. In Bob's case, enlightened self-interest would mean that retailers, consumers, and investors would reward them for making sure their supply chains were fair and equitable through Fair Trade.

Time would tell whether or not the bet would pay off.

BETTER COFFEE FOR A BETTER WORLD

I'D LOVE TO SAY THAT THE GMCR FAIR TRADE experiment was as simple as putting our label on their coffee packages and watching the sales go up, but it was more complex than that. Even in those early years, the specialty coffee market was cutthroat. GMCR was competing with hundreds of other brands for shelf space at grocery stores and for contracts with restaurants and other institutional buyers, from McDonald's to university cafeterias. In order for our Fair Trade line to be a success, we would need to get the sales reps at GMCR to buy into the concept. We had to sell it to the team who would be selling it to the stores. That's where T.J. Whalen came in.

T.J. was the vice president of marketing and sales at GMCR and the person responsible for leading the rollout of new product lines, including ours. Like Stiller, he wasn't 100 percent convinced that Fair Trade would be a big seller but was enthusiastic about the opportunity to test it. Fair Trade was still relatively unknown in the marketplace. Organic was the sustainability concept everyone was pushing, and it wasn't clear whether a label like ours could help them land more accounts. T.J. had a hunch that Fair Trade could work, but he knew it was a risk. "Like any company that's trying to figure out how to grow a product or a brand, we were making bets,"

T.J. reflected recently. "We were experimenting with different products and putting our chips down on a limited number of options, hoping they would grow."

At the time, GMCR was looking for a market differentiator. They were already selling organic coffee, but so were a growing number of their competitors. They needed a new hook. As T.J. describes it, "When a salesperson is trying to convince a retailer to take on a new item—and they've got literally thousands of other coffee brands they could choose from—they need a story to tell. What they tell a retailer in that first pitch meeting has to create an emotional connection that sticks with them. Fair Trade is ultimately trying to connect the consumer on one end of the value chain to the producers at the other end. We believed consumers were yearning for this connection and retailers would see the opportunity in it."

So T.J. and his team got to work creating a pitch for the Fair Trade and organic coffee they were selling. After a little tinkering, they came up with a particularly pithy slogan: "Better Coffee for a Better World." Not only did the tagline encapsulate the core value that both Fair Trade and organic had to offer (creating a better world through each purchase), but it also spoke to the higher quality that specialty coffee consumers expect. To this day, it is one of my personal favorites of all the sustainability taglines used by the companies we've worked with.

It was also effective.

T.J. and his sales team began pushing their "Better Coffee for a Better World" to retailers. They gave multimedia pitches, showcasing the social impact Fair Trade coffee had for farmers. They offered in-store advertisements extolling the virtues of Fair Trade and organic to consumers. Soon they landed their first big partner: Newman's Own Organics.

Newman's Own, started in 1980 by actor Paul Newman, had already established itself as a leading food company with the unique commitment to giving away 100 percent of its profits to charity. In 1993, Newman's daughter Nell Newman founded Newman's Own Organics as a division of the company, posing with her widely recognized father on the packaging. This would be their first foray into the world of coffee, in partnership with GMCR, and they agreed to make it 100 percent Fair Trade organic.

According to T.J., the Newman's Own Organics deal helped vault GMCR to a whole new level of relevance in the specialty coffee market. "Combining Newman's Own Organics with GMCR's Fair Trade allowed us to push into a much broader marketplace because it was so well-differentiated," T.J. explained to me. "We were now able to compel surprisingly big customers like Wild Oats, Hannaford, Safeway, and Kroger to carry our coffee. We even landed McDonald's, convincing the owner operators of every store in the northeast to sell and promote our Fair Trade organic coffee."

While T.J. can't say definitively that putting the Fair Trade label on their coffee compelled more customers to buy it, he's unequivocal in his conviction that it helped their business grow. "It turned out to have been a good bet." Part of this had to do with landing big accounts. But the benefits Fair Trade brought to GMCR also had to do with building customer loyalty to their brand, which is key to the long-term success of any business. "Once consumers bring that bag home, they have a chance to get to know what Fair Trade's all about. They read about the farmers who grew the beans while they're waiting for their coffee to brew. It gives them a different and more powerful emotional connection to the product than they get with many other coffees."

When T.J. started with GMCR in 2000, the company's annual revenues were around $90 million. By the time he left a little over a decade later in 2014, the company's annual revenues had grown to $4.5 billion. Of course, GMCR can't credit Fair Trade for all that growth. But our partnership did help them to establish themselves as one of the top sustainable coffee brands in the world during an era when sustainability was growing in its importance to consumers. Suffice it to say, our initial experiment worked, and GMCR dramatically expanded their business with us. By 2010, they were selling over sixty million pounds of Fair Trade Certified coffee, which made them the biggest Fair Trade coffee purchaser in the world—a title they have maintained to this day. During that decade, they generated $9.8 million in community development premiums for the farmers who grew their beans. Their impact won the company the "Humanitarian of the Year" award in 2011 from the nonprofit Medicines for Humanity (Cheesman, 2011). GMCR was living proof that companies could "do well by doing good."

AUTHENTIC FAIR TRADE?

WHILE OUR DEAL WITH GMCR HAD INSPIRED MANY COMPANIES to start working with us, it had the opposite effect on some others. Not long after the Newman's Own Organics deal, an alarming publication came across my desk. It was a copy of the coffee shop magazine *Arthur*, with a page earmarked for me to see. I opened up the magazine and saw a full-page ad personally attacking Paul Newman and Newman's Own Organics for sourcing their Fair Trade coffee from GMCR. The ad challenged Newman for getting his beans from a big company like GMCR that, it claimed, only certified a small percentage of their coffee as Fair Trade. The ad, it turns out, was paid for and written by Dean Cycon, the founder of Dean's Beans—a small, mission-driven coffee company that used to certify 100 percent of their beans as Fair Trade.

The fact that Dean had run the ad was particularly concerning to me. His company had been one of our early supporters, and Dean himself was a visible figure in the ethical sourcing movement. Before launching Dean's Beans in 1993, he spent over a decade as an environmental and indigenous-rights lawyer working on behalf of small farmers. Dean got into coffee in 1988 when he co-founded Coffee Kids, one of the coffee industry's first nonprofit development organizations. Then he shifted from the nonprofit to the for-profit world and started his company as a means of helping coffee farmers gain a fairer price for their product (Deans Beans, 2023). Dean was a Fair Trade partner in the truest sense of the word. So when he had a concern, I wanted to hear about it.

I followed up with Dean directly. I wanted to understand why he would put out what I considered to be such a divisive message within our fledgling Fair Trade movement. Dean is nothing if not blunt. He told me that he felt companies like GMCR shouldn't be allowed to use the Fair Trade label unless they were willing to certify a higher percentage of their supply. He was generally skeptical that big, publicly traded companies like GMCR really cared about our mission. How could a corporation intent on delivering quarterly profits to its investors really care about the plight of its farmers? By including them, he feared we would cease to be what Fair Trade promised to be. He believed GMCR, Starbucks, and companies like them were just practicing a form of greenwashing and thought that allowing them to wear the Fair Trade Certified label was a way of deceiving well-meaning consumers.

I tried to convince Dean that scaling up was good for everyone—that GMCR was not only friendly to the movement but an important part of it. We would never have the kind of social impact we both wanted until we could bring on large companies and provide benefits to the many farms they worked with. Unfortunately, our conversation didn't convince Dean to change his position. In fact, he doubled down on it. He was so passionate about the issue that he ran a second ad, this time in a bigger publication: the *Village Voice*. This one didn't criticize Newman but took a direct shot at Fair Trade USA. The ad was meant to "expose" the fact that many of our biggest partners were still certifying only a small percentage of their beans as Fair Trade. They even publicized the percentages for the three biggest companies we worked with: Green Mountain Coffee Roasters (12 percent), Starbucks (1 percent), and Seattle's Best Coffee (0.5 percent) (Walker, 2004).

While I obviously didn't agree with Dean, I could see his point. Over the years, we have had plenty of examples of companies who did just exactly as he feared. They came to Fair Trade to certify a tiny portion of their supply chain in order to use the label as "proof" to investors, consumers, activists, and the media that they were committed to sustainability. Then they never increased their commitment. Peet's Coffee, for example, started with Fair Trade in 2001 with a single blend and a token percentage and has maintained that level to this day. As discussed in the Introduction, we've never succeeded in growing our business with Starbucks either.

Is this greenwashing? Perhaps, in some circumstances. But in others it is quite the opposite. In reality the farmers growing even the small percentage of the beans sourced by these big companies experience the same benefits as the farmers growing beans for more mission-driven companies like Dean's Beans. They are paid the same guaranteed minimum price for their product and receive the same Fair Trade premiums.

And then there's the issue of scale. I wanted to partner with larger companies in part because they could help us dramatically grow the market for ethically sourced coffee in a way that smaller companies simply couldn't. For example, Starbucks' seemingly meager percentage of Fair Trade coffee represented one million pounds in 2003, which was four times more than what 100 percenter Dean's Beans certified that year (Walker, 2004). A big part of why Newman's Own Organics chose GMCR, for example, was that they had the capacity to supply such a big account, whereas a smaller company like Dean's didn't. By making our model more scalable for business, we could also scale our impact to a profoundly different level than where we had started. In order to do this, we needed to bring on partners with a whole new level of brand recognition and distribution capacity. I felt that getting in the door with bigger brands gave us a fighting chance to create real impact for more farmers. We were betting that they would begin to see the enlightened self-interest in Fair Trade and eventually grow with us. It had already started to happen with GMCR, who went on to become the top purchaser of Fair Trade coffee in the world.

Dean and I ultimately agreed to disagree, and while his company maintained their partnership with us in the short term, we eventually went our separate ways. To this day, Dean's Beans continues to practice its own flavor of ethical sourcing—but, in the industry, it's still a tiny, obscure player. While our respective approaches to achieving sustainability might differ, I have the utmost respect for Dean and others in the ethical sourcing movement who may share his skepticism toward big business.

MORE THAN JUST A NECESSARY EVIL

LOOKING BACK ON IT NOW, DEAN'S PROTESTS REPRESENTED A KIND of ideological split that was beginning to form in the Fair Trade movement during the early 2000s. As my old friend Jonathan Rosenthal of Equal Exchange told me at the time, "The difference is that you want to go mainstream, and these other companies don't." In my vision of Fair Trade and the larger ethical sourcing movement, in order to generate exponentially greater impact for farmers, workers, and their families, I wanted to reach a large, mainstream audience and not simply remain relegated to the specialty aisle of gourmet food co-ops. I dreamed of taking ethical sourcing from niche to norm.

Dean's view, on the other hand, reflected that of many traditional Fair Traders, including some of our early pioneering partners. They saw Fair Trade as a means of redistributing wealth from "First

World" consumers to "Third World" farmers. Fair Trade, in the way they practiced it, was an alliance between two key stakeholders: the farmers who grew their coffee and conscious consumers who wanted to do some good with their purchases. The businesses that bought and sold the beans, on the other hand, were viewed as less important middlemen between the two—a kind of necessary evil required to achieve our idealistic social and environmental goals.

But my view of Fair Trade, and ethical sourcing as a whole, had evolved. This shift led me to pursue a partnership with larger companies like GMCR and Starbucks, even at the expense of my relationships with some of our longtime supporters. I didn't see Fair Trade fundamentally as a means of redistributing wealth. Instead, I saw it as a way of transforming capitalism—creating a new way of doing business that benefited everyone involved: farmers, consumers, businesses, and the environment. The business world, in this context, is an important and equal partner, not a necessary evil. If we want to create a system of global commerce that sustains the families and communities it sources from, rather than draining and depleting them, we need to find creative ways of tapping into the enlightened self-interest of the business community. We need to embrace Michael Porter's model of shared value.

Some might call this position naive or accuse me of being a kind of corporate apologist. In fact, many have. But I don't claim that somehow the companies we partner with are all bastions of social responsibility and sustainability. Most are, but some are not. We have worked with plenty of companies over the years that may not yet have a grand vision for sustainability and ethical sourcing. Given the higher cost of Fair Trade, due to our minimum-price standards and mandatory premiums, many companies have simply not yet figured out how to scale with us.

But to me, that's precisely the challenge—not just for Fair Trade but for the broader ethical sourcing and conscious capitalism movements. I'm convinced that if we want to harness the power of business to tackle the world's biggest problems, we need to do it in a way that also creates new value for the business community, as we will explore in later chapters. It just won't work on a larger scale without it. We need to show that "doing good" is also profitable. Given the constraints inherent in capitalism, I don't believe it's realistic to expect companies to change overnight and go "all in" on sustainability initiatives. We have to meet them where they're at and bring them on a journey. It's a long-term transition, but ethical sourcing and sustainability are making major progress . . . and Fair Trade is an important laboratory for this next chapter of capitalism.

GOING TO THE SOURCE

WHEN YOU FIRST MEET GREG SPRAGG, YOU MIGHT BE SURPRISED to learn that he's a sustainability advocate. He's a button-down shirt kind of guy who has spent much of his career working in retail, starting with his teenage summer job bagging groceries. When I first met Greg in 2005, he was the executive vice president of merchandising for Sam's Club. If you're not familiar with the company, it gets its name from Walmart founder Sam Walton, who launched the members-only retail warehouse club as a competitor to Costco in the 1980s. Sam's Club—like their parent company, Walmart—was originally known more for delivering bulk discount prices to its members than for making a sustainability impact. But in the early 2000s, then CEO Lee Scott launched a broad campaign within Walmart to improve their sustainability record following public pressure from activists who were critical of their labor and environmental practices.

That's where Greg came in. Sam's Club started with us by certifying a portion of their private-label coffee, Member's Mark. With the blessing and encouragement of Sam's Club's then CEO Doug McMillon (who later went on to become CEO of Walmart), Greg worked with us to roll out the program, and we spent a lot of time together hammering out the details. According to Greg, this was a bit of a culture shift—for him personally and also for his merchandising team. As he recently put it to me, "A lot of us who grew up in the industry were just doing our best to sell merchandise at a profit. That was really our purpose. One of the things I appreciated about our relationship with Fair Trade back in those days is how you helped us to understand what it was that Sam's Club could do to make a difference in the lives of people—not just the customers we served, but the folks producing products we were selling on our shelves."

A big part of that educational process was a series of field trips we took with Greg and his team to the farms where their Fair Trade coffee was grown at the time in Brazil, Costa Rica, and Colombia. These "learning journeys" have always been an important part of our Fair Trade culture. They give our industry partners the opportunity to see and more deeply understand the profound human impact they are having in the communities we serve around the world.

One trip in particular stands out for both Greg and me. It was 2005, and we visited a farming community in Costa Rica. We toured the local school and visited the high-altitude farms where they cultivated some of Costa Rica's finest shade-grown coffee. We were invited to a very humble dinner by one of the farming families. I remember distinctly how Greg sat at their table and played games with their kids. When they offered him food, he gladly accepted it. The family worked so hard to show their gratitude for the effort Greg had made on their behalf, and he responded in such a beautiful and openhearted way.

"That trip was really, really meaningful for me," Greg now recalls. "It changed my perspective in terms of how I went to work every day and I started thinking more about our purpose as a company. We weren't just selling a bunch of coffee. That was just a by-product.

What we were really doing was helping people." Greg's face lit up as he shared his reflections. "I never really thought that a retail career could be thought of as noble. But in those moments when we were in that school and in that home and out in those fields, I changed my mind."

Greg's epiphany didn't just make his work more meaningful. It inspired him to become an advocate for Fair Trade within Sam's Club. He wanted to share the insights he'd gleaned from his trips to the field, so he created a presentation for the entire Walmart management team on the importance of having purpose as a company. "Fair Trade coffee was my product and I talked about it during every one of our virtual broadcasts with our sales teams. The message I wanted to get across was that we're not just in business to serve the small businesses who buy our products," Greg recalls. "We're in business to serve small-business people—everywhere. That includes the farmers."

Thanks to Greg's efforts, Sam's Club's commitment to Fair Trade grew over time. As he recalls, "Once I had a chance to tell the story internally, it wasn't really a difficult sell. And when the products sold well on the shelves, it became a whole lot easier. At the end of the day, no publicly traded business is going to do things out of the goodness of their heart. They are accountable to their shareholders." Greg says, "So the success, from a sales perspective, of the Fair Trade coffee was really the key." Greg's passionate advocacy helped convince Sam's Club to take a bigger risk with us, and as has often been the case, that bet paid off. They found their own enlightened self-interest.

Greg moved on from Sam's Club in 2009 and started a series of adjacent ventures. But more than a decade after he left Sam's Club, Greg's legacy still looms large within the world of Fair Trade coffee. Today, Sam's Club executive Alain Nzigamasabo continues to carry the torch, and he has made the Member's Mark line one of the largest Fair Trade private-label coffee brands in the world. The brand now sources 100 percent of its beans from Fair Trade growers and benefits thousands of small family farmers in Colombia and beyond.

Over the years, we've found that internal champions like Greg tend to make a huge difference in whether a company will simply dip their toes in the water of sustainability or grow into a much fuller commitment. As Greg says, "In retail organizations, leadership has to be bought in for responsible sourcing to work. Sam's Club wouldn't have done much with Fair Trade coffee if senior leadership hadn't been committed to sustainable business practices. Someone in that position has to see the real purpose."

PowerPoint decks of farmer-impact stories are certainly helpful. But experiential learning—taking someone like Greg to meet the farmers firsthand—can be deeply transformational for a business executive who is learning to lead with both heart and mind. Much has been written about the value of purpose in today's business world. In my experience, inspiration often tips the scale, giving leaders the courage to experiment with sustainability. Once the effort succeeds and the business case has been made, larger commitments usually follow.

REPUTATION MATTERS

WHEN THE HERSHEY COMPANY FIRST CAME TO US IN 2013, THEY had a big PR problem on their hands. A series of high-profile media reports had exposed a serious child-labor problem within the chocolate industry. The issues were centered in West Africa, a region that produces two-thirds of the world's cocoa, the primary ingredient in chocolate. Many of the farms that grew cocoa for the big chocolate brands, like Nestlé, Mars, and Hershey, were found to have a significant amount of child labor. And they were all taking major heat from the media, consumers, and even Congress.

According to reports by the US Labor Department, roughly two million kids worldwide were being put in harm's way as they labored on farms, working with dangerous pesticides and swinging machetes to clear fields (US Department of Labor, 2018). Plus, children working the fields usually dropped out of school at a young age. This limited their future potential and locked them into the system of generational poverty passed down to them by their parents.

Some of the kids working on farms are working for poor families with few options. Whether this kind of labor is morally justified is a complex judgment, one that no parent should ever have to make. But something even worse had driven Hershey to our doorstep: they were facing pressure from activist groups and the media about reports that a significant percentage of the chocolate industry's child labor actually fell into the category of trafficked or slave labor. These children were often migrants from outside the cocoa-growing regions who were "acquired" by unscrupulous farmers and forced to work long hours for little or no pay. According to reports, many of the farmers interviewed didn't want to use trafficked children on their farms but felt they had no choice. The prices paid to them by the cocoa middlemen were too low, and they needed a way to cut their costs. Their solution was to find the cheapest labor available, which in this case ended up being children (Whoriskey and Siegel, 2019).

Outraged by this horrific tragedy in cocoa supply chains, organizations like Global Exchange, Green America, and the International Labor Rights Forum mounted a national publicity campaign against the chocolate industry. They ran ads focused around Halloween and Valentine's Day when consumers were buying a lot of chocolate, shaming Hershey and other candy companies for their lack of effective response to the African child-labor situation. These campaigns built on a decade of organizing, which included a proposed congressional bill in 2001 aimed at forcing chocolate companies to prove there was no child labor in their supply chains. The bill never came to a vote, but the uproar about child labor in chocolate sparked a tremendous amount of heat for Hershey and other brands over many years.

Hershey needed to find credible solutions and also to protect their public image, and they thought working with us and Rainforest Alliance, which they also approached, was a good start. Cocoa was a natural fit for Fair Trade. Like coffee, cocoa is grown predominantly on small farms in marginalized areas of the world. And cocoa farmers are among the poorest in the world. The average income of a cocoa farmer in the West African nations of Ghana and Ivory Coast in 2021 was less than $1.50 per day, which often means that they rely on the whole family, including children, to work on the farm (Wageningen University and Research, 2021). Cocoa comes from pods grown on trees that take years to cultivate and are therefore deeply vulnerable to global price fluctuations. As with coffee, there is a significant market for specialty chocolate where price premiums for sustainability labels are easier for brands and consumers to absorb. As a result, Fair Trade chocolate was already being sold successfully in Europe and, on a smaller scale, in the United States under our label with pioneering brands like Guittard, Divine, Alter Eco, and Lake Champlain.

So in 2013 we partnered with Hershey, and because of their size, they quickly became one of our largest cocoa purchasers. We opened an office in Ivory Coast and certified dozens of cocoa cooperatives, representing thousands of small farmers and their families, who were selling to the traders that source for Hershey. As with Starbucks, Fair Trade made up a relatively small percentage of Hershey's total annual cocoa purchasing; yet it still represented significant volume, financial premiums, and impact for African cocoa farmers.

But there was something disappointing about the relationship. Unlike virtually every other company we worked with, Hershey initially chose not to put our label on any of their packaging. It seemed that they wanted to work with us for purely reputational reasons. Rather than directly engaging consumers, they wanted to show the media, activists, and investors that they had responded to the child-labor issue proactively through an "independently verified cocoa" program with Fair Trade USA and Rainforest Alliance.

Hershey's motives for working with us are not uncommon. Starbucks and Peet's initially came to us in the wake of activist pressure and media scrutiny around the humanitarian crisis in coffee in the early 2000s. Years later, many apparel companies sought our certification after the devastating building collapse in Bangladesh's Rana Plaza factory that killed 1,134 workers. Companies discover that they have some kind of social or environmental problem in their supply chain, receive public heat for it, and then come to Fair Trade or other certifiers to help fix the problems and clean up their public image.

To its credit, Hershey subsequently launched a comprehensive sustainability program called Cocoa for Good, which addresses responsible sourcing as well as fair treatment of women, youth, the environment, and other focus areas. Their latest annual sustainability report shows significant investment and progress across a range of issues. Unlike many companies, they are willing to make public their goals and future plans, as opposed to reporting only on what they're already doing. Eventually their approach to product labeling changed when they acquired Bark Thins and Lily's, two brands that use 100 percent Fair Trade cocoa and proudly display our label on the packaging.

My takeaways from the Hershey experience? First, investigative journalism and activist groups still have an important role to play in exposing the dark side of "business as usual." In cocoa, the consumer outrage that ensued when child labor and trafficking in the cocoa industry were exposed was key to motivating change. Sometimes companies need a little pressure—or a lot—to take the issues seriously and start to do better by the farmers and workers in their supply chains.

Second, some companies will join ethical sourcing programs like ours for purely reputational reasons. I believe we need to be comfortable with that. As long as those companies are playing by the rules, meeting rigorous standards, passing their audits, and creating real positive impact for thousands of farmers and workers, I'm less concerned about the motives that initially bring them to our movement. As we saw with Hershey, companies can pivot from a defensive reputational play to a more proactive, comprehensive approach to supply chain sustainability. Often, bigger change is just a matter of time.

Finally, even companies that start the ethical sourcing journey with a purely reputational goal in mind usually end up discovering the brand differentiation and sales value of product labeling. As consumer demand for sustainable products accelerates, the labeling trend will also continue to grow, even with mainstream brands like Hershey.

EMPLOYEE ENGAGEMENT

For Bob Stiller and GMCR, partnering with Fair Trade didn't just help their brand and sales. It also helped strengthen their company culture. "It was very motivational for employees," Bob told me, "because with social initiatives like Fair Trade, the more money we made, the more good we did in the world. That, in turn, boosted staff morale, pride, and retention. Our people were proud to work for a company that cares about doing good in the world." Bob's new book, *Better and Better: Creating a Culture of Purpose, Excellence, and Transformative Human Engagement,* is a great read on the tremendous value of employee engagement for business success and the power of sustainability initiatives like Fair Trade in supporting staff engagement.

It turns out that company values and culture are more important than ever for employees across much of the business world. According to a 2022 survey by Qualtrics, 54 percent of US workers say they would be willing to take a pay cut to work for a company that shares their values, and 56 percent wouldn't work for a company with conflicting values (Qualtrics, 2022). There are countless examples of purpose-driven companies, from Patagonia to Unilever, that have become sought-after destinations for talented employees due to their commitment to their company values.

My friend Scott Kerslake is a seasoned veteran in creating values-driven company cultures. Founder and former CEO of the Athleta athletic wear company, Scott also served for eight years as CEO of prAna apparel, where I first met him in 2010 when we helped them launch one of the first Fair Trade Certified clothing lines. For Scott, working with Fair Trade was a way to make sure that they were putting their values into practice and ensuring the workers in the textile factories that produced their clothing were paid and treated fairly. "It had a huge benefit for our employees. It made them proud that we took a stand for our workers and were willing to go the extra mile to help people." Scott, now a professor at the University of Oregon's Lundquist College of Business, is convinced that a company's dedication to its values drives performance. "When you develop a values-driven company, you attract like-minded souls. When someone finds a place that reflects their values, there's an incredible bonding experience. It creates a kind of flywheel effect in terms of cohesion and excitement and passion."

Companies are led by people—people with families, with hearts, and with values. Most of the business leaders I know want to bring their values into their work. They want to find purpose and meaning in their professional lives. So when a company makes moves toward doing the right thing, this appeals to everyone, from leadership to frontline employees. It gives them some measure of the uplifting feeling Greg Spragg had when he saw the good that simply selling coffee could do in the world. I believe that while it's sometimes hard to measure in quantitative terms, one of the most promising returns on any sustainable sourcing investment is the sense of pride and engagement it gives to employees.

CREATING SHARED VALUE

THERE MAY BE NO MORE ASTUTE ADVOCATE FOR THE POWER OF business to address social and environmental issues than Michael Porter, the distinguished professor at Harvard Business School whom I referenced earlier in the book. In fact, I still consider his 2011 *Harvard Business Review* article "Creating Shared Value" to be a great articulation of the ethos of Fair Trade and the broader ethical business movement. In the piece, Porter and his coauthor, Mark Kramer, challenge the business community to redefine its fundamental purpose by embracing what they call the "principle of shared value," which they define as "creating economic value in a way that also creates value for society by addressing its needs and challenges" (Porter and Kramer, 2011).

For example, they cite a case study from Nespresso (which also works with Fair Trade USA). The renowned specialty coffee company sources its beans from some of the most impoverished communities in Latin America and Africa. The economic instability of these regions was threatening the stability of their supply chains, so Nespresso decided to do something about it. They invested in the local farmers—launching technical-assistance programs, building processing facilities, and offering low-cost loans—and over several years were able to significantly improve the livelihoods of the farmers whose labor and harvests their business depended on. Viewed through Porter's lens, Nespresso created social value for their source communities and, in the process, improved the stability of their own business (Porter and Kramer, 2011). It was a win-win approach.

Porter's perspective is so powerful because, unlike me, he wasn't a sustainability advocate seeking a business solution. He was centered within the traditional, profit-driven world of business and saw the shared value of sustainability within that framework. Long before he talked about the social and environmental value of business, his work on competitive strategy was required reading in business schools worldwide. I remember reading his classic book *Competitive Strategy* during my MBA program at the University of California, Berkeley, in the 1990s. Through working with and analyzing the practices of companies around the world, Porter began to recognize that in order for businesses to effectively compete and thrive in the long term, they needed to redefine the narrow view that their sole function in society was to deliver short-term profits to shareholders. "We need a more sophisticated form of capitalism, one imbued with a social purpose," he writes. "But that purpose should arise not out of charity but out of a deeper understanding of competition and economic value creation" (Porter and Kramer, 2011).

The principle of shared value has been crucial to Fair Trade's evolution. In fact, I believe Fair Trade is one of the most successful examples of shared value at scale. We do not promote charity but rather represent a business solution to the issues of poverty and environmental degradation. We help producers, consumers, and businesses derive value from their interactions in the marketplace. Green Mountain Coffee Roasters, for example, gained value from their partnership with us by differentiating their products from those of their competitors and landing bigger retail accounts. The farmers who grew the beans received value through better prices and the twenty-cents-per-pound Fair Trade premium that they invested in their communities. The consumers who purchased "Better Coffee for a Better World" from GMCR not only enjoyed a great product but also got the emotional gratification of knowing their purchase contributed to the greater good.

Our theory of change is based on creating value for three key stakeholders: producers, businesses, and consumers. While the positive social impact Fair Trade has on producers may be obvious, the business impact unlocks its true potential for growth. I believe that models of ethical sourcing like ours must create real value for the business community and the consumer in order to usher in Porter's "new phase of capitalism."

This has certainly been the case for us. From the beginning, we were eager to partner with the business community to create value and drive impact. This led to significant growth for our organization as more and more companies signed up for Fair Trade, including mainstream retailers like Costco, Whole Foods, Walmart, Kroger, and Target. Usually, once these companies had a chance to pilot a Fair Trade program, test the shared value premise, and see the results, they chose to grow. But growth wasn't exclusively a function of enlightened business leaders like Bob Stiller "pushing" Fair Trade to the consumer. Just as important was the "pull" from conscious consumers who were demanding Fair Trade products and rewarding companies who offered them. We'll explore this fascinating phenomenon in the next chapter.

3

DO CONSUMERS CARE?

THE POWER OF ORGANIZING

IN THE FALL OF 2001, JUST THREE YEARS AFTER LAUNCHING THE Fair Trade Certified label, we received an unexpected call. A representative from Sara Lee's food service division was interested in learning more about our coffee program. This came as a bit of a surprise, to say the least. The food company was known more for its frozen cheesecakes, cinnamon rolls, and midwestern charm than for its interest in sustainability. While you may not think about Sara Lee when you think about coffee, they were actually one of the world's largest coffee roasters at the time, alongside Nestlé, Proctor & Gamble (Folgers), and Kraft (Maxwell House), which collectively sold over half of the coffee consumed in the United States. Like the other coffee giants, Sara Lee had become a target in the early 2000s of activists who were pushing for ethical sourcing in the face of low commodity prices and widespread media reports of suffering farmers. So they reached out to us.

Sara Lee's food service division supplied institutional buyers like corporate cafeterias, hospitals, and universities. It turns out that a group of five college students from one of their large accounts, the University of California, Los Angeles (UCLA), kicked off a campaign demanding that the university carry Fair Trade Certified coffee on campus. The student activists organized hundreds of their classmates and gathered over 1,000 signatures on their petition, urging UCLA to compel Sara Lee to convert to ethically sourced coffee—or seek another supplier that would. Their pressure worked. Sara Lee came to us and eventually certified a line of their Superior brand coffee, focused specifically on their many university accounts (*Daily Bruin*, 2001). As one of the student organizers, Christine Riordan, said at the time, "Our organizing, together with other campus campaigns, played a key role in motivating Sara Lee, one of the world's largest coffee companies, to begin offering Fair Trade Certified coffee. We were inspired by the fact that our efforts here at UCLA were connected to the larger Fair Trade movement."

Around the same time, another group of activist students organized a campaign at Columbia University in New York, this time with a different result. At the time, Columbia dining halls served Starbucks coffee, and students were demanding that the coffee giant convert all of their campus brew to Fair Trade—or else. Inexplicably, Starbucks denied their request, so the university decided to meet the students' demands and switch suppliers. They found that Green Mountain Coffee Roasters (GMCR) was more than happy to scoop up the account, serve Fair Trade coffee in Columbia's cafeterias, and support the switch with flyers and signs proudly touting their positive farmer impact. Adding insult to injury, the media coverage of the incident was embarrassing to Starbucks because it made them look insensitive to the needs of both farmers and consumers.

Starbucks lost the Columbia University account but learned and evolved quickly. Within months, Starbucks was proactively shipping

Fair Trade coffee to hundreds of its university accounts to get ahead of further activism and account losses. For the fledgling student movement, supported by organizations like Global Exchange and Oxfam America, the victories at UCLA, Columbia, and other colleges led to the formation of the United Students for Fair Trade, whose explicit mission was to build awareness and demand for Fair Trade products on campuses nationwide.

The campus activists at UCLA and Columbia, along with many others around the country, are a great example of the power consumers have to drive change in the ethical sourcing movement. Consumers represent the third key stakeholder of the Fair Trade movement, along with producers and businesses. While all three are equally important for the model to work, consumers are often the engine of growth. In some cases, this has taken the form of applying direct action on behalf of Fair Trade, as with the university students. In others, consumers have become brand ambassadors, helping to raise awareness and build demand by spreading the word. The Lutheran and Catholic churches, for example, have actively supported serving Fair Trade coffee and tea after Sunday service in churches nationwide for many years, building awareness of the simple ways we can all make a difference in the world.

More often, however, the consumer isn't organized or visible. Our understanding of consumers comes from surveys, focus groups, and sales data reflecting purchasing behavior after the fact. "Consumer behavior" is *our* behavior—the sum of all the purchasing decisions, large and small, that we each make on a daily basis. Without a doubt, the impact of expressed consumer preferences and purchasing decisions is huge in shaping corporate decisions around product offerings. This is reflected in the growing market share of products with social and environmental attributes, from organic tomatoes to free-range eggs. It's also reflected in the proliferation of product certifications and labels around issues such as non-GMO, animal welfare, and carbon neutrality. Clearly, consumers increasingly want more information about the food they eat and the products they buy. Conscious consumers, as we now call them, are those of us who want to make sure that the way we shop is not having a negative impact on the planet. We are a segment of the market that has grown dramatically over the last three decades, fueling the accompanying growth of the ethical sourcing movement as a whole. And Corporate America is paying attention.

THE RISE OF THE CONSCIOUS CONSUMER

BEFORE THE 1990S, "CONSCIOUS CONSUMERS" WERE A TINY, NICHE market. Think hippie baby boomers who shopped at food co-ops, boycotted Walmart, and went out of their way to buy the most ethical products possible. These were the diehard consumers who helped get the early ethical sourcing movements, including organics and Fair Trade, off the ground. They were willing to pay more for sustainable products, often sacrificing their own personal preferences—accepting blemishes on their organic apples, buying only the blends of coffee available with Fair Trade labels, and sacrificing stylishness for sweatshop-free apparel.

But over the last three decades, the conscious consumer movement has expanded well beyond its early crusaders. Thanks to pioneering companies like Whole Foods and Patagonia, conscious consumerism has now become fashionable and connected to quality. Sustainable shopping has started to overcome some of its stigmas. Environmentally friendly, ethically sourced, cruelty-free products are no longer associated with lower quality, less choice, and even higher prices. Ethical consumption is going mainstream.

A 2020 consumer survey by the IBM Institute for Business Value and the National Retail Foundation found that three in four consumers say they consider sustainability when choosing between brands. The same study found that 73 percent of consumers indicated traceability of products was important to them (IBM Newsroom, 2020). A 2022 study by Simon-Kucher & Partners that surveyed 11,700 people across nineteen countries found that 89 percent had shifted their purchasing behavior toward more environmentally sustainable products over the past five years. The study also found that the leading reason for the shift cited by those surveyed (64 percent) was a sense of responsibility (Simon-Kucher Newsroom, 2022).

The trend toward more conscious consumption has apparently accelerated since the onset of the Covid pandemic in 2020. A 2020 study by the World Economic Forum found that 86 percent of consumers want more sustainable and equitable products in the post-pandemic world (Russo and Markovitz, 2020). And a 2021 study by the Stifel Institutional Group found that four out of five consumers said they wanted to shop more sustainably, with seven in ten saying that they cared more than they did a year ago (Stifel Institutional Group, 2021).

We've seen a similar growth trajectory in consumer attitudes in our movement. A 2022 study conducted by the Natural Marketing Institute, for example, found that Fair Trade Certified is now the third most recognized sustainability label in the United States behind organic and non-GMO. Sixty-five percent of American consumers recognize the Fair Trade Certified seal (76 percent among Millennials), which is more than double the amount in 2008. One in three shoppers says it influences their purchasing decisions (43 percent among Millennials). This growth in consumer awareness and interest is a big reason why more and more companies are offering Fair Trade Certified products each year across many different categories.

I recently spoke with Michael Pollan, author of *The Omnivore's Dilemma* and a neighbor in my Berkeley, California, community. As he has been one of the world's leading writers on food over the past few decades, I wanted to get his take on the rise of the conscious consumer. "The whole word 'consumer' has a connotation of self-ishness and self-interest," he reflected. "But in the conscious consumer movement, we're combining our identity as consumers with our identity as citizens. That's a very powerful idea."

While Michael believes that conscious consumption alone isn't enough to transform the food system, he was eloquent on the impact it's had. "The phrase, 'voting with your fork' has been very compelling for a lot of people. It has such a positive vibe compared to a lot of other social justice and environmental movements, because there's something you can easily and actively do. So people can feel really good about it." I agree with Michael's take, especially in a world where the problems often seem to outnumber the solutions. In the face of the many challenges we face, conscious consumption gives us a simple, concrete way to help that doesn't cost much time, money, or energy to embrace.

This growing demand for more sustainable products has nudged many companies to get on board with ethical sourcing. Today, the average consumer walking down the aisle of their local grocery store or shopping online is exposed to a wide variety of labels across many different categories. If you're concerned about farmer and worker livelihoods, there are seals like Fair Trade Certified, Fair for Life, and the Equitable Food Initiative. When it comes to environmental certifiers, there are even more: USDA Organic, Rainforest Alliance, Forest Stewardship Council, Marine Stewardship Council, and Green Seal. There are animal welfare organizations, like the Animal Welfare Institute, which certify products as vegan or cruelty-free. And there are general "ethical business" certifiers like B-Corp, which give their seal to companies that meet a broad array of social, environmental, and governance criteria.

Many brands are now seeking product certifications like ours because they see an opportunity to differentiate themselves from their competition and tap into the conscious consumer trend.

Consumer research indicates that most shoppers tend to be skeptical of companies (especially large corporations) making claims of virtuous practices (Fernandes, 2023). This skepticism has led to growing demand for third-party certifications that can independently validate the credibility of corporate claims. And there's money to be made in offering certified products. According to GreenPrint's 2021 Business of Sustainability Index, 64 percent of Gen X consumers said they would spend more on a product from a sustainable brand, and that figure jumps to 75 percent among Millennials (GreenPrint, 2021). Across all studies of the market for sustainable products, Millennial and Gen Z consumers index particularly high in their expectations that companies will do no harm to society and the environment. I believe this gives us a glimpse of our collective future, one in which ethical sourcing and sustainability are the norm, not the exception.

PUSH VERSUS PULL

As profound as all this growth has been, I don't think we can conclude that consumer demand alone is what has driven the shift in corporate behavior. It's more complicated than that. There's a famous quote by the late Steve Jobs about building the Apple brand that, in my experience, also describes this delicate balance between the companies and consumers involved in the ethical sourcing movement: "Some people say, 'Give the customers what they want.' But that's not my approach. Our job is to figure out what they're going to want before they do. I think Henry Ford once said, 'If I'd asked customers what they wanted, they would have told me, "A faster horse!"' People don't know what they want until you show it to them. That's why I never rely on market research. Our task is to read things that are not yet on the page" (Atens, 2021).

Growing consumer demand for ethically sourced products has definitely made companies more interested in partnering with sustainability certifiers or developing in-house programs. But in many cases they're not making those moves because their consumers are actively demanding it. Grocery stores aren't necessarily being inundated with request cards from consumers asking for Fair Trade bananas. Most brands we work with don't come to us after consumers start posting Fair Trade requests on their Instagram pages. Rather, most companies are "reading the tea leaves" of the marketplace, analyzing consumer research, watching their competitors, and anticipating that if they offer ethically sourced products, consumers will reward them for it.

That was the case with GMCR, for example. They made a bet that by adding Fair Trade to their brand promise, they'd be able to differentiate themselves from their competition. They weren't being pulled by consumers to go Fair Trade. But their consumers eventually rewarded them for their decision by buying their Fair Trade coffees in greater quantities once they were available. This "corporate push versus consumer pull" dynamic has been at play in the evolution of the ethical sourcing movement from the very beginning and will continue to shape it moving forward.

FAIR TRADE CAMPUSES, CONGREGATIONS, AND TOWNS

Today, you can get a Fair Trade Certified version of many products, from bamboo bedroom furniture to Nicaraguan rum. But did you know that there are also Fair Trade cities, congregations, and universities? Starting in the small town of Garsang in northern England in 2000, a movement of communities across the United Kingdom began officially declaring themselves as "Fair Trade Towns." The movement soon grew to include other institutions like universities, schools, and congregations, buying Fair Trade products and implementing policies to support the mission.

In 2006, the Fair Trade Towns movement came to the United States, starting with Media, Pennsylvania, just outside Philadelphia, and soon followed by dozens of towns and institutions around the country. In 2008, Fair Trade USA decided to officially sponsor and fund the growth of these local campaigns as a way to spread awareness and build grassroots support. The Fair Trade Campaigns movement has grown steadily ever since. By 2024 there were more than 230 campaigns around the country. They encompass approximately 100 universities, including UCLA, Arizona State University, and the University of Houston; 50 towns, including Chicago, Los Angeles, Milwaukee, and Boston; and numerous schools and congregations from multiple faiths.

SWEATSHOP COFFEE

IMPORTANT PLAYERS IN THE PUSH-PULL DYNAMIC OF FAIR TRADE, especially in the early years, were the activist groups, like the students at Columbia and UCLA, who helped shine a spotlight on the need for ethical sourcing models like ours. Today, Fair Trade is more widely known. (As discussed earlier in the chapter, roughly two-thirds of American consumers recognize our label and have a basic understanding of what it means.) But it wasn't always that way. In the early days after we launched, few people had heard of us, and even fewer understood what we represented. We needed a lot of help to generate a broader understanding of just why Fair Trade was needed for products like coffee. A big piece of this public education came from the activist community.

In the late 1990s and early 2000s, the global coffee community was in crisis. The price fetched by a pound of coffee beans in the international market was depressed for an extended, seven-year period, hovering at or well below $1.00 per pound. The tragic result: millions of already marginalized farmers were forced into poverty. The crisis sparked a massive wave of immigration from Latin American countries into the United States and made front-page headlines in newspapers around the world. Coffee companies were taking a lot of heat for it, especially Starbucks and other emerging specialty coffee brands.

At the time, the anti-sweatshop movement was already popular. Activist organizations like the Worker Rights Consortium, Clean Clothes Campaign, and Global Exchange were running pressure campaigns against companies like Nike and GAP, exposing low wages and deplorable working conditions in the factories from which they sourced their products. But as Deborah James, who was global economy director for Global Exchange at the time, points out, "People weren't making the connection between the coffee they were drinking and the kinds of exploitative labor practices we were seeing in the apparel industry. In those early days, Fair Trade represented a solution without a clearly defined problem, because most people didn't know that coffee farmers were being horribly exploited."

So in the fall of 1999, Deborah spearheaded the "Roast Starbucks" campaign and called for the company to use Fair Trade in every one of their stores. The effort included a petition-signing effort at Starbucks locations around the country and a significant letter-writing initiative. They coined the phrase "sweatshop coffee" to help connect consumers to the grim reality of how their coffee was produced. The campaign connected the dots for the public about the need for Fair Trade, and there was a significant response. By the spring of 2000, days before Global Exchange's planned National Day of Action with coordinated protests at Starbucks locations nationwide, Starbucks decided to partner with us.

But the impact of the activist pressure didn't stop there. Global Exchange sounded the alarm and called on student organizers on college campuses across the United States to launch their own campaigns and get Fair Trade coffee into their university cafés. At the same time, Global Exchange started campaigns against a handful of other companies, pressuring Peet's, Seattle's Best, and Proctor & Gamble to add Fair Trade coffee to their lines.

According to Liam Brody, the coffee and trade program director at Oxfam America in the early 2000s, the "sweatshop coffee" campaign represented a new kind of strategy that focused not just on exposing corporate wrongdoing but also on encouraging a positive alternative that consumers could support. Liam, who has become a brother to me over the years, was responsible for leading the coffee arm of Oxfam's global "Make Trade Fair" campaign. The campaign gave Oxfam, at the time primarily focused on humanitarian relief and development work, a novel market-based solution for addressing global poverty. It represented a shift from boycott to "buy-cott," encouraging supporters to buy more responsible products, which made a big splash, with celebrity partners like Coldplay's Chris Martin helping spread the word. As Liam says, "It represented a sea change, even for an international development organization like Oxfam, because we were promoting purchasing opportunities for people to take direct action and make a difference. It really sparked a transformation in the development community toward embracing enlightened capitalism and social entrepreneurship as a whole new approach."

For Liam, the impact of the campaign went well beyond Starbucks and the other targeted brands. "It was really a rallying cry for everyone to do more—from consumers to governments to brands," he told me recently. "Even though we knew that many major brands might not convert to 100 percent Fair Trade, the simple act of calling for it began to accelerate the shift to a more just, inclusive, and sustainable way of doing business." Those early activist campaigns were instrumental in putting sustainable coffee on the map, building momentum, and bringing more and more companies on board.

The initial pressure from organizers like Deborah and Liam sparked a kind of chain reaction. Liam left Oxfam in 2004 to take a job as director of sustainable coffee at Green Mountain Coffee Roasters. By that time, the landscape had already changed dramatically. As Liam said, "In 2000, there were less than a million pounds of Fair Trade coffee sold in the U.S. But fast-forward a couple of years later, GMCR alone was purchasing over 4 million pounds of certified coffee. The market really took off, and activism played a key role."

To this day, I give those early activists so much credit for helping raise awareness among consumers and companies alike about the need for models like ours to address global poverty. This created an important sense of urgency and a kind of moral imperative that drove real changes in the industry. As with every other aspect of this journey, it has taken collaboration, and sometimes conflict, between different stakeholder groups to help build the ethical sourcing movement.

IT FEELS GOOD TO DO GOOD

IF THE GOAL OF CONSCIOUS CAPITALISM IS TO CREATE SHARED value for all the stakeholders involved, this begs an important question: What's in it for the consumer? The value to producers and businesses is more straightforward. But what value does someone derive from buying an organic cotton T-shirt or non-GMO milk or a Fair Trade Certified chocolate bar? What do consumers get out of the deal?

For some ethically sourced products, particularly organically certified ones, the answer to this question is a little clearer. People often buy organic food because they believe it's healthier. A 2021 study published in the *PLOS One* journal found that perceived health benefits were by far the biggest motivator for consumers to purchase organic products (Gundava and Singh, 2021). But the equation is different when it comes to social sustainability labels like Fair Trade. When a consumer makes a purchase that they know will have a net positive impact on the people and communities that made the product, there's apparently nothing in it for them, materially speaking. It's an act of altruism—of care, compassion, and solidarity. They're often paying a higher price for an ethically sourced product so that someone they've never met and never will meet—the farmer or worker—can have a better life.

This logic, in a sense, flies in the face of traditional notions of consumption. It contradicts Adam Smith's economic theories holding that we are all purely self-interested beings acting only for our own benefit. But in truth, despite all this, consumers often do prefer socially responsible products that benefit others. We can see this in the data laid out thus far in this chapter, not to mention in the growth of the ethical sourcing movement as a whole and the popularity of iconic mission-driven brands like Patagonia, Ben & Jerry's, TOMS shoes, and Warby Parker.

A growing body of research on the neuroscience of altruism and kindness illuminates why we exhibit these behaviors. John Ballatt and Penelope Campling, for example, in their book *Intelligent Kindness: Reforming the Culture of Healthcare*, explore the evidence for the impact that kindness can have on the human brain. Individual acts of kindness, they find, release both endorphins and oxytocin and create new neural connections (Ballatt and Campling, 2011). In other words, it feels good to be kind. Dutch historian Rutger Bregman also writes about this phenomenon in his book *Humankind: A*

Hopeful History, arguing that humans are fundamentally decent and wired to do what they believe is the right thing in their dealings with others (Bregman, 2021).

In 2023, 69 percent of Americans donated to charity. Sixty-three million people in the United States, or 23 percent of the total population, volunteered their time and energy for a nonprofit organization. Almost seven million people donate blood every year in this country, and most will never meet the recipient of their donation (Non-Profit Source, 2024). There is abundant evidence that people care.

This research and data resonates with me. I believe the evidence around the psychological benefit we get when we behave with kindness and caring toward others translates to our behavior as consumers. When we buy products that seem more ethical or good for the world, we feel good about ourselves. We feel a sense of purpose, connection, and belonging. These are powerful emotional needs that are increasingly motivating us as consumers to seek products that resonate with our values and how we want to perceive ourselves.

At this point, I can hear the pessimist in me saying, "That's bullshit." Or wishful thinking, at best. Skeptics might suggest that altruism and kindness are optional behaviors that will always yield to self-interest. They might dismiss ethical purchases as a kind of emotional salve that privileged people occasionally use to ease their guilty consciences. Because they're harder to measure, the emotional benefits of conscious consumerism are still not well understood. But to deny these benefits ignores something brands and corporate marketers have long known: psychological benefits matter. Feeling good about ourselves is an important factor motivating many of our purchasing decisions, far beyond the realm of sustainability.

Think about how companies advertise cars, apparel, cosmetics, and smartphones to us. It's all about status, beauty, excitement, or coolness. These are all psychological benefits. So when we buy things, we're acquiring more than just their physical product features and functionalities. We're also getting a lot of intangibles and an array of emotional benefits that actually may be as important as the tangible product features themselves.

I believe it's the same with ethically sourced products. When you buy a bag of coffee that you know was grown by farmers who were paid fairly for their work and were able to keep their kids in school, you get a little hit of goodness. When you buy a pair of jeans sewn in a factory where you know workers had safe working conditions and were treated well, you get an ego boost for being a "good person." You may also feel more empowered to do something about the many problems in the world that matter to you. The simple truth is that feeling good about our purchases can help us feel good about ourselves—and that benefit can be a powerful motivator.

In a 2021 United Kingdom–based study published in the *Social Policy and Administration* journal, a team of researchers from the London School of Economics found that consumers reported significant benefits from purchasing Fair Trade products. In particular, they talked about the benefit "resulting from the feeling of doing the right thing" as one of the main reasons they purchased Fair Trade items. In fact, the more they had to "sacrifice," in terms of paying extra for Fair Trade products, the greater the emotional benefit they expressed. From all of this, the researchers concluded what conscious capitalists all intuitively know: "Market transactions can no longer be construed simply as private actions for reciprocal private gain; the transaction is imbued, at least for the ethical consumer, with some objective of public or social benefit" (Le Grand, Roberts, and Chandra, 2021).

I posed this question about the value consumers derive from altruistic purchasing to my friend Tristan Lecomte, founder of Alter Eco (a pioneer of Fair Trade products in France) and Pur Projet, an international reforestation and sustainable-development company. Tristan, who has built a career on understanding the motives of conscious consumers, was quite eloquent on the point. "When you buy

Fair Trade products or plant a tree or do something good for your community, you can really feel this heartwarming effect. There's a sense of pride inside of you. I think Fair Trade opens consumers up to a window of compassion for other people within the supply chain. It's really a call for solidarity, compassion, and caring for others. To be Fair Trade is to touch people's hearts and make them resonate deeply with the products they buy."

Tristan also pointed to research showing the neurological benefits of altruism. For example, research done by the Mind and Life Institute, co-founded by the Dalai Lama, has found that the centers of the brain that light up for feelings of compassion are also responsible for happiness. In other words, practicing compassion might literally make us happier. A team of researchers at the University of Georgia published a study in 2016 mapping the neurological effects of altruistic behavior. They found that "altruistic behaviors engage many different parts of the brain, proof that such actions have tangible and measurable effects on our psyche." Specifically, the study found "that engaging in altruistic behavior has both psychological and physical benefits, including easement of anxiety/depression, self-reported improvement in general well-being, and lower likelihood of developing serious illness" (Filkowski, Cochran, and Haas, 2016).

All of this research makes sense. Human beings aren't instinctually "lone wolves"; nor are we independent agents acting solely out of self-interest all the time. We are wired for connection. We evolved in families, tribes, and communities. In our modern lives, we continue to be deeply involved in complex social and cultural networks. Yet, in our globalized economy, we often lack a direct connection with many of the basic ingredients of our lives. Think about it. Go to the kitchen and open up your refrigerator. Do you know where the food in front of you was grown or who grew it?

One of the most powerful elements of buying ethically sourced products is that it gives us a chance to connect with the source and story of so many objects in our lives. Retailers know this. It's why many produce sections in grocery stores today now have pictures of farmers. Or why there has been an explosion of interest in farmers' markets around the United States over the past quarter century. Many of us yearn to be connected to the source of our food or our clothing. We want to know more about the real people that make our products. We would like to think that we have helped make their lives better or at least done them no harm through our purchase.

I posed this question to Michael Pollan about the value we derive from connecting with the people who grow our food.

Narrative changes everything for people. They want to know the story behind how their food is produced. In most cases, they can't meet the farmer. We now have a very long, opaque food chain. Making it more transparent feels good. It's less anonymous. We've lost track of who the people are on the other end of the chain, because they're so far away. In an era where we don't have a lot of time, and with this huge distance between us, labels like Fair Trade and organic represent a helpful substitute when we lack a direct connection to our farmer. We rely on these organizations to guarantee that we're getting what the label says we're getting. So it's a storytelling medium as much as anything, and people will pay for a good story, especially around their food.

Of course, products with ethical certifications like Fair Trade can't perfectly fulfill this desire for connection. They are, as Michael suggests, a substitute for a more direct connection. But they help move us in that direction. They make us at least think for a brief moment about the people across the supply chains that bring products into our lives. They add faces, real or imagined, to the often faceless system of global commerce. This is a real, emotional benefit to consumers, one that more and more of us are seeking.

EMPOWERING WOMEN

While the plight of the average smallholder farmer around the world is dire, it's particularly bad for women. In many agricultural communities, women and girls are often treated as second-class citizens. They have fewer job opportunities than their male counterparts, and most end up dropping out of school at a young age. They have less access to capital, because their names are often not on the deeds of their farmland, and they therefore have no collateral. Most have limited prospects for improving their lives.

A wealth of research shows that dealing with global poverty must include empowering women and girls. That's why our movement has always made gender equity a priority. Fair Trade standards are designed to prevent gender discrimination, increase female participation in producer organizations, and empower more women to access the benefits of Fair Trade. We require that the elected leadership of producer organizations reflect the gender balance of the membership; in most of our certified groups, 30 to 40 percent of the board or Fair Trade committee members are women. Most Fair Trade producer groups also offer credit, savings, and training programs aimed specifically at helping women achieve greater economic independence. With income comes greater independence and a voice in the local community.

On a personal note, I'm incredibly proud that PRO-DECOOP, the Fair Trade coffee cooperative I started in Nicaragua, has been very successfully led by Nicaraguan women ever since I left in 1994.

QUALITY AND PRICE ARE KING?

IMAGINE WALKING DOWN THE COFFEE AISLE OF YOUR LOCAL GRO-cery store and surveying all the different options before you. What are you looking for? What kind of roast do you prefer: dark, light, or medium? Is there a particular origin whose flavor profile you like? Are you a fan of Kenyan coffees or Colombian? Do you have a particular affinity for a local roaster, or do you prefer a major brand like Starbucks or Folgers? How important is the price?

When we shop, each of us has our own personal calculus for making decisions. Everyone prioritizes their criteria differently, and our preferences can shift from one day to the next. For some, quality is most important. For others, it's price. Many care most about other product features like origin or style. For a growing number of consumers, things like organic and other sustainability certifications are crucial.

Yet even the most educated, responsible shopper is unlikely to buy the most sustainable option on every trip to the store. There are many reasons for this. One of the biggest is price. Even though a lot of research indicates that consumers will pay more for sustainability, there's still the question of how much more. There's also the issue of availability. Most people won't make a special trip to another store to buy a sustainable brand, so it must be convenient and available at the stores where people normally shop.

As industry pioneer Seth Goldman, founder of Honest Tea and Just Ice Tea, said to me, "Fair Trade and other sustainability labels are often tiebreakers for consumers. When given the choice between two otherwise equal options, most will choose the one with a sustainability seal. But the key here is giving the consumer options." For example, if you're a fan of Darjeeling tea but can't find one with a sustainability seal on it, you may still go with that origin because your flavor preference is what's most important to you.

Then there's the issue of quality. This was particularly challenging for us in the early years, when a stigma associated with Fair Trade coffees suggested they were of lower quality. I have to admit that some of this lower-quality reputation was deserved. Some of the farmers we worked with were so poor and marginalized that they didn't always deliver the best-quality product. It makes sense. If you're a farmer struggling to put food on the table, you're not going to have the resources to invest in growing the highest-quality crop. Fair or not, we took the criticism seriously.

Quality is everything in the coffee industry. The world of specialty coffee roasters tends to be very elite. Roasters take a lot of pride in their craft and work hard to develop the "perfect" blends using just the right combination of coffees, often sourced from different regions around the world. The more we could familiarize our farmers with the specific flavor profiles that roasters were looking for in their final product, the better equipped they would be to deliver the quality the market was after. So, in the mid-2000s, we deployed our fundraising team to raise millions of dollars to invest in farmer education and infrastructure. These funds were used to train farmers in better cultivation techniques such as harvesting only ripe red coffee cherries. Training and on-farm infrastructure improvements helped farmers adopt proper de-pulping, washing, and fermentation techniques as well as effective drying and storage. All these efforts improved the final quality and value of their coffees.

We also joined forces with other international development organizations and helped co-ops in Africa and Latin America build "cupping laboratories." This was simple, low-cost infrastructure where they could sample their coffee in real time and learn to discern the different flavor profiles and qualities required by the market. Typically, someone from the community would get trained as a professional "coffee cupper" and work in the co-op's cupping lab, managing quality control for all the coffee they grew and sold. These were sought-after positions within the co-op, and it was often the young women in the community—the bright, promising daughters of coffee farmers—who ended up winning them. They went through rigorous training and often went on to earn their "Q-grader" certificate, essentially a certification of their taste buds. We would organize annual buyer trips to visit the cooperatives, giving them a chance to cup different coffees together and "calibrate" their assessments. All this helped improve the co-ops' ability to train their farmers around the importance of quality. And, without a doubt, by developing the capacity to taste and score their own products, the co-ops dramatically increased their market power and revenue. Before, they were selling blind. Now, they could negotiate better prices and capture the full value of their investment in quality.

We wanted to make sure that the improvements in the quality of our farmers' coffee also led to a better reputation throughout the coffee world. So we encouraged our farmers to enter every quality competition they could. These events, attended by many of the leading roasters and coffee luminaries, provided a great opportunity for us to combat the stigma associated with our coffees. The most widely known series of competitions is the Cup of Excellence. Each major coffee-growing country hosts the contest each year, with expert jurors providing blind cupping evaluations and ratings of samples from thousands of producers. The winners are publicized online, in an online auction, and in the coffee trade magazines. Within a few years of entering these competitions, Fair Trade producers started to consistently win or place in the top five. It took a long time—the better part of a decade—but eventually we were able to transform our reputation for "low quality" in the coffee world. We were able to deliver on GMCR's promise of "Better Coffee for a Better World."

But as much progress as we've made—in coffee and other product categories—there's still a long way to go. In the attempt to bring ethically sourced products to the mainstream, we continue to face a complex set of purchasing criteria. We continue to be a "tiebreaker" for many people. So in order to grow in the marketplace, we need to also address consumers' other priorities. We need to strive to make sustainable products more affordable. We need to expand the variety, style, functionality, and convenience so consumers don't have to make a big sacrifice for sustainability.

Of course, I believe that conscious consumerism will continue to rise. The data, as we've discussed, is clear on this. Sustainability will continue to become more and more of a priority for companies and consumers. But for ethically sourced, sustainable products to become the norm and not just a market niche, we can't ask consumers to make a big personal sacrifice to buy these products. We must make sustainable products more competitive on quality, price, variety, and availability. The "tiebreaker choice" must be effortless.

GREENWASH AT YOUR OWN RISK

No conversation about consumers is complete without a discussion of the phenomenon of "greenwashing." The term was originally coined by environmental activist Jay Westerveld in a 1986 essay about the hotel industry. While the word "green" implies a focus primarily on environmental issues, the term "greenwashing" is applied broadly across a range of sustainability claims. Simply put, a company is accused of greenwashing when it makes claims about the social or environmental impact of its practices or products that are either unfounded or overblown (Edwards, 2024).

Thanks in large part to the rise in activism and conscious consumerism, there's never been more public scrutiny of a company's sustainability initiatives than there is today. According to Athleta founder Scott Kerslake, "So many companies are now 'virtue signaling' around sustainability and using the term so loosely that customers are getting smarter." There's data to back up Scott's comment. GreenPrint's 2021 Business Sustainability Index found that 53 percent of Americans "sometimes" or "never" believe companies' environmental claims (GreenPrint, 2021).

This is especially important to the younger generations, for whom authenticity is of the utmost importance. Generation Z consumers in particular have a strong sensitivity to overclaiming and "performative" behavior. They gravitate toward brands that they perceive as sincere about who they are and what they do, and they move away from brands that aren't. They don't necessarily expect companies to be perfect bastions of sustainability, but they do demand honesty. I believe the companies that will thrive in this environment will be those who strike the right tone about their sustainability claims, educating consumers with accuracy, humility, and authenticity.

I see greenwashing and corporate misinformation as serious threats to our progress. But it's also a kind of "success problem" of activism and conscious consumerism. As we've discussed in this chapter, there's greater demand for sustainability among the general public than ever, and with it comes more pressure on companies to perform. In many cases, the business community has met this demand with sincere and impactful sustainability initiatives, like implementing models of ethical sourcing to clean up their supply chains. In other cases, their efforts have been halfhearted at best or even deliberately fraudulent. But the very fact that companies feel like they're on the hook to do something about sustainability is an indication of the growing power of our movement. No longer can companies simply stand on the sidelines and admit that they don't care about the impact of their practices. In the information age, there's more transparency and accountability than ever, and consumers are often quick to penalize companies for indifference.

According to a study by the *Harvard Business Review*, consumers respond "harshly" to companies that fail to meet their stated social responsibility goals (Ioannou, Kassinis, and Papagiannakis, 2022). Some of this has to do with perception, and consumer criticisms may not always be fully warranted. But many greenwashing claims are deserved. A 2021 study conducted in the European Union, for example, found that 42 percent of green claims were "exaggerated, false, or deceptive" (European Commission, 2021). Whether real or imagined, greenwashing is becoming a bigger issue for the business world. BlackRock, United Airlines, Phillips 66, and other big companies are increasingly warning investors about risks from more scrutiny of their claims of sustainability. According to a Bloomberg Law study, at least fourteen major S&P 500 companies cited greenwashing as a business risk factor in their 2023 annual reports, up from only five in 2022 (Ramonas, 2023).

We obviously take accountability seriously. It's a big part of our own brand promise. Through our annual auditing practices, we make every effort to ensure that the supply chains of companies wearing our Fair Trade Certified label are in compliance with our rigorous standards. We are also proud members of the International Social & Environmental Accreditation & Labelling (ISEAL) Alliance, the global standard and oversight body for independent sustainability certifications like ours. ISEAL's Codes of Good Practice provide a globally recognized framework defining best practices for credible sustainability systems. As ISEAL community members, we commit to continually improving our standards, certification, and impact evaluation systems through participation in ISEAL's learning, collaboration, and innovation programs.

In our commercial relationships, we put a lot of emphasis on clarity and truth in advertising. We don't want brands that use our seal to misrepresent its meaning. That's why we only allow companies to put our label on the specific products that meet our standards. Further, we have a clause in all our contracts with brands and retailers giving us the right to approve or reject their advertising, packaging, press releases, and online content related to Fair Trade. When they send us copy for approval, if we feel they've exaggerated their impact or commitment, we make them fix it. That said, it's a pretty rare mistake among our industry partners; most are extra careful and accurate in the way they advertise their Fair Trade products.

While I think that greenwashing is and will continue to be a crucial issue in the ethical sourcing movement as a whole, I've found that greenwashing accusations can often be misapplied. In fact, over the years, some critics have mistakenly called our Fair Trade label a form of greenwashing. For example, as discussed in Chapter 2, some have suggested that if a company is only committing a small percentage of their supply chain to Fair Trade, then inherently they are using our label as a form of greenwashing. Whole Foods has been similarly criticized for not exclusively selling organic produce. The argument, as we've discussed, is that these companies have no intention of truly transforming their supply chains. They just want to engage in the minimum activity necessary to create a kind of "halo effect" that shines a more sustainable light over their entire brand.

But can we really call this greenwashing? I think not. We've found over the years that it's crucial to allow our industry partners to start small, dipping their toes in the water, to see if our model works for them. These initial tests have often grown into something much more significant and impactful. To me, greenwashing occurs when a company misrepresents their commitment to sustainability. They make big claims without backing them up. But in my experience, the companies that only do the minimum don't tend to make big claims. In fact, many companies know that overexaggerating their commitment to Fair Trade would likely bring about public criticism and shaming, which they want to avoid.

Take Peet's Coffee, for example. After certifying a single coffee blend with us in 2001 in response to activist pressure, they haven't grown their Fair Trade coffee offering in over twenty years. One could speculate about their motives. Perhaps they cynically did only the minimum effort to keep the activists away. Or perhaps they found other sustainability partners that better meet their needs. Importantly in this context, however, Peet's hasn't done anything to make themselves appear more committed to Fair Trade than they are. Our label is not part of any of their advertising or branding, in stores or on packaging. In fact, my guess is that most Peet's consumers today have no idea that the company has any Fair Trade coffee at all. Of course, I'm disappointed that after all these years, we haven't been able to do more with Peet's. But I don't think it's greenwashing, just a missed opportunity.

THE END OF CONSCIOUS CONSUMERISM?

"IN THE NEXT GENERATION, THERE WILL BE NO SUCH THING AS A conscious consumer."

The statement took me aback, especially considering who made it. Guillaume Le Cunff is the CEO of Nespresso and a longtime friend and partner. He was speaking to me via Zoom from his office on the shores of Lake Geneva in Switzerland, where the global specialty coffee company has its headquarters. I asked him to explain his prediction.

"I recently had an 'a-ha' moment during a meeting with a group of MBA students," he recounted. "We were discussing the importance of sustainability in the purchasing decisions of their generation— namely Gen Z—and their perspective was illuminating."

Guillaume, who is both brilliant and eloquent, paused for a moment, as if still unpacking the philosophical consequences of his "a-ha." "We built Nespresso's brand based on delivering customers an emotional experience. It's a moment of indulgence with their coffee, a treat. It's a 'me' moment, essentially a one-way street. But that's no longer enough for this generation. They now see the brand experience as a two-way street. The 'feel good moment' now requires that you're also giving something back. It has to include an impact moment. For them, the value in a cup of coffee is 50 percent what's in the cup and 50 percent what's happening outside of the cup."

I could relate to Guillaume's perspective, and not just because of my reading of the research. My son Emiliano is a Millennial, and my daughter Camila is the quintessential Gen Z-er. They have grown up in the conscious consumption era and reflect many of the attitudes of their generation. I love talking about these issues with them, and I always learn a lot from their perspectives. In essence, the transparency created by technology and the internet has made young people the most informed consumers in history. As such, for many of them, sustainability isn't an added bonus. It's a baseline expectation.

"Sustainability is no longer a preference," Guillaume continued. "It's a decision tree. If you don't include it in your brand promise, they won't buy it. They'll no longer be your customer. They'll simply move on. End of story. Sustainability has become the new standard for their generation."

Guillaume admitted that his epiphany wasn't yet completely confirmed by consumer research. It was a hunch based on a combination of his interactions with the MBA cohort and his years of experience in the industry. But it was a deeply educated opinion, and one that got me thinking. Could we truly reach a point in the future where sustainability is the requirement and expectation of all consumers?

It's plausible that many corporate sustainability practices that are today optional may tomorrow be required by law. Already in the European Union we're seeing legislation obliging larger firms to integrate human rights and environmental impact into their management systems. The new laws on corporate sustainability set obligations for companies to reduce their negative impact on human rights and the environment, such as child labor, slavery, pollution, and deforestation. Companies will soon have to integrate "sustainability due diligence" into their policies and risk-management systems, including publicly available descriptions of their approach, processes, and code of conduct (European Parliament, 2023). We will see how such policy initiatives unfold in the years ahead and how long it takes for the United States to follow suit.

In the meantime, it's clear to me that voluntary, market-based approaches to sustainability will continue to be our greatest hope for scalable solutions to the social and environmental challenges of our time. In this theory of change, consumers will continue to play a critical role, now and for the foreseeable future. Whether it's organized students demanding sustainable food choices on campus or the micro decisions we all make each time we shop, I'm convinced that consumers have more power than they know to bend the arc of the global economy toward justice.

4

FAIR TRADE FOR ALL

SANTIAGO'S SON IS A FARMWORKER

ONE OF THE MOST REWARDING ASPECTS OF THE WORK I DO IS GOING to the field and visiting the farmers and workers who grow and make Fair Trade products. The context for these visits varies. Sometimes I'm leading a group of business leaders like Greg Spragg from Sam's Club or Ron Rankin (one of our most generous philanthropic supporters) on a tour of the farms and factories so they can see for themselves the impact our work has on the lives of so many people. Other times, I'm taking a side trip to visit an old friend among the many producers I've gotten to know over the years. These visits always reconnect me with the heart and soul of the Fair Trade mission. I get a chance to rediscover my own passion and sense of purpose.

During one of these field trips back in 2008, I had an experience that, in many ways, shaped my perspective on the future of our movement. I was leading a tour for a group of coffee company representatives at my old pal Santiago Rivera's finca in the northern Nicaraguan highlands. After the tour concluded and my colleagues departed, Santiago and I had some time to catch up. It was a balmy December afternoon, and we headed back to his rustic clay-and-wood home nestled in the forested village surrounded by the coffee fields where he and his fellow farmers had their plots. We sat on his front porch and watched the sun set, sipping black coffee made of the beans his wife Hermelinda roasted and ground for us with her own hands. The enormous trees above us were full of brightly colored orchids and tropical birds paying homage to the sinking sun with songs so elaborate they sounded as if scored by human composers.

As we were getting to the bottom of our cups, a familiar face appeared from around the corner of the house. It was Santiago's youngest son, Armando, now in his late teens and looking more like a grown man than the boy I remembered from past visits. He greeted me with a big hug, and we got to chatting about what had happened in each of our lives since we last saw each other. Unlike his sister Yolanda, Armando hadn't chosen the schooling route. He had dropped out when he was sixteen. I could tell by his clothes that he had followed in his father's footsteps, laboring in the fields. When I asked him if he was working with his father, he fell silent. Both he and Santiago exchanged a look. I was confused, so I asked him to explain.

They told me that Armando wasn't able to work with his father. Santiago's oldest son, Mercedes, was already working on the farm, and the operation wasn't big enough to support both sons. So Armando had to find work elsewhere. He didn't have the resources to buy land and had few other prospects for work in the area, so his best chance to earn a living was to apply his lifetime of training as a "coffee kid" to someone else's operation—a large coffee estate nearby. He and his fellow farmworkers were earning roughly $3 per day working for someone else and had little hope for a better future. While the Riveras had benefited significantly from the premiums their Fair Trade coffee had brought to their family, it wasn't enough to change their fortunes overnight. Times remained tough in the region, and many young people like Armando needed a job—whatever job they could find.

This hit me pretty hard. I had hoped that the kinds of Fair Trade programs we'd implemented in the region would be a bigger help to the next generation of coffee kids. The long-term goal of Fair Trade is to help break the chains of generational poverty so that farmers and their children can, over time, build a better life. Sadly, I knew there wasn't much we could do to help someone in Armando's position. As I discussed earlier in the book, large estates like the one he was working on were historically excluded from Fair Trade certification by the farm-size limitations in our standards, which meant he couldn't enjoy the benefits his father had. We couldn't provide the same modest-yet-important Fair Trade premiums that small farm owners received to the hired farmworkers who made the large estates run.

We had, in essence, created a divide between farmers and farmworkers. Ironically, the latter group arguably needed our help the most. Farmworkers were both cash and land poor. They didn't even have the buffer of owning their own land and growing some of their own food, like Santiago did. They were truly the most marginalized members of rural society. Armando's circumstances were far from unique. In many of the villages around the world where Fair Trade products are grown, much of the population still works as day laborers on large farms. In fact, only an estimated 10 percent of the world's coffee is grown on farms that meet our basic Fair Trade requirements: that they be less than ten acres in size and part of a formal cooperative. We had, in the early days of the movement, kept large estates out of the model in order to level the playing field and give the small farmer a fighting chance to compete in the global marketplace. But it was becoming painfully clear with the passage of time that our approach was systematically excluding the poorest of the poor.

If the goal is to break the cycle of generational poverty within producer communities around the world, how could we, in good conscience, exclude the majority of them from our model? In my mind, our mission was calling us to open our doors to farmworkers like Armando in order to create more value, drive more impact, and become more inclusive.

TIME TO SCALE

MY EXPERIENCE WITH ARMANDO CAME DURING AN INTERESTING time for Fair Trade USA and underscored a desire to expand the model that had been growing for years. Since our inception in 1998, we'd accomplished a great deal. We'd certified nearly a half billion pounds of coffee in our first decade. We were certifying farms in over seventy countries and, by our estimations, had touched the lives of over one million farmers. Through all of this, we'd achieved a huge socioeconomic impact, cumulatively generating over $125 million in Fair Trade premiums for producer communities by 2008. On the market side, we'd also grown significantly. The Fair Trade Certified label was recognized by 35 percent of US consumers and adorned products in over 200,000 retail stores across North America.

We'd also received a lot of public recognition for our efforts, particularly in the area of social innovation. First, in 2000 I received the Ashoka Fellowship, which elevates promising, early-stage social entrepreneurs. Then, the Schwab Foundation for Social Entrepreneurship, sister organization to the World Economic Forum, named me one of the world's Outstanding Social Entrepreneurs in 2001 "for pioneering systemic solutions to global poverty" and invited me to speak at the forum's annual meeting in Davos, Switzerland. A few years later, I received from Jeff Skoll and the Skoll Foundation their Award for Social Entrepreneurship, which came with a much-needed $1 million prize to support our work. *Fast Company* magazine honored me with its "Social Capitalist" award four years in a row (2005–2008) and even put me on the cover of its January 2007 issue. Fair Trade USA and I continued to receive recognition over the years. We got press attention from places like the *Washington Post*, *Wall Street Journal*, Fox Business, and CNN. Each time I or the organization get recognized in this way, I feel pride and gratitude for the work we've done together but also a sense that it means something for the cause. A few minutes of airtime on a network like that could feel to viewers like a small thing, but to me it's a payoff for years of hard work by the incredible team at Fair Trade USA.

Yet, despite all this growth and recognition, I also felt a kind of healthy dissatisfaction with our progress. Sure, we were certifying a significant volume of coffee, but it still only accounted for less than 5 percent of the US market. And coffee was by far our biggest product. We had entered new product categories as well, including fresh produce, flowers, cocoa, tea, and even sugar. But those programs were fledgling. We had even partnered with some big mainstream brands, like Dunkin' Donuts, Ben & Jerry's, PepsiCo, and Dole. But we remained mostly a label for specialty products aimed at only the most educated conscious consumer. It was starting to feel too small.

My vision for Fair Trade has always been to transform capitalism. I never subscribed to the "small is beautiful" mentality, and I never wanted to remain a market niche. I've always seen the potential to grow our model and have a meaningful impact on global poverty. For me, it's always been about the mission, about reaching as many people and improving as many lives as possible. I want to transform how companies do business in such a way that they can no longer take the well-being of farmers and workers in their supply chains for granted. I want the world's consumers to think about who produces the goods they buy on a daily basis and help ensure they are compensated fairly for their hard work. I want to help empower producers and communities around the world, improving their lives and giving them hope for their future. In order to achieve a dream as big and impactful as that, I knew that we would need to take our Fair Trade model to scale, making it a case study of successful systems change and a catalyst for scale in the broader ethical sourcing movement. In order to do that, we would need to make the necessary adjustments to make it scalable.

Our attempt to get all of Starbucks' business happened soon after my visit with Santiago and Armando. In a very real and personal way, both experiences strengthened my resolve to make our model more inclusive. As I laid out in the opening story of this book, our failure to land the Starbucks deal was rooted in part in our inability to evolve the Fair Trade model. The members of our international umbrella organization, Fairtrade Labeling Organizations (FLO), were unwilling to expand the standards to allow farmworkers on larger farms (and small farms that weren't part of co-ops) into the Fair Trade fold. Such a shift was perceived as too big a threat to the organized smallholders and cooperatives that we had always championed. Starbucks was unwilling to adapt to our existing standards, and FLO was unwilling to evolve in order to achieve the kind of breakthrough scale that a partnership like that would enable.

I believed, and still believe, that FLO was wrong. Since the beginning, both a mission and a market logic have guided every strategic decision we've made at Fair Trade USA. It was becoming crystal clear to me and my colleagues that there was now a strong mission and market motive for expanding the model. On the mission side, refusing to allow large farms and those that weren't already affiliated with co-ops to be certified as Fair Trade was putting us on moral thin ice. In our quest to protect small farmer cooperatives, we were ignoring the poorest of the poor—farmworkers like Armando, who made up the majority of the labor within the world's supply chains not only for coffee but for many other products as well. On the market side, it was becoming increasingly obvious that our unwillingness to expand the model was also compromising our potential for growth. If companies like Starbucks couldn't certify their entire supply chains, there would always be a hard cap on our growth. This would make working with larger companies and going mainstream almost impossible.

So we decided to try, yet again, to negotiate with FLO and other stakeholders in hopes of expanding the model. Over the course of several years, we had a series of meetings to try to reconcile the competing perspectives and reach some kind of common ground. I still remember the words of my dear friend, Merling Preza, who succeeded me as general manager of PRODECOOP back in the early 1990s. "Brother," she said at a gathering of the FLO board, "you're dead wrong on this one. If we let plantations into the system, our cooperatives are doomed. Fair Trade is for smallholders. The farmworkers are someone else's problem."

These gatherings failed to help us reconcile our differences, which went beyond strategy and technical considerations and increasingly reflected a deeper, more ideological division. It began to feel like we were fighting over the very soul of our cause. And my colleagues and I were starting to see that it was time for a bold move.

This was a challenging period for me. I had many conversations with trusted friends, partners, and board members about how to bridge what was becoming an insurmountable gap between Fair Trade USA and FLO. I remember one particularly impactful conversation with my friend and mentor John Mackey, co-founder of Whole Foods. During a hike in the redwoods of Marin County, I described the pushback I was getting about opening up the standards to include more types of producers. John and Whole Foods have been some of our biggest supporters over the years, and he shared my frustration with the unwillingness of many within the Fair Trade movement to embrace a bigger vision. At one point, he turned to me and said, "Fair Trade should be for everybody. Fair Trade is a universal set of standards for labor and the environment and some economic mechanisms to ensure that the trade between the different parties is fair. If any given corporation or producer is willing to play by those rules, then why shouldn't they be allowed?"

He had a point, of course—one that I understood deeply and that was reflected back to me through many conversations with people like John. What mattered most, to me, was our social impact—not the size of the producers we worked with or whether they were part of a co-op. The more farmers and farmworkers we included in the model, the more lives we could improve with our impact. But my colleagues at FLO and many of the producer co-ops themselves just didn't agree with this perspective. I remember John saying to me at one point, "If you can't persuade them, break away and do your own thing. If you don't, you run the risk of losing your relevance."

He was right. I believed the evolution of the conscious capitalism movement was trending toward more inclusion and mainstream participation—of producers and companies. I also believed our value and credibility within this broader movement—as an independent third-party certifier of ethical practices—were at risk if we continued with such a limited scope of beneficiaries. It was like we'd doubled down on a protectionist model aimed at shoring up the co-ops at the expense of everyone else in the village. For an organization like ours, deeply committed to social justice and "walking the talk," this felt dangerously close to hypocrisy. I feared that our window of opportunity for greater relevance and impact would close and that organizations with lower standards would step in to capture the growing corporate demand for ethical sourcing programs.

So we decided to split from FLO (now called Fairtrade International). Notably, FLO is a membership organization of independent nonprofits, like ours, with their own boards, governance structures, and customer bases. FLO has also brought producer representatives into its governance structure. FLO members all agree to adhere to the same standards and share key functions, including auditing and certification, but they are distinct entities. In our case, we've always had independent legal status as a US nonprofit corporation, our own board, certification label, and funding base, and hundreds of contractual relationships with US companies. We had built the US Fair Trade market and movement with very little support from FLO and the European Fair Traders. So splitting off was easier than one might expect. In 2011, we formally resigned our FLO membership, and to elevate our new direction, we announced our bold vision for the future: Fair Trade for All.

THE ROAD TO $500 MILLION

THE SPLIT WITH FLO WAS DIFFICULT FOR BOTH ME, PERSONALLY, and for our organization. There were lots of logistics to work out and lots of criticisms hurled our way. But as we developed our plan to move forward independently, we began to see how the shift could give birth to a whole new chapter in the Fair Trade movement with much greater impact for far more families around the world. We began setting some bold goals: within five years, we aimed to create $500 million in cumulative financial impact for producers, roughly triple what we'd achieved in our first decade. This would require a dramatic increase in the overall sales of Fair Trade Certified products. To accomplish this ambitious goal, we rolled up our sleeves, took advantage of our newly won freedom to innovate, and started to make some serious changes.

First off, we would need to create new standards for larger farms that helped make sure their workers had better conditions, wages, and premiums. By including bigger farms, we could encompass more of the industry's existing supply chains and product formulations. In time, this would make it easier for more and larger companies to work within the Fair Trade ecosystem.

Second, we would need to allow and offer certification to small farmers who weren't part of cooperatives but were selling to processors, traders, and other aggregators. This would allow us to expand our mission of supporting more and more of the 500 million smallholder farmers throughout the world, whether they were in a co-op or not.

Third, we would need to continue to adapt our standards to fit other industries, like seafood, apparel, and produce, where the dynamics are quite different than for coffee, tea, and chocolate. By doing this, we could give consumers more ways to find and support our label. We dreamed of the day when consumers could buy not only our certified coffee and other core products but eventually Fair Trade salmon, yogurt, furniture, and blue jeans. Our vision was to create a kind of "Fair Trade lifestyle" that gave consumers an option to buy a certified product on every aisle, in every store.

We also took the opportunity to develop and strengthen our own infrastructure. We raised $25 million in philanthropic support from a variety of foundations, including an incredibly generous $11 million personal donation from Green Mountain Coffee Roasters' Bob Stiller and his wife, Christine. We viewed these funds as "venture philanthropy" and used them to build out our programs for impact at scale. For example, we expanded our training programs to help farmers improve their productivity and quality. We invested a significant amount in consumer-education campaigns, helping to grow the overall demand for Fair Trade products. We also started developing better mechanisms for tracking our impact, so that our industry partners had greater transparency in their supply chains and could better communicate the value of Fair Trade to their stakeholders.

The years following the launch of Fair Trade for All in 2011 were a thrilling time at Fair Trade USA. We were standing on the shoulders of what we and others had done up to that point and leaning ambitiously forward into what we hoped would be a high-growth future. But it wasn't all fun and games. Not surprisingly, we also received criticism from the traditional wing of the Fair Trade community, which didn't agree with our decision to split from FLO and expand the model.

THE BRAWL

ONE OF THE MOST VOCAL CRITICS OF OUR NEW DIRECTION WAS ONE of our oldest partners, Equal Exchange. As you may recall from Chapter 1, the company and their co-founder, Jonathan Rosenthal, helped me get my start with Fair Trade back in Nicaragua in 1990. So when they turned against us publicly, it hurt.

In the spring of 2012, not long after our split with FLO, Equal Exchange ran a full-page ad in the *Burlington Free Press* going after Green Mountain Coffee Roasters (GMCR). The ad included an open letter to GMCR with the following message: "We wish to congratulate you for your past deeds, but we now urgently request that you withdraw your support for the certification agency Fair Trade USA" (Sherman, 2012). Ironically, for all their scathing criticism of our new direction, Equal Exchange never stopped using our certification, and some of their coffees carry our label to this day. Fortunately, GMCR was a public supporter of Fair Trade for All and our staunch ally, so, if anything, the criticism only served to strengthen our relationship with them.

Companies like Equal Exchange weren't the only ones to attack our new direction. FLO established a new affiliate in the United States, called Fairtrade America, whose strategy was simply to go after our industry partners and try to convince them that we were no longer credible because we had left the FLO system. Their efforts weren't very effective, but they were able to pull away a handful of companies, including Starbucks, Ben & Jerry's, and Wholesome Sweeteners (which later came back to us). Emotions have cooled in the decade plus since the "divorce," but you can still see evidence of it on your grocery shelves today. While about 90 percent of Fair Trade products in the United States bear our little green-and-black Fair Trade Certified label, you'll still find a few here and there with the green-and-blue label of FLO. While this may seem confusing, from my perspective competition is a good thing. No single organization should have a monopoly on Fair Trade standards and sourcing. In fact, the overall growth of sustainability labels in the market suggests that consumer confusion is not a major problem.

Somewhat surprisingly, the split within the Fair Trade movement received a decent amount of press at the time. The August 2012 issue of the *Nation* included an article titled "The Brawl over Fair Trade Coffee," featuring interviews with many of our detractors. "For Paul, it's all about volume," said Jonathan Rosenthal. "And that means getting the big guys on board." Matt Early, founder of the Wisconsin-based company Just Coffee, highlighted the predominant critique of Fair Trade for All. "Cooperatives cannot compete with plantations on the economy of scale. . . . We saw almost all of this coming nearly ten years ago—the pandering to corporate coffee, them wanting to change their rules to dumb down standards in order to get the big boys more involved" (Sherman, 2012).

These criticisms were painful. Even now, more than a decade later, my stomach gets tied up in knots when I read these comments and reflect on the heated debates we had in the early days of Fair Trade for All. I could see the protectionist logic behind their arguments. In fact, a part of me empathized with them. They echoed a similar sentiment to the arguments that Dean Cycon made against our partnership with big companies like GMCR and Starbucks years earlier. Many of us had spent the better part of our lives fighting against "business as usual" to demand a fairer share for the little guys at the other end of the supply chain. We had witnessed the callousness with which many multinational food companies had done business in producer communities around the world—treating farmers as nameless, faceless production units and making business decisions that wreaked havoc in their communities. There was a legitimate fear that by allowing large farm owners into the model and adapting to the supply chain needs of large corporations, we would be letting the fox into the henhouse and disadvantaging the smallholder once again. There wasn't a lot of trust that these companies, and now us, would keep the interests of the "little guys" at the forefront.

But at the same time, it was obvious to me that the traditional Fair Trade model not only wasn't scalable from a business perspective but was increasingly losing its moral authority because we excluded so many families who needed our help. The FLO label would ensure protection for the types of producers who were allowed in their ecosystem, but I didn't believe it would succeed in the mainstream market. I felt like it was time for the Fair Trade movement to evolve. Clearly, as Marshall Goldsmith said in his best-selling book, "what got you here won't get you there." If we wanted to make a truly significant impact on global poverty, we were going to need to find a way to work with farms and factories of all kinds. And we would need to collaborate with integrity with the giant companies who dominate retail—maintaining the high level of rigor in our standards and certification, without watering down the impact that had made Fair Trade such a powerful force for good. If we couldn't evolve, I was certain that we would remain a small, niche movement making only a marginal difference.

Several years after the split, a former consultant to our organization, Manel Modelo, published an in-depth study of the Fair Trade for All split in the *Stanford Social Innovation Review*. Modelo sums up the conflict between the two sides as a tension between a consumer-focused approach versus a producer-focused approach:

The fair trade movement was founded to benefit small producers of coffee and other commodities—most of them located in developing countries of the Global South—by integrating them advantageously into a global export market. Yet as the movement has evolved, it has come to place a considerable emphasis on tailoring its efforts to the needs and aspirations of consumers in the Global North. In theory, fair trade can flourish on the basis of a win-win relationship between producers and consumers. In practice, however, tensions can emerge between those in the movement who emphasize the "fair" part of fair trade (for them, the interests of the producers are paramount) and those who emphasize the "trade" part (they prioritize the need to reach consumers). (Modelo, 2014)

While I agree with Manel's take to a degree, I also wonder if he's creating a false dichotomy. I don't believe that ethical sourcing requires an exclusive or preferential emphasis on one stakeholder (the consumers and, by extension, the companies) or the other (the producers). We have shown that it's possible to develop a win-win platform where all stakeholders benefit. It doesn't have to be a zero-sum game. That's what multi-stakeholder capitalism is all about. We create shared value for everyone involved.

In the case of Fair Trade for All, by opening up the model to include larger estates, we were able to extend the labor and environmental standards of the Fair Trade model to a much larger group of farmworkers and their families without watering down the standards themselves. We were able to direct our premiums to the laborers working on those estates and give them the power to choose how those funds would be invested in their communities. From a workers' rights perspective, Fair Trade is not just about improving wages and conditions; it's also about empowerment, engagement, and voice. As such, it can be transformational in the lives of workers. For the companies, we allowed them more ways to "do the right thing" within our model. Different companies could certify more types of products as Fair Trade in order to gain the market distinction that comes with our label. (Notably, many agricultural products, such as fresh produce, sugar, and tea, are grown predominantly on large farms.) By certifying their existing supply chains, regardless of farm size, we would make it easier for more companies to come on board. For consumers, more ethically sourced products would become available, giving them more opportunities to feel good about their purchases. To me, Fair Trade for All is rooted deeply in both mission and market logic.

Ultimately, I'm a pragmatist. I believed we needed to experiment, learn, iterate, and demonstrate—with humility—that our new direction would truly lead to growth and impact. Time would tell if we were right, and we would always course-correct to continue perfecting the model, based on our results.

EXPANDING THE PIE

IN THE COFFEE INDUSTRY, BLENDS ARE EVERYTHING. COFFEE roasters test and perfect just the right combination of beans and roast levels to develop the unique flavor profile customers want. This profile makes customers come back again and again for a certain company's "breakfast blend" or "French roast." Coffee is generally sourced through trading houses, which often import large batches pooled from hundreds of different farmers, including co-ops, independent smallholders, and large estates. This makes for complicated supply chains that take years to establish, so coffee roasters are usually reluctant to disrupt them.

Working with blends has been an ongoing issue for our certification process. In order for a certain coffee blend to be labeled as Fair Trade Certified, we require that 100 percent of its beans come from certified producers. This presents a challenge for roasters, because it limits their blending options. These limitations were, historically, exacerbated by the fact that Fair Trade standards didn't allow participation by large estates or independent smallholders, which make up the vast majority of coffee producers globally. So the requirement that roasters only use co-op coffee met with a lot of resistance, and many simply refused to go along with it. This made it difficult for us to increase the demand within the industry for Fair Trade Certified beans and eventually led to the emergence of a competitive concept, so-called Direct Trade, which is farm-size agnostic.

One of the most illustrative examples of this dynamic was the Allegro Coffee Company, owned by Whole Foods and the exclusive roaster of its private-label coffees. Allegro sourced the beans for one of their top-selling blends, Espresso Bel Canto, from a variety of farms in Brazil, Guatemala, and Ethiopia. Allegro cared about sustainability, but because the Brazilian coffee was estate grown, they couldn't certify Espresso Bel Canto as Fair Trade. That meant that none of the farmers or workers received Fair Trade premiums, even though the other two-thirds of the blend was sourced from certified smallholder cooperatives. It was a frustrating situation for all involved.

But this all changed after the 2011 split. We worked with a 568-acre farm called Fazenda Nossa Senhora de Fatima in the state of Minas Gerais in Brazil, one of the world's premiere coffee-producing regions, to make it the world's first ever Fair Trade Certified coffee estate. The farm was owned and operated by Ricardo de Aguiar Rezende and his wife, Gisele—both of whom were third-generation coffee farmers—and had 110 employees. Ricardo was also an agronomist and had spent decades as a pioneer in agroforestry, planting shade trees across the estate and establishing habitats for native flora and fauna. Fazenda already had several ecological certifications, including being 100 percent organic, but as one of their employees pointed out, Fair Trade "is the first one that focuses on us, the workers" (TriplePundit, 2012).

Once we certified Fazenda in 2012, Allegro's entire Espresso Bel Canto supply was now eligible for Fair Trade. This meant that not only would Fazenda's farmworkers all receive our impact premiums, but so would the many co-op farmers from Ethiopia and Guatemala who supplied the majority of the beans for the blend. It was a perfect example of how expanding our standards actually increased the number of small co-op farmers who could benefit from Fair Trade—a truly win-win situation for all involved. Rather than cutting into a fixed share of the market for Fair Trade Certified coffee, as our detractors had feared, by including the Fazenda estate, we actually grew the market itself. By allowing the whole blend to be certified, we were able to meet the demand and increase the industry's ability to implement Fair Trade coffee as a whole, benefitting farms of all sizes and types that met our standards. According to the latest reports in 2022, Allegro was up to 80 percent Fair Trade Certified across the entire brand.

As for the workers on the Fazenda estate, their benefits were similar to those of the small farmers who grew coffee for Allegro. They formed a committee of farmworkers who voted democratically on how to invest their premiums. After they sold their first two containers of Fair Trade Certified coffee a few months into the program, the workers received a $7,250 premium payment. They chose to invest the money in eye and dental care for the workers and their families. This allowed some of the older workers on the farm to receive their first pair of eyeglasses, ever.

COOPERATING WITHOUT COOPERATIVES

The "Borderlands" of southern Colombia have, over the last three decades, established themselves as one of the premiere coffee-growing regions on earth. The area, which encompasses the states of Cauca and Nariño, gets its name from the fact that it is located on Colombia's border with Ecuador. Its high-altitude tropical climate makes it ideal for the cultivation of Colombia's two most important cash crops: coffee and coca. In fact, the states have become one of Colombia's primary coca-producing areas, a reality that has brought significant violence and unrest to the region (Sheridan et al., 2015).

At the same time, the Borderlands' 40,000 coffee-farming families are known for producing some of the world's finest coffees, attracting the attention of both Starbucks and Nespresso, which collectively purchase much of Cauca and Nariño's beans. But despite the success of the coffee industry as a whole in the Borderlands, the majority of its farmers still live in poverty. The region's coffee farmers are predominantly smallholders working plots that are, on average, less than 2.5 acres in size (Sheridan et al., 2015).

For a variety of reasons, these smallholders are primarily independent and not organized into co-ops. In many areas of the world, cooperatives are a significant benefit to farmers, allowing them to band together, share resources, and achieve economies of scale that help them compete in the global marketplace. But in conflict zones like Cauca and Nariño, farmers often fear joining cooperatives because they can become targets of violence.

Before making the Fair Trade for All shift, we were unable to certify independent smallholders like those in Cauca and Nariño. Our standards made it mandatory that small farmers join a cooperative in order to get certified. But in the wake of our split from FLO, we established the Independent Smallholders Standard (ISS), which afforded the same price guarantees, premiums, and benefits to independent smallholders, who would organize themselves into local committees to make decisions about how to invest their Fair Trade premiums. One of our first ISS pilot projects was in Nariño and Cauca, which we launched in 2013 with Nespresso. We started with 100 farmers, including some in the conflict-ridden community of Samaniego, an area that had rarely been visited by foreign buyers.

The beauty of Fair Trade premiums is that they motivate a kind of collaborative, organized structure, even for those farmers who aren't co-op members. In this case, the farmers formed community-based committees to decide how they wanted to invest their premiums and worked closely with Nespresso and the Colombian Coffee Federation (our local partner) to carry out their vision. What did they choose? Clean water.

Clean drinking water was a serious issue in the Borderlands. Much of the surrounding forestland was rapidly being cut down and converted to ranches to feed the global demand for beef. The communities downstream of those ranches experienced a significant drop in water quality as cattle farming expanded. Almost 95 percent of these citizens had access to running water that was gravity fed from the streams and springs in the highlands above, but the majority of that water supply was contaminated. We conducted a survey and found that over half of the region's farmers said their water was polluted, and 25 percent indicated that at least one family member had suffered from a water-borne disease.

The farmer committees hired an engineer who designed low-cost water-treatment facilities to be built within the local aqueduct system that fed the coffee-producing communities. The first facilities were completed in 2017 and have since expanded throughout the region. By 2023, the water-treatment system was providing clean drinking water to over 15,000 households in Nariño and 11,000 in Cauca, in addition to all the schools, community centers, and health facilities (Rice, 2024). To date, we estimate the overall impact to have reached roughly 65,000 people.

The clean-water initiative in Colombia's Borderlands has become one of Nespresso's celebrated sustainability achievements. As their CEO, Guillaume Le Cunff, recently told me, "I'm super proud of what we've accomplished in southern Colombia. When I read the latest report about water sanitation and the health improvements it's led to in the region, I got emotional. It's becoming very concrete."

That's what I love about the story. It's a concrete result. It shows the real, material benefits of investing in the infrastructure of a marginalized community. And it's a shining example of why it's been so important for us to include these independent small farms in the Fair Trade model. According to a study by the International Coffee Organization and Enveritas, there are approximately 12.5 million small coffee farms globally, and only a small percentage are in co-ops (less than 10 percent) (Browning, 2019). By opening our doors, I believe we can eventually bring tremendous benefits to the majority of these farmers who need our support. That's a very real manifestation of the kind of inclusive vision on which Fair Trade for All is based.

GROWING INTO PRODUCE

IF YOU LOVE BERRIES, YOU'VE PROBABLY HEARD OF DRISCOLL'S. Their iconic cursive-font brand can be found on plastic clamshells of strawberries, blackberries, blueberries, and raspberries in virtually every grocery store in the United States. Founded in the late 1800s by Ed Reiter and his brother-in-law Dick Driscoll during Central California's "Strawberry Gold Rush," the company has grown to be the largest berry distributor in the world (Goodyear, 2017). Headquartered in Watsonville, California, not far from their original strawberry farm, they now work with a network of independent growers and harvesters in twenty-one different countries and sell their berries in forty-eight countries around the world.

Unlike most multinational agricultural corporations, Driscoll's is still a family-run company. Ed Reiter's grandson, Miles, was CEO of Driscoll's from 2000 until 2015 and then reassumed the position from 2018 to 2023. His daughter, Brie Reiter Smith, serves as vice president of product leadership for the company, and his son is one of their strawberry farmers. They are about as close to berry royalty as it gets. So when they approached us in 2015, we were thrilled to take the meeting.

At the time Driscoll's was in the midst of a significant PR crisis. They were facing boycott campaigns from activist groups fighting for better pay and working conditions at two of their suppliers, including one in the small community of San Quintin on Mexico's Baja Peninsula. A group of worker activists went on a twenty-eight-day media tour publicizing what they considered to be unfair conditions up and down the Pacific coast, ending at Driscoll's headquarters in California (Yu Hsi Lee, 2016). The company knew they had a serious issue on their hands and wanted to do something about it.

This was a few years after our split from FLO, and we were now in a position to explore collaboration with Driscoll's, which sourced its berries from large farms employing seasonal farmworkers. It would be a good test case for our farmworker standards, which we had already begun to roll out with several other large produce operations, mostly in Mexico. The farmworker standards were designed to ensure safer working conditions, better benefits, and higher wages on larger farms. The beneficiaries of the impact premiums were the workers themselves, who organized Fair Trade committees, conducted community-needs assessments, and voted democratically about how to invest these funds in their communities.

I'm very proud of our efforts to improve peoples' lives on these farms. Many agricultural workers have some of the most difficult labor conditions on earth: long days with little to no rest, exposure to toxic chemicals, no access to water or restrooms, and substandard housing for migrant workers. Our farmworker standards tackled all these issues. Admittedly, our standards sometimes simply require that the labor laws on the books in any given state or country be respected. But the key difference is that we make sure our farms are actually in compliance with the law through our rigorous auditing practices. In most countries where we operate, even in the United States, labor laws are loosely enforced, if at all.

We launched our pilot berry program with Driscoll's in January 2016, starting with a test case on a few of their strawberry and raspberry farms in Baja California, Mexico. The program was aligned with Driscoll's internal "Global Labor Standard" but brought the unique benefits of Fair Trade. We worked closely with the Driscoll's team, led by Soren Bjorn, who was the head of their North American operations at the time and has since been named CEO of the company. As Soren recalls, "It was quite challenging in the beginning. Our vision has always been to be the world's biggest berry company, enriching the lives of everyone we touch. But your team challenged us to think differently about our business. We weren't being sensitive enough to the specific needs of our growers and farmworkers."

When I asked Soren recently about the biggest impact Fair Trade had on Driscoll's in the beginning, he didn't talk about the business or PR benefits; he focused first on how our model strengthened and elevated their existing standards through the impact of premiums.

When we went out and surveyed farmworker families, the biggest problem we heard about was the lack of water storage. Baja California is a very arid region and there isn't a consistent supply of running water to households. Their water only runs a few times a week, so families essentially have to wait until they hear the water running and then fill up as many storage receptacles as possible to use for everything—drinking, cooking, and cleaning. The problem is that you can't predict when the water will run, and it often happens when kids are in school and parents are at work; so no one is around to fill up the containers.

In that first year, Driscoll's farmworkers voted to invest their premiums in new water storage tanks that would turn on automatically when the water started to run. During that initial period, Driscoll's installed over a thousand of them in homes across the region, purchased with funds from Fair Trade premiums. It had a huge impact on the community, Soren says. "The water situation in Baja is hard for us to relate to here in the developed world where we take running water for granted. But it was their number one concern. I went down to see some of the tanks installed and it was amazing to see the sense of relief it gave the families. It was all over their faces."

Suffice it to say, the initial experiment with Driscoll's was a success from the perspective of everyone involved. Not only did the berries sell well, but Driscoll's was able to show their critics that they were willing to work on improving working and living conditions through the continued evolution of their standards and their partnership with us. By listening to their workers, they were able to address a core need of the community and dramatically improve relationships with their growers and labor force.

But even after the boycott ended, Driscoll's wasn't done. In fact, they soon expanded their Fair Trade operations to include all of Baja California. Today, every Driscoll's berry grown in Baja is Fair Trade Certified, which represents roughly 10 to 15 percent of their total volume. Since they launched the program, Driscoll's has sold millions of crates of Fair Trade Certified berries to US retailers. Their certified farms employ over 6,500 workers and now generate over $1 million in premiums for the community each year (Driscoll's, 2024). Driscoll's has become the employer of choice in the region. As Soren said, their "Fair Trade farms help raise the bar for everyone. If you have a Fair Trade farm right next to a farm that isn't Fair Trade, most of the workers are going to want to go and work on the Fair Trade farm. They know they're going to be treated better. They know there are programs in place that will give them a stronger voice about what goes on the job."

After their initial investment in water storage, the Driscoll's farmworkers shifted their focus to health and education. For farmworkers in the area, there are limited options for health care, so many basic needs often go unmet. Starting in 2017, Driscoll's workers voted to invest their premiums in a series of community health fairs, or *ferias de salud*, held throughout the region, which helped address a health-care access challenge. During these events, doctors, nurses, and medical students provide specialized care to thousands of workers and their families, including gynecology, dental exams, and eye care (Driscoll's, 2024).

Education has also been a priority. Many farmworker children can't afford the basic supplies required to attend school, and they often drop out at young ages. Driscoll's Fair Trade committee has addressed this problem directly by buying and distributing backpacks full of school supplies every year to local children in need. These include everything from crayons and pencils to notebooks and scissors (Driscoll's, 2024).

One of the more invisible benefits of the Fair Trade berry program has been its influence on Driscoll's operations globally. As Soren pointed out to me, "Looking back, we learned a lot from Fair Trade. Now, at every community we operate, we conduct a formal community-needs assessment that is then used to prioritize projects and activities we invest in using what we call our community engagement funds, which are similar to our Fair Trade premium fund." This kind of feedback is music to my ears. When we're able to encourage companies to not only participate in Fair Trade but evolve their business practices on a broader scale, we start to have a much bigger impact. This kind of ripple effect has been a crucial component of growing our footprint in new industries.

All of this was made possible by the evolution of our standards. Had we simply stayed put, we wouldn't have been able to work with a company like Driscoll's, and they wouldn't have had the opportunity to do better by their workers through our program. It has also given us the opportunity to make an impact in the broader produce industry, which is dominated by large farm operations. Unlike coffee and cacao, which still have a significant number of smallholders, the vast majority of fresh produce, from tomatoes to pineapples, is grown on big farms. With our farmworker standards in place, we can now offer their workers the protections, benefits, and premiums of Fair Trade.

A WHOLE NEW ERA

STARTING IN 2011, THE FAIR TRADE FOR ALL CAMPAIGN USHERED in a whole new chapter—one that I think of as Fair Trade 2.0, characterized primarily by a more inclusive approach and a widening of our scope. It has been a time of rapid expansion, both within the industries we were already a part of and into new categories altogether. During this time, we launched our factory standard and started certifying apparel and home goods. We soon brought Patagonia and other brands on board to make Fair Trade Certified apparel, and West Elm began sourcing Fair Trade rugs and furniture. Seafood and other products soon followed. All this came with significant impact. In 2015, we generated over $59 million in total premiums, more than double what we had done in 2011 ($23 million).

With all this growth, we had to make a lot of changes to the way we operate. We had to deal with the greater complexity of managing many new product categories and all their attendant requirements. And not all of these ventures have been successful. We'll explore all of this and some of the lessons of failure in the next chapter.

5

FROM FARMS TO FACTORIES TO FISH

DEEP OR BROAD?

ONE OF THE PERENNIAL QUESTIONS WE'VE FACED SINCE WE launched Fair Trade for All in 2011 concerns breadth versus depth. The vision of Fair Trade for All was all about scaling Fair Trade and, with it, the entire ethical sourcing movement. We wanted to expand beyond our niche into the mainstream market. We wanted Fair Trade to become a household name in the way that organic had and, in the process, to make a significant impact on global poverty and sustainability. We envisioned shifting the way food systems work on a grander scale. Naturally, there were competing ideas about how to do that.

Some on our team thought the best path forward was to focus on "going deep." This meant doubling down on our core products like coffee and chocolate and growing our market share from a small fraction to a significant percentage. For example, in coffee, we'd attempt to grow from roughly 5 percent to more like 20 or 25 percent, as has been done in some of the smaller European markets like Switzerland and the United Kingdom. We could use the changes to our rules afforded by Fair Trade for All to bring in bigger brands and certify larger volumes within the industries where we already had traction. This, the argument went, was the most efficient way to scale up. We would be adding more energy and resources to our existing infrastructure rather than building new programs for products with which we had less experience. Ideally, we could reach a tipping point within our biggest categories like coffee and chocolate and start to expand our business with mainstream brands like Folgers, Maxwell House, Nestlé, Hershey, and Mars.

"Going deep" also meant focusing on ways to have more social impact within the producer communities where we were already working. Most of our one million certified producers only sell a small percentage of their total production to Fair Trade buyers because of limited demand. They are forced to sell the rest on normal commercial terms with no certification or premium. In 2023, for example, the Coffee Barometer, a leading coffee industry report published by Ethos Agriculture, found that only 25 percent of global Fair Trade coffee production was sold to a Fair Trade buyer for a premium (Panhuysen and de Vries, 2023). This meant that farmers who complied with Fair Trade practices only got paid premiums for a fraction of their harvest. Therefore, by focusing on growing industry and consumer demand for Fair Trade products within our existing product categories, we could presumably channel more premiums and more impact back to our current producer community—rather than trying to benefit new ones.

On the other hand, some on the team felt the best approach would be to "go broad" and expand our scope to as many new product categories as possible. We imagined a "Fair Trade lifestyle" opportunity whereby consumers could walk through any Whole Foods, Target, or Walmart and find Fair Trade Certified products in every aisle—in the usual places, like the coffee and chocolate sections, of course, but also in the dairy, seafood, canned goods, and apparel sections. "Going broad" would enable us to engage a much wider range of leading sustainable brands that were eager to partner with us. It would also help to raise Fair Trade's overall brand awareness and give consumers more options to act on their values through their purchases. Consumers who, for example, didn't drink tea or coffee could still support the movement through their purchases of yogurt or blue jeans. Then, as they became familiar with the concept, their interest might naturally grow, and they might seek out a Fair Trade version of the other products in their lives. From an impact perspective, this approach would allow us to take the powerful benefits of our model to new kinds of producers in new communities around the world, unleashing ripple effects of change that we could only imagine.

Both strategies have merit, but we've definitely chosen to go broad in this phase of our journey. This means when "lighthouse brands" come to us and want to partner to enter a new industry or market segment, our first inclination is to say yes. Naturally, we have a formal process for evaluating new product and geographic opportunities. First and foremost, there must be a mission fit, a social need that our model addresses. We also look for market fit, meaning there must be expressed demand from one or more brands or retailers wanting to pioneer the new product. Finally, there must be seed funding—either from philanthropy or corporate coffers—to incubate the initiative. If these criteria can be met, we'll prototype and test certification of a new product, aiming to learn, refine, improve, and eventually grow.

This approach has allowed us to be agile and responsive to the growing demand for ethical sourcing across industries. It gives us permission to enter wildly new product categories, communities, and countries, as we will explore in this chapter, learning so much along the way. It means we can reach, empower, and improve the lives of entirely new, completely deserving producers. Yet every year we revisit the "depth versus breadth" debate, looking at the product choices we've made, the way we've deployed our limited resources, and the social return on those investments from an impact perspective. I wouldn't be surprised if, based on what we learn over time, we eventually modify our approach to this important strategy question.

The years following the split were, in many ways, a kind of coming-out party for us, as we dove headfirst into a wide variety of product categories that we had either only dipped our toes into or that were completely new to the Fair Trade program. We certified factories that produced apparel for prAna, Patagonia, and J.Crew and furniture for West Elm, Pottery Barn, and Target. We certified coconut smallholders in the Philippines producing coconut water for PepsiCo. We launched a seafood initiative with Albertsons/Safeway to protect fishermen and processing-facility workers. We expanded our fresh produce offerings dramatically, working closely with Whole Foods and Costco. We certified sugar for PepsiCo's new hipster soft drink line called Caleb's Kola (which eventually failed). We certified a range of ingredients for products like Lärabar (General Mills), Popcorn Indiana, and Cascadian Farm. We even tested more obscure products like quinoa, spices, rum, and soccer balls. This constant experimentation has continued to this day, as we're always in the process of exploring new opportunities to adapt the model and innovate for impact.

But with every new product category, there has been a significant learning curve. We've had to adapt and tailor the model to fit new supply chain processes. We've had to streamline redundancies when certifying farms and factories that already had strong social auditing practices. We've had to learn new industry dynamics, profit drivers, and politics. Through all of this, we've done everything we can to keep producer impact at the forefront of our efforts, maximizing premiums and applying our rigorous auditing practices to ensure all workers are treated fairly and safely. To be honest, it hasn't always worked. Some programs have died on the vine while others are considered "maintenance" categories that have limited potential for scale and therefore get little of our organization's attention.

This chapter explores some of the more salient new product "experiments" that emerged in the wake of Fair Trade for All and the lessons learned, starting with one of the most complex and rewarding: factories.

FAIR FACTORIES

WITHIN EVERY NEW INDUSTRY WE'VE GENERALLY STARTED WITH A pioneering company that aligned with our values and also saw value for themselves in certification. For apparel, one of those pioneers was prAna—the outdoor company started in the early 1990s with a mission to "make clothing with a higher purpose." Scott Kerslake, whom we met in Chapter 2, was prAna's CEO when we first started working with them in 2010. "When we had the chance to work with Fair Trade, we saw it as a monumental opportunity," Scott reflected to me. "No other major apparel companies were doing Fair Trade at the time and we realized we could be the first." We were hoping that the growing awareness of the Fair Trade label in other categories would have a spillover effect into apparel. Scott agreed. He said, "The thing you all had going for you at that point was the level of brand equity you'd been able to develop. Everyone knew Fair Trade coffee and chocolate. So we saw a huge opportunity to be a first mover in apparel."

But launching our apparel program wasn't as simple as applying the same standards we used for food products to clothing companies. We had to adapt the model completely. That's where my dear friend and colleague Heather Franzese came in. Now driving responsible sourcing for a large US retailer, Heather led the incubation of our apparel business from 2009 to 2012. Heather, who is now based in Hong Kong, has a rare combination of big-picture vision and operational skill that has helped her successfully navigate the complicated reality of textile supply chains. In fact, few people know as much about this world as her. When I asked her recently to recount the launch of our apparel program, she articulated our motivations simply. "We had seen the success of the model in food commodities and wanted to be able to expand impact and enable a Fair Trade lifestyle. Apart from food, what else is a daily necessity? Everyone wears clothing. We wanted to make it possible for people to live their values beyond just what they eat."

The apparel industry was particularly ripe for a new approach to "social compliance" and ethical sourcing. While the anti-sweatshop movement of the 1990s had forced the industry to make some changes, the plight of the average garment factory worker was still far from acceptable. The demand for cheap clothing from "Fast Fashion" brands like Zara and H&M perpetuated an environment where many workers were paid far below most definitions of a living wage and in some countries worked in unsafe, substandard conditions. Sweatshops were still common in the industry. So Heather and the rest of our team got to work with prAna, Indigenous Designs, and a few other pioneering companies to put together a program for certifying apparel.

Unlike those of simpler food commodities, apparel supply chains often include two very distinct production systems: an agricultural component and a factory component. With cotton-based apparel, for example, we had an opportunity to benefit the farmers growing the cotton, which was more in our wheelhouse. But we also needed to certify the factories where fabric was cut and sewn into clothing like blue jeans and T-shirts. This required some evolution on our part. As Heather pointed out, "There was a massive difference between a farm and a manufacturing environment, in terms of the workers' needs and economic situation. So we approached our factory program initially as a kind of experiment—a learning lab."

In 2011, we partnered with one of prAna's suppliers, the Chetna Coalition, which is a cooperative of nearly 9,000 small-scale cotton farmers in India. They were already 100 percent organic at the time and quickly demonstrated that they met Fair Trade standards as well. By the end of the year, prAna was selling its first Fair Trade Certified cotton product, a women's T-shirt called Soul T.

Then, in 2012, prAna was able to certify the factory where the Soul Ts were manufactured, the Liberian Women's Sewing Project, founded by the extraordinary social entrepreneur Chid Liberty. The approximately thirty women working in the project were able to earn 30 percent more than the average worker in Liberia, in addition to the Fair Trade premium. As Heather explained,

> After thirteen years of civil war and in a country with 80 percent unemployment, the impact was huge. Not only did they support their extended families on this income, but when I talked to these women about how they wanted to use the money, invariably they mentioned literacy classes, computer training, childcare, and health clinics—things that benefitted the broader community. The fact that consumers could buy a prAna T-shirt that directly contributed to the future of these women and their community was a giant step forward for the people of Liberia.

prAna, of course, didn't stop there. They have been a committed partner to Fair Trade ever since and stayed on with us even after they were acquired by Columbia Sportswear in 2014. They have now certified eleven factories around the world, including in countries like Thailand and Vietnam. Through the sales of Fair Trade products, prAna has generated premiums that have touched the lives of over 26,000 workers throughout their supply chains. They even posted a bold public pledge on their website: to go 100 percent Fair Trade by 2028 (prAna, 2024).

Sadly, in early 2024, prAna quietly informed us that they planned to drop Fair Trade certification by the end of the year. It turns out that after several years of lower profits due to the post-pandemic economic downturn, they were looking to cut costs, and Fair Trade premiums were one of the items on the chopping block. It goes to show that even the most pioneering companies aren't immune to economic pressures that can make ethical sourcing more difficult from a profit-and-loss standpoint. This setback for the movement also raises questions about the staying power of sustainable, light-house brands when they are acquired by larger, publicly traded com-panies with less commitment to ethical sourcing. While we're sad to see them go and wish they could muster the wherewithal to stay the course with us through tough times, we're grateful for the pioneering role prAna played in our factory program.

A DOMINO EFFECT

NOT ONLY WERE SCOTT AND THE WHOLE PRANA CREW GREAT partners in piloting our apparel program, but they also soon became brand advocates for us to others in the industry. When I spoke with Scott for this book, he shared an illustrative story. Not long after prAna began working with us, he attended a leadership summit hosted by their biggest client, REI. The Seattle-based outdoor com-pany hosted 500 or so people, including representatives from every brand they sourced from, to come together, meet each other, and share stories and strategies. "During the event, I had the chance to get up in front of everyone to speak about prAna and I was wearing our first Fair Trade men's T-shirt," he recounted proudly. "Instead of going through the typical bullshit about our company, I got on my soapbox about Fair Trade. I told everyone 'This is a Fair Trade T-shirt. It sells for this amount. Here's what our margin is. You can do this too.' I was trying to convince everybody that it was possible to actually have supply chains like this that benefit workers."

When I asked Scott how his speech went down with the crowd, he laughed. "Half the crowd was like, 'What is this guy doing?' and the other half applauded." When I asked him if it helped him get the shirt into REI, his answer was simple: "Hell yeah! The thing about REI is that they have this natural instinct toward community because they're member owned. Plus, they really looked to us as being on the cutting-edge of the whole social sustainability thing." Scott would be the first to admit that his Fair Trade stump speech may not have inspired many other brand reps at the conference to come on board with us. But I'm positive that prAna under Scott's leadership did create a wave of influence in the industry. This is the way it has always worked. After a pioneering company takes a risk and shows that it can be done, others follow. Today, REI is a major supporter of Fair Trade and other sustainability initiatives.

It didn't take long for us to develop a strategic alliance with one of the apparel industry's most respected and iconic brands: Patagonia. By then, Heather Franzese had handed off our apparel program to the brilliant Maya Spaull Johnsen, who architected the Patagonia partnership and many others and led our Fair Factories program until her tragic death in 2022.

Needless to say, Patagonia was a natural fit for us. Their founder, Yvon Chouinard, was famous for his commitment to building a business with purpose. As he wrote in his 2005 autobiography, *Let My People Go Surfing*, "What we take, how and what we make, what we waste, is in fact a question of ethics" (Chouinard, 2005). And Chouinard wasn't just talk. In 1985, he promised to donate 10 percent of Patagonia's profits to environmental causes. In 1996, their commitment grew to a donation of 1 percent of total sales. This led to the birth of a new nonprofit called One Percent for the Planet, which helps other businesses make similar commitments (Patagonia, "1%

for the Planet," 2024). That same year, Chouinard transitioned the entire company to organic cotton (Patagonia, "Cotton for Change," 2024).

But while Patagonia was a leader in their commitment to protecting the environment, they had room to improve on the social dimension of sustainability. As Cara Chacon, who served as their vice president of social and environmental responsibility from 2010 to 2021, pointed out,

> Back then, Patagonia was really passionate about the social side, but we didn't really have a credible, customer-facing way to show our commitment to workers in the supply chain. We found that partner in Fair Trade USA where their program enabled us to expand our work in social responsibility by adding the financial premium to workers, as well as show our customers that commitment through the certification label that is attached to the product you buy. Adding that element to our brand was a game changer for us, both in evolving our impact and messaging. It also added balance to the environmental and branding work we were doing.

For Patagonia, the big wake-up call came around the issue of living wages. For decades, consumers had benefited from the low-wage workers in the developing world who sewed their clothing. Many of these workers were being paid below what they needed to make a decent living. The concept of a "living wage" has been an important issue in the apparel industry for years. In essence, it is the amount of income an individual or family requires to afford a decent standard of living, including access to things like nutrition, clean water, housing, health care, and education. Our team dedicated a tremendous amount of time and energy to researching this issue. As Heather Franzese recalls, "We did a ton of analysis to figure out what the actual living wage should be in some manufacturing countries, predominantly in Asia," she said. "At the time, a group called the Asia Floor Wage Alliance calculated that the average living wage in countries like India and Vietnam was two times the minimum wage. In some places, it was more like six times."

This wage gap had an impact on the thinking of Patagonia's leadership team. As Cara pointed out, "We didn't feel comfortable making huge profits off of clothing, when the workers were making wages that were not on par with a basic needs wage. That didn't sit well with Patagonia's executives and ownership." The thing about worker wages in the apparel industry is that they are very difficult to increase. It's such a competitive industry, with such small margins, that it's rare to find factory owners who are able and willing to pay their employees more than the legal minimum wage. Similarly, few apparel brands are willing to pay factories anything extra to ensure that workers receive a living wage. In the Fair Trade model, companies are required to pay premiums directly to a fund that is managed by a democratically elected committee made up of workers. In this way these premiums supplement the wages workers earn from their employers and begin to close the income gap.

As Cara said of our proposal to them, "When they pitched it to me, I immediately saw how the premiums could be a first-step model to help improve the low-wage situation in a real, tangible, and measurable way. Even in situations where it wasn't possible to increase their pay, the premiums could give workers a direct cash infusion, or a product or service that would help enhance their livelihoods. We saw it as a good way to show our commitment to living wages even though we weren't entirely clear about how to get there at that time."

We started our Patagonia partnership in 2013. One of their first suppliers to get certified was the MAS Active-Leisureline facility in Sri Lanka, which was already known within the industry for its commitment to social and environmental sustainability. It was a great starting point. MAS workers manufacture a wide variety of apparel for different brands, but for Patagonia their specialty is surfing shorts.

In a "behind-the-scenes" story written for a Patagonia catalog, surfer Dave Rastovich described what it's like inside a Fair Trade factory: "At MAS, the workers show us pictures of a recent celebration when their Fair Trade premium money was used toward daily staples, a choice made by the democratic workers' committee. The stoke on their faces was plain to see as they told the story of receiving a 50-kilogram delivery of rice, baby formula and flour, paid for out of their benefit fund. For an industry that has much room for improvement, this is what the start of doing better looks like" (Rastovich, 2017). The premiums, as Rastovich pointed out, had a significant impact on the workforce, which was predominantly female. This had a huge positive impact on their household income. It didn't fully bring these workers to a living wage, but it went a long way, and the Fair Trade standards also required the factory to improve wages over time. As Heather put it, "We saw premiums as a transparent economic benefit to workers and a kind of bridge to a living wage."

So did Fair Trade contribute to Patagonia's success as a business? According to Cara, it helped increase the strength of their brand. "Fair Trade definitely contributed to Patagonia establishing itself as one of the most responsible companies in the world. We were already receiving a lot of accolades for our environmental initiatives, but after Fair Trade we could see an even greater amplification of goodwill and press towards the brand. By 2024, over 90 percent of Patagonia's products were Fair Trade Certified, and they had contributed approximately $31 million in premiums to the workers."

CROSS-POLLINATION

PARTNERING WITH PATAGONIA WAS A MAJOR MILESTONE FOR FAIR Trade. That same year, another headline-making opportunity emerged when Jim Brett, the visionary president of West Elm, approached me at the Clinton Global Initiative annual meeting in New York. Jim had a bold proposition: he wanted West Elm, part of Williams-Sonoma, Inc., to become the first international home furnishings retailer to offer Fair Trade furniture and home goods. Fortunately, our factory standard for apparel was easily applied to West Elm's home goods supply chains, so this expansion was fairly straightforward for us to execute. Within a few months, we hammered out a groundbreaking partnership plan that included producing and certifying thousands of items—from rugs and linens to sofas and beds—all sourced from dozens of factories around the world. The Clinton Global Initiative, where Jim and I first met, gave us the stage a year later to announce major public commitments to growth and impact over the next few years. Later, other Williams-Sonoma brands, such as Pottery Barn, would join the Fair Trade initiative and help generate over $15 million in cumulative premiums by 2023, improving the lives of more than 25,000 workers and their families.

Often we see a kind of ethical sourcing cross-pollination among our industry partners, either through direct, pre-competitive collaboration between companies or when executives from one company move to another and bring Fair Trade with them. Such was the case with J.Crew. In the summer of 2017, Jim Brett left West Elm to become CEO of J.Crew. The day the news went public, I called Jim to congratulate him, and then I jokingly asked how long I had to wait before we could start talking about Fair Trade at J.Crew. "Give me a year and we'll talk," he said. Three months later, Jim called me back.

At the time, the J.Crew Group's uber-successful Madewell brand was led by CEO Libby Wadle, who has since become CEO of the J.Crew Group. Part of Jim and Libby's due diligence in bringing Fair Trade to J.Crew back in 2018 was to learn from Patagonia's experience. Libby remembers learning about Fair Trade apparel from a Patagonia representative whom they invited to speak at one of Madewell's town hall meetings. "He shared with us Patagonia's journey—what they'd learned and how they ran their business. It was an eye-opening experience for us. And it definitely helped inspire us to bring Fair Trade to Madewell."

Like Patagonia, Madewell was already invested in sustainability. Through their denim trade-in program, they offered all customers a $20 store credit for any pair of jeans that they returned to the store. The old denim was then shredded up and recycled into insulation used in homes built by Habitat for Humanity. As Libby says, "Fair Trade was the next step for us beyond environmental sustainability. Madewell has a values pillar around people and community, and Fair Trade gave us a chance to lean into it." Both Madewell and J.Crew came on board with us, initially focusing on denim, which represents a substantial percentage of Madewell's business.

We started by certifying a factory in Vietnam called Saitex, founded by industry luminary Sanjeev Bahl, who was already known for his strong commitment to sustainability and wasn't sure that the additional audit to achieve Fair Trade certification was necessary. This was a common response from many high-performing factories we've worked with. As Heather Franzese says, "Large brands already do their own labor standards auditing in their factories. So in addition to social auditing, we really focused on the Fair Trade difference, which is the direct premiums to workers and the opportunities for workers to have a voice." Saitex eventually saw the value our premiums provided their workforce and wholeheartedly embraced the model. "Fair Trade was able to supplement livelihoods and cover expenses that workers had a hard time saving for," Heather pointed out. "They could help pay for childcare or health insurance to cover the workers and their families."

The Saitex experiment soon proved successful, and both J.Crew and Madewell expanded their business with us. Today more than half of J.Crew and Madewell's denim is Fair Trade Certified, and their bold public goal is to reach 90 percent by 2025 (Madewell, 2024). We eventually expanded with them into certifying chinos and cashmere, which are also slated to reach 90 percent Fair Trade by 2025 (J.Crew, 2022). Since first partnering with us in 2018, they have become one of our biggest apparel partners—and they've kept the domino effect going, helping to inspire other companies to come on board.

MORE THAN JUST AN AUDIT

One of the key benefits that many of our factories have cited is the improved transparency between management and workers that our Fair Trade committees facilitate. It turns out that a lot of worker issues don't always come to the surface during a typical factory audit, even if it's a stringent one. Heather Franzese shared a particularly powerful example. "At one of the Fair Trade factories in Sri Lanka, women were calling in sick a lot because they didn't have sanitary pads during menstruation every month. As a result, they were missing out on wages, and the factory's productivity was hindered. The women were embarrassed to talk about it. But when the Fair Trade committee was established, it created a kind of opening for them to share. The company soon connected the dots, and the workers invested some of their premiums in providing sanitary pads. A regular audit would not have surfaced something like that."

LOSING LEVI'S

OUR FORAY INTO APPAREL WASN'T WITHOUT ITS SETBACKS. ONE OF the biggest came early on, during our conversations with Levi Strauss about the possibility of developing a Fair Trade line, which would have been a huge boost to our apparel program. Levi's was so interested in the program that they gave us a $500,000 grant through their corporate foundation to help us develop our factory standards. We were thrilled to be partnering with such a large and credible player in the industry and saw it as a huge opportunity.

Unfortunately, not everyone felt the way we did. A group of anti-sweatshop activists, including the Worker Rights Consortium (WRC) and United Students Against Sweatshops (USAS), were developing their own approach to ethical sourcing, which they considered to be more effective. The activist groups were originally formed to pressure colleges and universities across the United States to ensure that their official T-shirts and sweatshirts were sweatshop-free. In 2011, they took their activism a step further. They partnered with the leading supplier of college-logo apparel—a South Carolina company called Knights Apparel—to create an experimental "living wage" factory in the Dominican Republic. The factory, called Alta Gracia, paid its 120 workers three and a half times the prevailing minimum wage—a figure they determined through their own research to be the living wage for people in that region (Greenhouse, 2010).

This is where the Alta Gracia approach differed from ours. As described in the previous section, Fair Trade standards aim to get workers to living wage over time, but in the short term, we don't set or mandate living wage. Rather, we address the "wage gap" through our premiums and require companies to gradually improve conditions and pay overtime. But WRC and USAS felt this was insufficient and were concerned that Levi's would partner with us and then avoid committing to a living wage. When they got wind of our conversations with Levi's, the activists called the head of social responsibility and reportedly threatened to attack them publicly if they partnered with us. This was difficult for us. Somehow we had become the target of their activism, even though we were both ultimately trying to do the same thing: improve the working conditions and livelihoods of workers.

As Heather recalls, "We all wanted the same thing: decent jobs for workers that pay well and where workers have a voice." The conflict was over the pathway to getting there. We were taking heat from many of these activists because our Fair Trade standards didn't require factories to unionize or pay what they defined as a living wage. "Their expectation was that factories producing Fair Trade Certified clothes should require a union and pay a living wage from day one," Heather said. "Our response was that in a market-based model like Fair Trade, engaging consumers and building a market for ethically sourced products would support higher wages over time."

Ultimately, Levi's decided to back away. In spite of the significant philanthropic investment they'd already made in helping us to develop the Fair Factories program, our label has yet to make it onto a pair of their jeans. While no one from the company has officially admitted that they bowed to pressure, it's very likely that the threat from the activists played a role in their decision. Perhaps Levi's simply chose to play it safe. In any event, it was a huge blow to our early efforts in apparel, showing that activism can sometimes be a double-edged sword.

"It really came down to a difference in our philosophy of change," reflected Heather. "Our thinking was that we were creating a movement that would build towards a deeper impact, supported economically by the consumer through the transparency of the label." Change, in our view, is progressive over time. But some of the activist community didn't see it that way. They wanted to set a higher standard and make it mandatory from the beginning. While I could empathize with their goals, I felt their position on Fair Trade was self-serving. Why focus on undermining the growth of Fair Trade, a program aiming to achieve the same end goal? Why not combine forces or take a more open posture toward experimenting with multiple approaches to worker well-being?

Unfortunately, the Alta Gracia apparel factory in the Dominican Republic and its experiment with living wages ultimately failed. The company never managed to expand beyond their single 120-worker factory. The Covid-19 pandemic led to a dramatic decrease in demand for their products. As students shifted to online learning, Alta Gracia's primary customer base—bookstores at colleges and universities—stopped making orders. The factory couldn't weather the storm and closed its doors in 2021 (Legrain, 2021).

To me, the Covid-related closure of the Alta Gracia factory is less revealing than the fact that it did not become a model for other factories. The company was never able to create a larger customer base outside their university bookstore market niche, and I suspect their higher labor costs probably made it difficult for them to compete with lower-cost alternative apparel, especially for student consumers on a budget. Without a communication strategy or label that could help them tell their living wage story effectively, many college students may not have even known how these T-shirts and hoodies were different.

Of course, we can only speculate about how their business model might have succeeded in other circumstances. I believe the existence of a higher-wage model was not implicitly a threat to Fair Trade's efforts to make more incremental change. Similarly, I wish that we could have simply agreed with the activists that Fair Trade was not a threat to the Alta Gracia experiment. I also think this case illustrates how the commitment to higher standards like a living wage, when pursued without an effective strategy for addressing market realities, can end up failing. We would all benefit from some rigorous, in-depth research into the Alta Gracia experience as I'm sure there are important lessons there for the broader ethical sourcing movement.

The living wage issue is growing in importance across industries. Increasingly, companies are being asked to take a position and demonstrate a willingness to act. Fair Trade standards call for employers to improve wages over time, and our goal is to eventually achieve a living wage for all farmers and workers. However, recognizing the economic realities of our industries, our model takes a gradual approach to the issue. Living wages will not come overnight, unless through legislation. So advocacy and policy work are essential but also slow. In the meantime, Fair Trade has found a transparent way (through our impact premiums) to deliver tangible financial benefits to workers without dramatically increasing costs for farms and factories, while we work to grow enough consumer demand for ethically sourced products to support higher wages in the future. We're optimistic, but we're also realists—navigating hard market realities, learning and refining our approach along the way, and playing the long game of social change.

PROJECTS VERSUS BONUSES

ONE OF THE INTERESTING WRINKLES WE DISCOVERED AS WE adapted our model to factories and large farms was that workers tended to invest their premiums differently than small family farmers. Because they don't own the factories and estates where they work, unlike farmers who own their land, workers have no reason to invest in production-related infrastructure. While in many cases workers would invest their premiums in community-based projects like health clinics or daycare centers, numerous worker committees voted to use their premiums to purchase home goods like rice cookers and washing machines that helped close the gap between their weekly wages and the income they needed to improve their families' lives.

One great example came from a rug factory in northern India. As you will recall, West Elm was the first home goods company to partner with us. Today, they offer everything from Fair Trade Certified sheets and comforters to nightstands and dinner tables, but we launched our program with them at a single rug factory in Panipat, India. Located sixty miles north of New Delhi, Panipat is often called the "City of Weavers" for its rich history of textile manufacturing, and the Raj Overseas rug factory we certified is one of its biggest.

After the Fair Trade program was implemented, the workers elected their Fair Trade committee and conducted a needs assessment. They surveyed the entire workforce and found that transportation—to and from work and around town—was a major expense for the employees. So the committee chose to invest their premiums that year in bicycles for all 300 workers in the factory, which they bought at a wholesale price. At the time, it seemed like a great project and an interesting example of how wholesale purchasing can enable workers to stretch their premiums further to address specific needs.

But then a funny thing happened. A year later, we did a survey of the workers to find out how impactful the bicycles had been in their lives. It turned out that almost a third of them had sold their bicycles for cash. As committee president Muhammed Yunus shared when we met on my visit to the factory a few years later, "Some people needed the money for other, more pressing needs and sold their bicycles as a way to get it. Who could blame them?"

The Panipat story highlights an issue we continue to encounter with our premiums. Many workers prefer cash bonuses over community investments, especially if they are migrant workers who have come from other regions. In fact, many studies done over the past decade within the international development community suggest that short-term "cash transfers" when combined with long-term community investments may be the most effective way to combat global poverty (Matin, 2022). While our official policy at Fair Trade USA is to encourage workers to prioritize premium investments in projects over bonuses, experiences like Panipat have taught us that our approach to worker well-being needs to be open and adaptable to the specific needs of each group of workers themselves, both in agriculture and industry. We need to trust that they know their own interests best.

THE FUTURE OF SUSTAINABLE APPAREL

I'M PROUD OF WHAT WE'VE ACCOMPLISHED THUS FAR IN OUR FAIR Factories program, the brands that have joined us, and the workers whose lives we've helped improve. But we're really nowhere near having the kind of impact we want in the industry. Currently, less than 1 percent of all apparel purchased by US consumers on a yearly basis is Fair Trade Certified. So how do we effect change on a larger scale? Many people have a lot to say on this topic—some I've interviewed for this book—but there may be no more astute observer of the future of sustainable apparel than my friend Ryan Gellert, CEO of Patagonia.

When I asked Ryan to speak about the state of the industry today, his reflections are those of a sustainable apparel visionary who is frustrated with the pace of change.

[Twenty-eight] years ago, Patagonia switched to using 100 percent organic cotton at a time when less than 1 percent of the world's cotton was organic. At the time there was no real market for it, and we put our business at risk because we believed it was the right thing to do. Fast-forward nearly three decades and if you just look at how frequently the term is used in marketing campaigns, you'd think that there's been a dramatic increase in the amount of organic cotton grown globally. But in reality the number hasn't changed. Today, less than 1 percent of the world's cotton is organically grown. It's similar with Fair Trade. It just hasn't scaled in the way that it needs to. So that's the real barrier that needs to be broken.

It's true. Like so many of our product categories, scalability has been elusive within Fair Trade apparel. But there are ways to begin to move the needle. One that Ryan highlights is bringing in more of the brands that source from our Fair Trade Certified factories but have yet to partner with us. We certified roughly 150 factories around the world in 2024, going through the painstaking process of auditing them and bringing them into compliance. Yet the majority of the brands that source from these factories aren't yet using our label or paying workers the premiums. As Ryan points out, "Collectively, Fair Trade has made it awfully easy for the apparel companies at these already-certified factories just to come in and do zero work except for writing a check for the premiums. So they don't have much excuse not to sign up."

That's very true; yet the free rider problem persists. Of course, because our staff regularly visit the factories, we know the names of all the brands sourcing from those factories, Fair Trade or otherwise, because we can see their labels in the sewing rooms. Naturally our apparel team is actively pitching those brands on the benefits to their business of joining the Fair Trade program, noting that the hard work of getting the factories certified has already been done. The pitch is that this is easy, and the time is now.

Ryan isn't optimistic that many of these brands will come on board, at least in the near future. "There's a quote I often use, which is stolen from Winston Churchill: 'Americans will do the right thing as soon as we've exhausted every other option.' I think the same is true of many business leaders, especially in the fashion industry."

Maybe he's right. If so, the question is, how do we get more of these companies to see ethical sourcing as their best option? Perhaps it will come through further activism and media exposure of the persistent labor issues in the fashion industry. Maybe it will come through increased consumer demand for "ethical fashion."

Ryan says that it could be the employees in the apparel industry who help accelerate change. "I think every person working in the apparel space doesn't love this part of the business. They aren't happy with the average working conditions within the industry. There's some nuance, but I don't think anybody is comfortable with that. So I think there is an opportunity to speak to employees and customers about the fact that there's a better way, and it's accessible. Doing so will put pressure on the leadership within companies by creating an environment where people are clear that this is an issue and that there are, in fact, solutions like Fair Trade."

In any case, I still believe that Fair Trade will have a meaningful impact in the apparel industry. To do so, we'll have to continue to innovate, learn, and co-create our model with the fantastic companies and other stakeholders who have helped build this movement and claimed it as their own.

A WHOLE NEW KETTLE OF FISH

MUCH ATTENTION HAS BEEN GIVEN TO THE ENVIRONMENTAL impact of the seafood industry. Overfishing, for example, has been a highly publicized issue for decades. According to the 2022 "State of the World's Fisheries and Aquaculture" report of United Nations Food and Agriculture Organization (UNFAO), only 65 percent of global fisheries are being "fished within biologically sustainable levels" (UNFAO, 2022). There has also been a lot of attention given to animal rights issues in the open oceans, particularly to the "harvesting" of whale populations and the impact of tuna fishing on dolphins (which led to the "dolphin-safe tuna" movement).

But the crisis in our global fisheries isn't just ecological. There's a less-publicized human component as well. Much as in other extractive industries, poor labor conditions and low wages are rampant in fisheries, particularly in the tuna industry. In 2019 the Business & Human Rights Resource Centre conducted a survey of the biggest tuna brands in the industry and published a landmark report with a shocking title: "Out of Sight: Modern Slavery in Pacific Supply Chains of Canned Tuna." The report found a disturbing level of worker abuse within Pacific tuna fisheries, which make up 60 percent of the global market. The abuse includes forced labor, child labor, low wages, dangerous workplace conditions, and substandard housing. In the most extreme cases, workers were reportedly isolated on ships or remote islands and essentially trafficked between the companies running the fishing operations. The report also found that 88 percent of the companies had no real transparency in their supply chains and therefore weren't in a position to address the issues directly (Business & Human Rights Resource Centre, 2019).

Given these labor issues, the seafood industry has been on our radar for years. From 2014 to 2016, thanks to generous grants from the Moore Foundation, Rockefeller Foundation, Disney Worldwide Conservation Fund, Walton Family Foundation, and Packard Foundation, we were able to develop the first ever Fair Trade seafood program, which we piloted in partnership with Safeway (owned by Albertsons Companies). These philanthropic leaders had been concerned about the environmental and social impact of fisheries for many years and saw Fair Trade as a promising approach.

We launched our pilot program in 2014 with an association of 120 small tuna fishermen in Indonesia's Maluku Islands. These are some of the most skilled fishermen on earth. They use small boats propelled by handmade kites that capture the wind to help them pursue the yellowfin tuna that are their livelihood. They then use single-hook handlines to haul in the massive fish, which are six feet long on average and often weigh over 400 pounds. It's grueling work and also quite risky as the fishermen often spend days in small boats out on the open ocean pursuing their catch.

To support the program, we developed our Capture Fisheries Standard, which included rules for both the fishermen who catch the fish and the factory workers who process them. The fishermen cooperatives received premiums reflecting a percentage of their "dock-side" pricing, while the factory workers received a percentage of the factory gate price. One of the first investments they made with their premiums was to buy compasses to help fishermen navigate their way home through thick fog and bad weather.

According to Darcie Renn, who was senior director of sustainability and corporate social responsibility for Albertsons Companies at the time, the program gave them an opportunity to "wrap their arms around the seafood supply chain." Safeway partnered with one of their suppliers, Anova Foods, and launched the Natural Blue tuna brand, which had our label on the packaging. According to Darcie, who is now vice president of sustainability for the Alterra Mountain Company, the Fair Trade Certified tuna sold well. "We were first to market, so it gave us something unique to push out in our marketing and social media. It gave us a whole new way to talk about our seafood sustainability program that gave it legitimacy and credibility."

Safeway soon expanded the program to include twenty-one different fishing groups representing over 500 fishermen in the Maluku region. They now have three different Fair Trade Certified seafood items on their shelves in partnership with Anova, including my personal favorite: their delicious frozen wild-caught ahi tuna steaks.

PRESERVING ECOLOGICAL AND HUMAN COMMUNITIES

NOT LONG AFTER LAUNCHING THE STANDARD, WE MOVED INTO another area of the seafood industry: wild-caught shrimp. We partnered with Del Pacifico to build a program for their blue shrimp fishermen in the Altata Bay of Baja California's Sea of Cortez. These fishermen use some of the most environmentally sustainable practices in the whole seafood industry. They hand-catch the large blue "peel-and-eat" shrimp from small boats called *pangas* that are manufactured locally, and they use primarily wind and tides to drift their nets. The nets themselves, called *suriperas*, are highly effective at minimizing "bycatch," which is the inadvertent capture of sea life other than the shrimp themselves.

Like so many other kinds of producers around the world, the fishermen of Altata Bay struggle to make ends meet. These coastal towns and villages are primarily dependent on fishing for their livelihoods and are therefore vulnerable to market fluctuations. As one co-op member, Maria Rodriguez, pointed out, "shrimp basically supports the whole community." Rodriguez, who works on the processing side of the shrimp business sorting blue shrimp from brown ones on the docks after the catch, says that Fair Trade has helped to give their community more hope for future generations. "By doing this I've been able to educate my kids and give them more opportunities" (Jurgensmeyer, 2020).

One of the biggest points of pride in our seafood program is its integration of environmental and social sustainability, which are deeply intertwined in the shrimping industry. Blue shrimp are dependent on delicate aquatic ecosystems to thrive, and when their habitat suffers due to pollution or illegal fishing, productivity dwindles. Our standard stipulates that at least 30 percent of the premiums must be invested in environmental projects. In the Altata Bay, one of the big projects these funds have supported is the restoration of the native mangrove ecosystem that supports the blue shrimp population. The Fair Trade program also helps to control overfishing by regulating how often certain areas of the bay are harvested and mandating "rest" periods for shrimp populations to recover.

QUINOA, SOCCER, AND RUM, OH MY!

The Fair Trade for All era was full of new product-line development—a journey that took us in some unique and interesting directions. For example, we partnered with a brand called Near East (owned by PepsiCo) to certify the quinoa that goes into their various blends. Our standards channel premiums to the small farmers who grow the ancient grain in the high-altitude fields of Bolivia, Ecuador, and Peru.

In 2012, we partnered with soccer ball company Senda Athletics to help them source their line of products from a Fair Trade Certified factory in Sialkat, Pakistan. Pakistan, it turns out, produces 70 percent of the world's soccer balls, and by certifying one of the many manufacturers in the region, we hope to create a ripple effect within the industry.

We even got into the spirits industry, first with the pioneering company Fair, which makes vodka, liqueurs, and other adult beverages. Later came a partnership with Flor de Caña rum. The 130-year-old rum company distills what it calls "the world's first spirit to be carbon-neutral and Fair Trade Certified" in their facility at the base of Nicaragua's San Cristobal volcano. We certify the sugarcane that is used to make the rum, ensuring better conditions and premiums for their farm-workers. I might have had a bit of Flor de Caña during my eleven years in Nicaragua, so I was happy to see them join the movement.

AN ISSUE OF SCALE

OUR SEAFOOD PROGRAM HAS EXPANDED OVER THE YEARS. WE'RE now certifying a variety of products, from Maldivian skipjack tuna to Alaskan salmon. We've also expanded our standards to include aquaculture, or farmed fish. The mere fact that we have a presence in seafood is a big win for us. We want consumers to have more and more ways to express their values through their purchases. As one of our former partners, Peter Handy of Bristol Seafood, pointed out to me recently, "Seafood consumers are considerably more engaged and ask more questions about the source of their food than other segments. People generally care more about where their fish came from than they do their mustard or asparagus." So it's important for Fair Trade to play a role in the industry.

Unfortunately, our growth in seafood has been particularly slow. Safeway has been an enthusiastic partner, but their Fair Trade business has stalled somewhat. They still carry only three certified products, and their volume within each of those categories represents a relatively small percentage of their total sales. Similarly, while our partnership with Del Pacifico has helped us make a dent in the Mexican shrimp industry, that segment of the market is only a tiny fraction of the shrimp industry globally. Despite a lot of effort, we just haven't had the success in seafood that we have in some of our other new products, like berries or apparel.

There are a lot of reasons why this may be the case. One thought is that seafood customers just don't care as much about the human impacts of seafood fishing as they do about the environmental impacts. As Darcie Renn says, "Many companies don't want to talk a lot about the social impacts of seafood because they're afraid to scare customers away. They can highlight the positive difference that a can of Fair Trade tuna makes, but they don't have anything to contrast it to." In other words, they're afraid to educate consumers about the value of Fair Trade, because they're afraid it will make them ask more questions about the seafood industry and the plight of fishermen as a whole.

Another issue with our seafood model has to do with how we set it up in the first place. As in the early days with coffee, our standards focus on the small-scale fishermen and community fisheries rather than the big vessels that dominate the industry. Part of this is because the foundations that supported the development of the program in the first place had a particular interest in these small fishermen who hand-harvest their fish and are part of local co-ops, often referred to as fishery improvement projects. At the time, they saw a gap in the sustainability initiatives in the industry, given the focus of the Marine Stewardship Council, the Monterrey Bay Aquarium, and other ocean sustainability leaders on the environmental issues. This led some of the funders to support a program like ours that would focus on social issues and support the smaller fishermen.

Unfortunately, as time has gone by, the big headline media stories about modern slavery in the fishing industry have focused on the big fishing operations (Tickler et al., 2018). For retailers connected to these scandals in the media, the pressure is to address labor issues on the big boats, and that's not where Fair Trade is focused. So it's possible that we will need to shift our attention to addressing and verifying labor conditions on the big boats if we want to be more relevant in the industry.

Finally, perhaps the biggest obstacle preventing Fair Trade from growing in seafood may be an issue of scalability. When I asked Darcie Renn about why Safeway hasn't grown their Fair Trade business much over the years, her answer was simple. "When a company like Safeway develops new products, they really want to make it available in more than just a few market locations. They want to offer it everywhere—to supply all 2,300 stores consistently with no interruptions." That's a pretty high bar for any supplier. It's a kind of supply-versus-demand, chicken-and-egg situation. Can we certify enough Fair Trade fisheries to land big accounts that require a certain volume? And how can we get that volume of supply certified without those accounts?

Peter Handy, CEO of Bristol Seafood, also spoke about scale, but in a slightly different way. Peter had recently decided to stop working with Fair Trade USA, and I was curious to learn why. His answer was illuminating. Peter is a Wharton graduate who went to work on Wall Street before purchasing the Maine-based seafood-processing and -distribution company in 2016. He's passionate about sustainability, but he's also a former financial services guy, and his business acumen drives his decisions at Bristol. "We certified one product as Fair Trade," said Peter. "It was our New England sea scallops, which represent only 3 percent of our business. We had roughly ten boats dedicated to Fair Trade." It turned out that this small segment of their business was a big success. After adding the Fair Trade Certified label to their scallops, their sales jumped by 40 percent in the first ninety days, despite the fact that they increased the price to cover the premium. Peter attributes that growth entirely to our label.

But, in the end, that wasn't enough for Bristol. As Peter says, "I'm a big believer in Fair Trade. I just don't think it was right for my business. I needed a certification that I could apply to our whole operation." The thing about Bristol is that they certify a wide variety of products from different locations around the world, including Canada, Japan, Argentina, and Peru. They felt that the cost of sending teams to all their locations to implement our Fair Trade standards in each of their supply chains was just too high. So they stuck to the 3 percent that their New England sea scallops represented, which sold well, but the benefit ended up not being worth the cost and hassle of applying the standards across their other products. As Peter says,

In our situation, the uncompromising standards of Fair Trade collided with the reality of the wild-catch fishing industry, which is completely different from most workplaces. Fair Trade has all these requirements around the number of hours employees can work consecutively, work schedules, etc., which are critical to the integrity of the standards in most industries. But these are what workers in wild fisheries sign up for. They work in these big spurts. They'll put in 18-hour days on the boat for seven days in a row and then they'll take 10 days off. So we had to put in a tremendous amount of extra effort to make exceptions to the rules and explain the limitations to our employees. In the end, it just wasn't worth the administrative burden, and the fishermen didn't support the restrictions.

When I asked Peter if he thought Bristol's lack of fit with the Fair Trade model was particular to them or an industry-wide problem, he had an interesting take, which speaks to one of the core challenges of expanding into niche categories.

I think we are more representative than unique. Part of the challenge is how small the seafood category is. Seafood is a $100 billion industry in the US, which is how much money people spend on dog food and treats. Of this $100 billion, about 70 percent of it is sold to restaurants, where there is no branding. Then, of the roughly 30 percent that's sold at retail, half of it moves through the fresh service space, which also has no branding. So you're left with about $15 billion in seafood that is packaged and has the opportunity to carry your label. It's just a really small part of a relatively small industry. So even if you got a 50 percent share of the packaged seafood category, you'd still probably sell more Fair Trade bananas.

Peter's comments pose an interesting challenge to our "go broad" strategy. Is it worth our expanding into an industry with seeming structural limitations like seafood? Would we have greater success and impact by doubling down on products that are closer, structurally, to our bread-and-butter programs, like coffee?

GOING DEEP, STRATEGICALLY

WHEN I REFLECT ON THE PAST DECADE-PLUS SINCE WE LAUNCHED the Fair Trade for All chapter and expanded into all these new product categories, I can see how much we've evolved. We've learned some valuable lessons, not only for the future of Fair Trade but also for the ethical sourcing movement as a whole.

First off, it's become clear that there is truly no one-size-fits-all solution within ethical sourcing. As we've moved between industries and geographies, we've learned that we have to be adaptable. Some elements of our standards are universal, like no slavery or child labor. But other elements vary from one product to the next, depending on the specific conditions faced. For example, we realized early on that our fisheries standards needed a requirement that all boats carry first aid kits. Many of our fishermen spend days far out in the open ocean, and if there is an accident like a cut, they may not have enough time to return to shore for proper medical treatment. By contrast, we don't require our coffee farmers to bring first aid kits with them into the field each day, because most of them work close to home where they can get treatment more quickly in the event of an injury. So our universal standard is worker safety, but it's been executed differently in different environments. I believe that balancing this dedication to having strong standards with a willingness to adapt them is key to our continued relevance and growth.

The second lesson we've learned is that going broad has, to an extent, been successful as a consumer-awareness strategy. Not all of our new product experiments have met growth expectations. But as we've offered consumers a wider variety of products and opportunities to see the Fair Trade Certified label, we've dramatically grown their awareness. Between 2011 and 2024, consumer awareness of our label grew from 34 to 65 percent. While we've not yet achieved our vision of having a Fair Trade product in every store and on every aisle, our reach is far greater than it was a decade ago. Fair Trade is no longer viewed as just a coffee program. True, you can't get a Fair Trade Certified iPhone yet, but you can get a soccer ball, cashmere sweater, and bedside table with our label on it. You can cook a meal using multiple Fair Trade products and ingredients. Slowly but surely, the Fair Trade lifestyle opportunity is becoming a reality, accompanied by significant growth in consumer recognition.

This expansion has led to the third, and perhaps most important, lesson from this era. In our efforts to go broad and experiment with many different products, we've now determined which industries we believe have the most growth potential over the next five years. As we move into the next chapter of Fair Trade, we've decided to maintain our breadth but to begin focusing more on depth within a few specific categories: coffee, fresh produce, and apparel. It's in these industries that we see the most potential demand and impact in the near future. There are several dimensions to this.

First of all, there is a strong and publicly visible need for ethical sourcing within each of these industries. In coffee, produce, and apparel, producers continue to struggle with significant social and environmental challenges. These issues are highly publicized and have received relatively more attention from activist groups and the media. So there's greater public awareness of the problems that ethical sourcing models like ours can address.

As a result of this social need and public awareness, there is also greater industry energy to tackle the problems. In coffee, produce, and apparel, there is a broader understanding that sustainability is important. Different companies are using different approaches— some more genuine and effective than others—to act on that understanding. We've found that ethical sourcing models like Fair Trade work better when the industry is already engaged. That makes it easier for us to identify and partner with lighthouse brands and create a domino effect once we've established ourselves.

Finally, we've learned that it's important for our particular solution to be a good fit for the particular problems of the industry. In coffee, produce, and apparel, our model tends to work well. It's easier to apply at scale within those industries, and the perceived benefits to companies and consumers are more obvious. In other industries, like seafood, for example, some stakeholders don't see our approach as directly addressing the biggest perceived problems: environmental damage and slave labor on big ships. With our three areas of emphasis, on the other hand, the connection between what Fair Trade provides and what those industries need is more direct—in the eyes of companies and consumers.

Will a strategic focus on these three industries ultimately allow us to dramatically increase demand, market share, and impact in the years ahead? That will be a guiding question for the next phase of Fair Trade. As always, success will depend in part on our ability to innovate, adapt, and deliver shared value with excellence. We see so many emerging opportunities for ethical sourcing in the years ahead. But perhaps our greatest contribution will now come from focusing on a few big wins, from a product category perspective, that create a powerful demonstration effect for other initiatives in the ethical sourcing movement.

6

BRINGING ETHICAL SOURCING HOME

NOT JUST A "THIRD WORLD" ISSUE

HISTORICALLY, THE PREVAILING VIEW IN THE ETHICAL SOURCING movement was that efforts should prioritize the poorest countries in the developing world. In fact, the original philosophical model of Fair Trade rested on the premise that wealthy consumers in Europe and North America should help poor artisans, farmers, and workers in the so-called Third World by purchasing products that ensure producers get their fair share. Because of this developing-world emphasis, little if any attention was paid to the plight of producers in the developed world. In fact, the earliest versions of our Fair Trade standards explicitly excluded producers from these wealthier countries, including the United States—an exclusion still made to this day by FLO, now known as Fairtrade International.

Over the years, I and many others in the ethical sourcing world have come to see this as a false dichotomy. It is true that absolute poverty levels are more severe in many developing nations and that producers there may face harsh conditions that are less common in wealthier countries. But poverty is also relative, and evidence abounds that farmers and workers are struggling everywhere in the world, including in the wealthiest countries, where their wages may be better but the costs of housing, food, and other essentials are also higher. Issues like low wages, poor benefits, dangerous working conditions, child labor, poverty, and hunger are global issues. And we continue to face them right here in the United States.

In the wake of our Fair Trade for All campaign, we began to look toward expanding our model to include farmers and workers in the United States. For the first time, we had the freedom to explore how we might "bring Fair Trade home" in support of domestic producers. Starting in 2014, we began interviewing stakeholders, learning about the relevant issues, and developing initial ideas about standards. The more we learned, the more we saw a need for Fair Trade's premiums and protections here at home.

PROTECTING THE DOMESTIC WORKFORCE

IN FEBRUARY 2023, *NEW YORK TIMES* REPORTER HANNAH DREIER published an explosive piece of investigative journalism illuminating a disturbing trend within the US migrant worker population. Titled "Alone and Exploited: Migrant Children Work Brutal Jobs Across the U.S.," the article exposed the dramatic rise in children migrating to the United States and being forced into dangerous work situations by their "sponsors." As she writes, "Largely from Central America, the children are driven by economic desperation that was worsened by the pandemic. This labor force has been slowly growing for almost a decade, but it has exploded since 2021, while the systems meant to protect children have broken down" (Dreier, 2023).

The system breakdown she refers to has to do with the checks and balances that the US Department of Health and Human

Services (HHS) is supposed to provide minors who enter the country on their own. Due to a massive influx of immigrants—Dreier reports 250,000 unaccompanied children in the two years prior to publication—the HHS has been unable to satisfactorily vet the "sponsors" who are supposed to care for these children. This has left these minors more vulnerable to predatory labor contractors, and even family members, who offer sponsorship to children at a steep price. "Far from home, many of these children are under intense pressure to earn money," Dreier writes. "They send cash back to their families while often being in debt to their sponsors for smuggling fees, rent, and living expenses" (Dreier, 2023).

Sadly, these young people end up forced into a wide variety of dangerous jobs to make ends meet. In many cases, they work in jobs that ban child labor or toil far more hours than allowed by law. Dreier spent months investigating the story and spoke to hundreds of children: twelve-year-olds working as roofers, underaged workers in slaughterhouses, children tending the ovens that bake granola bars, and kids clocking overnight shifts sawing boards in a mill. The incidence of workplace injury within these particular industries was higher for children. "Adolescents are twice as likely as adults to be seriously injured at work, yet recently arrived preteens and teenagers are running industrial dough mixers, driving massive earthmovers and burning their hands on hot tar as they lay down roofing shingles" (Dreier, 2023).

Unfortunately, the dynamics of child labor that Dreier's report exposed have been part of the US agricultural industry for decades. And it's not just children. Migrant workers, who often have less protection than other workers, make up a large percentage of the US workforce on farms. As Michael Sainato wrote in a 2021 article for the *Guardian*, "It's widely understood that there's severe underenforcement of labor law in the agricultural industry, leading to widespread abuses of workers" (Sainato, 2021). As a result, these workers are often subject to particularly difficult conditions. Sainato writes, "Workers in America's agricultural fields are regularly subjected to abuses ranging from high occurrences of sexual assault and harassment, wage theft and safety issues including injuries, fatalities on the job and exposure to hazardous chemicals" (Sainato, 2021).

Even workers who are afforded the proper working conditions by farms and factories that are in compliance with labor regulations aren't exactly thriving. Perpetually low wages make it difficult for many to make ends meet, and they are forced to work long hours to pay the bills and send money home to their families. According to the 2020 National Agricultural Workers Survey, the average farmworker's family income was between $25,000 and $29,000, and 44 percent of families with at least six members fell below the poverty line (Gold et al., 2022). Many farmworkers typically live in overcrowded, substandard housing and struggle to access basic health care and education for their children.

When you look at the state of the US workforce in these more vulnerable industries, particularly its migrant workers, a different picture begins to emerge about who really needs and deserves the protections and benefits of Fair Trade. The plight of our nation's farmworkers, while maybe not quite as dire as that of workers in other areas of the world, is still concerning. Years of budget cutting have left the Occupational Safety and Health Administration, the federal agency responsible for enforcing workplace safety standards in the United States, without sufficient inspectors or resources to adequately investigate workplace safety violations, especially in agriculture (Berkowitz, 2019). Lax enforcement of these and other labor regulations and exemptions for farms with fewer than ten employees create a real need for the kind of supply chain transparency and auditing that Fair Trade provides. For low-wage workers, our premiums could help close the gap between what people make today and what they need to make for a decent living.

SAVE OUR FARMS

THE IMPETUS FOR BRINGING FAIR TRADE HOME WASN'T JUST ABOUT protecting US workers. It was also about helping farmers, who have a long-standing place in the cultural heart of this country. Like many others, I grew up with a love for the family farmer that was rooted in my own family history.

I remember my mother, Ruth, telling me stories about her childhood on a small farm on the plains of Oklahoma during the 1920s and 1930s. Like so many "Okies" during that Dust Bowl and Great Depression era, her family struggled to put food on the table. My grandparents were so poor that the family ate mostly cornbread, beans, and greens, and Mama often went to bed hungry as a child. It was truly a *Grapes of Wrath* upbringing. Mama was the first person in her family to graduate from high school, and she would go on to get her doctorate and become a successful psychologist, but she never lost her connection to that hard life on the farm. Because of her stories, I've always felt sympathy and a deep connection to farming folk. In fact, it's a big reason why I chose to study rural economic development in college and look for work in that area after graduation.

Family farmers are a cultural icon in the United States and are often romanticized. You can experience this as you drive through many regions of the country and see billboards and bumper stickers with slogans like "Save Our Farms." You can see it in the contemporary "Buy Local" movement that inspires so many of us to get our produce from the friendly folks at our neighborhood farmers' markets. In the United States, we love the mystique of the hardworking family farmer.

Yet, while love for the small farmer is still strong in the United States, the actual agricultural landscape has changed dramatically over the last century. In fact, the US farmer today is somewhat of a dying breed. Since 1935, when the number of farms in the United States peaked at 6.8 million, there has been a dramatic trend toward consolidation in the agricultural world. Thanks to increased mechanization, farms have gotten larger, and the number of farmers has decreased significantly. By the 1970s, there were less than three million farms in the United States, and that number has continued to decrease to our current level of roughly two million, with an average farm size of over 400 acres (USDA, Economic Research Service, 2024).

At the same time, farmers have struggled economically. Between 2013 and 2018, the prices for corn, wheat, dairy, beef, and other products dropped precipitously. As a result, the average net income among US farmers fell nearly 50 percent (US Department of Agriculture, Economic Research Service, 2024). The US government has attempted to address this economic decline through subsidies, but these have primarily benefited the largest farms and agribusinesses. According to a CNBC report, the top 5 percent of trade bailout recipients in 2018 and 2019 received nearly half of the $28 billion total paid to all farmers, which has accelerated bankruptcy in the agricultural industry (Heeb, 2020).

The dire state of the family farmer in the United States began to reveal to us a unique opportunity to make a positive impact with our Fair Trade model. By certifying farms in the United States, we could start to provide a concrete, financial reward for those who dedicated themselves to sustainable practices. Domestic farmers could get premiums to benefit their workers and also improve the safety and efficiency of their operations. As a result, farmers could capture the benefits of a more stable and productive labor force. Overseas, farms that invest in their workforce through Fair Trade premiums have experienced bottom-line benefits like improved worker retention, increased productivity, lower recruitment and training costs, and stronger commercial relationships with their buyers. We believed the same would be true on domestic farms.

We also saw the potential to tap into the "Buy Local" and "Buy America" movements that have been important to US consumers.

While there are no official certifications associated with "local," and while local does not necessarily mean "sustainable," most shoppers have an intuitive sense that buying local is good. There are reduced emissions, for example, from not having to transport goods over long distances. There are also the perceived benefits of investing in your local community. It's a sense that the money you spend on locally produced goods will support your friends and neighbors—and benefit the community as a whole.

In the United States, Fair Trade has historically been associated with faraway places, but we began to see an opportunity to change that perception. If we could align our brand with the US consumer's love for buying local, we could open up a new market for Fair Trade products. Much as we found historically with other labels, such as organic, piggybacking on the "Buy Local" and "Buy America" trends offered us an opportunity to continue to grow the customer base for Fair Trade products.

SI, SE PUEDE!

In the United States, we have a strong history of farmworker activism led by people like Cesar Chavez and Dolores Huerta. Starting in the 1960s, Chavez and Huerta began advocating for the rights of the millions of migrant farmworkers who labored to grow our food. Chavez, a first-generation US citizen raised in a family of migrant laborers, used his $1,200 life savings in 1962 to found the United Farm Workers of America (UFW), the country's first and most important union of farmworkers (Chavez Foundation, 2024). Chavez and Huerta are not just giants in the farmworker movement but are widely recognized as two of our nation's key civil rights heroes. In the early 1970s, Chavez, Huerta, and the UFW led the highly publicized "La Causa" movement in which millions of consumers refused to buy California-grown table grapes. The boycott eventually led to the passage of California's Agricultural Labor Relations Act of 1975, the country's first law that protected farmworkers' right to organize (Lee and Michelena, 2021).

Chavez and Huerta have been personal heroes of mine since college, and they have done as much as anyone to improve the livelihoods of farmworkers. In the decades since Chavez and Huerta founded UFW, there has been a tremendous amount of progress in the US farmworker community. UFW was in large part responsible for the ban on spraying pesticides while workers are in the fields; mandatory rest breaks, bathrooms, and handwashing facilities; and the first comprehensive union health benefits for farmworkers and their families. Nevertheless, the persistence of below-poverty wages, poor housing, and unsafe conditions on many US farms underscores the need for further effort. As Cesar Chavez always said, "Si, se puede!"

EXPANDING THE GROWING SEASON

ONE OF THE BIGGEST MOTIVATIONS FOR US TO EXPAND INTO THE United States came from the produce industry. Some of our retail partners, especially Whole Foods, were pushing us to develop a more consistent supply of Fair Trade Certified fruits and vegetables. In the produce industry, having a year-round supply is crucial, and companies generally achieve this by sourcing from the United States and Latin America. Harvest seasons differ across growing regions, so retailers tend to get their produce from different countries at different times of the year. Previously, we had no Fair Trade standards in place for domestic producers, which meant that our retail partners could only source certified produce from outside the United States. This created issues during the periods of the year when most produce was being sourced domestically due to seasonality.

In 2015, we finally added a domestic module to our agricultural standards. We piloted the program on a bell pepper farm in British Columbia called SunSelect that grew produce distributed by the Canada-based company Oppy, which in turn supplied a variety of retailers, including Whole Foods. The program was a success and allowed Whole Foods to source and offer Fair Trade Certified peppers year-round, not just when the Mexican harvest was coming in. The Canadian bell pepper pilot served as a proof of concept, and we were now ready to expand, looking toward the United States.

NORTH AND SOUTH OF THE BORDER

THE FIRST US-BASED PRODUCER WE APPROACHED WAS RICARDO Crisantes, a third-generation farmer and co-owner of Wholesum with his brother Theo. Wholesum grows organic tomatoes, squash, cucumbers, bell peppers, and eggplant on their array of farms located on both sides of the border between Arizona and the Mexican state of Sonora. Ricardo is no stranger to sustainability. His grandfather Miguel Crisantes Gatzionis, a Greek immigrant to Mexico, started farming in one of Sinaloa's prolific agricultural valleys in 1928. His father, Theojary, got a degree from the University of California, Davis, and then joined the family operation in the 1960s. He had read Rachel Carson's *Silent Spring* in college and was interested in reducing his farm's dependence on chemicals. It took some time, but he eventually became an early adopter of organic cultivation methods in the 1990s. As Ricardo put it, "It became more logical to farm in accordance with nature instead of fighting against it."

As with many of our produce partners over the years, the original introduction to Wholesum came from Whole Foods, where they had already been selling certified organic produce for years. As Ricardo puts it, "If Whole Foods comes to you and says, 'Hey, we think there's value for you in Fair Trade,' you pay attention." Wholesum originally partnered with us in 2012 to certify a portion of their Mexican operations, starting with tomatoes. Their commitment to Fair Trade grew dramatically over the years. Today, they are one of our biggest vegetable producers, selling 67 percent of their produce as Fair Trade Certified (Packer, 2022). In fact, Ricardo has become such a big advocate for Fair Trade that he agreed to join our board in 2017 and was eventually elected chair.

When we first approached Ricardo about certifying his operation on the US side of the border, it was an easy yes for him because he'd already experienced significantly positive results on their Mexican farms. Using Fair Trade premiums, his workers in Mexico had invested in school buses for their children, received medical vouchers for dental and vision care, built a community soccer field and a computer center, and even funded a tortilla factory that sold tortillas back to the community at cost. In the fall of 2016, we certified Wholesum's tomato farm in Amado, Arizona, just north of the border. After only a few months of production, the 130 workers received their first premium check in the amount of $30,000 (Romeo, 2017). More came soon after that. The US workers were thrilled, not only with the extra income they received from the premiums but also with the empowerment that being a part of the Fair Trade committee gave them. "I think the biggest impact I've seen is that farmworkers gain a sense of hope for the next generation," says Ricardo. "They are able to better provide for their children and give them more opportunities for the future."

But Ricardo soon began to notice a difference in how premiums were invested by his US-based workforce. "The farmworkers in Mexico and the US had different needs, so they invested in different projects." In Mexico, for example, workers tend to vote to spend their premiums on more basic infrastructural needs: home improvement projects, school nutrition programs, a school bus, and so forth. But for workers on his Arizona farms, many of his workers' basic needs are covered. "The workers on our Arizona farm have never made any investments in education, because education in the United States tends to be more accessible and higher quality. Parents feel confident that their children are getting a good education."

Instead, the farmworkers at Wholesum's Arizona operations have invested in projects more suitable to their particular needs. For example, they've launched a home-improvement project where workers can apply to receive up to $1,000 to spend on major appliances or home improvement products. They've also launched a transportation project where workers are shuttled to and from work by vehicles funded by both the premiums and Wholesum. Finally, given the high cost of health insurance in the United States, workers have chosen to fund affordable health-care programs for both workers and their families.

The autonomy that different producer communities have to choose how they invest their premiums is such an important feature of our model. It speaks to our belief in the empowerment and self-determination of the producers we serve. Every group of workers and farmers is required by Fair Trade standards to conduct a participatory needs assessment each year and then vote on how their premiums will be spent to address those needs. This tends to lead to better outcomes than if some well-intentioned but paternalistic company or charity determined the project from outside the community. This grassroots approach also makes our model more adaptable and effective in any culture, country, or industry where we're involved. This feature has proven meaningful to our expansion into the United States.

The success of Wholesum's Arizona operation created a solid template that we could use to certify other domestic farms, and the program soon grew. Since 2017, we have added many more products, including Washington-grown apples, Canadian blueberries, squash grown in California, and coffee from the Hawaiian island of Kauai.

PAYING FAIR TRADE FORWARD

One of Ricardo's favorite Fair Trade stories took place far away from his farms in northern Mexico. In 2013, several states in central Mexico were devastated by two different hurricanes (Ingrid and Manuel) that moved through the region within weeks of each other. The increase in rain from the storms caused dramatic flooding and mudslides throughout the region, and many of the already marginalized communities got hit the hardest.

Many of the workers on Wholesum's farms originated from central Mexico and wanted to support their home communities. When the Red Cross put out a request for funding, they had an idea. They collectively decided to donate $30,000 of their premiums—representing a significant percentage of their overall budget that year—to help hurricane victims hundreds of miles away. For Ricardo, it reinforced the power of the Fair Trade promise. "They were willing to forgo their own funds to help communities on the other side of the country," he said. "It just goes to show that people who are shown generosity tend to show generosity themselves."

THE CURIOUS CASE OF KVARØY
ARCTIC SALMON

GOING DOMESTIC WAS PART OF A LARGER SHIFT FOR US: WE OPENED up to producers in developed nations everywhere. We added organic apples from New Zealand and red kiwis from Italy. As we discovered with Ricardo's farm in Arizona, the socioeconomic environments in these countries differed significantly from those in the majority of the countries where we work. But there was still a need for the protections and benefits of ethical sourcing. That has created interesting opportunities to adapt our model.

Take the case of Kvarøy Arctic salmon. Kvarøy Arctic is a third-generation, family-owned salmon farm based on the small island of Kvarøy (pronounced "KWA-ray") in northern Norway, above the arctic circle. It's about as far away from civilization as you can get—an eight-hour journey from Oslo requiring a train, a taxi, and two boat rides. It was founded in 1976 by Alf Olsen and his son Geir and is now run by Geir's three children, Ida, Germund, and Havard, and son-in-law Alf-Goran Knutsen. Nearly all of Kvarøy's 100 residents are connected to the fishery in some way, creating a true family atmosphere around the company. As such, Kvarøy Arctic has always made the community a top priority. They pride themselves on producing some of the best, sustainably sourced farmed salmon in the world. So they were a natural fit for Fair Trade.

But Kvarøy is located in one of the most socially stable nations on earth. Norway and other Scandinavian countries are famous for their investments in social programs. Poverty levels in the country are remarkably low, in part due to the many social safety nets in which Norwegians have invested for generations. So unlike a farm in Honduras or Vietnam, where our Fair Trade premiums often "fill in the gaps" for basic necessities that local infrastructure can't provide (like clean water, education, and health services), the workers in Kvarøy already have a fairly high standard of living. Yet Kvarøy

Arctic still wanted to partner with us so they could showcase their social sustainability to their seafood customers. They felt that the Fair Trade Certified label would provide a significant brand differentiator for them in a highly competitive farmed-salmon market. So in 2021 we certified their farm and several of their processing facilities, also based in Norway.

Our partnership with Kvarøy initially went smoothly, but two years in, an important wrinkle emerged in relation to our Fair Trade premiums. Kvarøy, like many producer companies, passed on the cost of the premiums to the retailers who bought their product. Soon they started to get pushback from some of those retailers, and as a result, Kvarøy asked us to get rid of the premiums for their product. They argued that their employees actually didn't need the premiums, due to the relatively stable socioeconomic conditions in the region where they're based. According to the company, their employees were already so fairly compensated—by the company and Norwegian society—that the premiums simply weren't necessary.

After much discussion, we chose not to approve Kvarøy's request to forgo the premium. But the issue raised some interesting programmatic questions for us about how we might adapt our model to wealthier nations like Norway in the future. For example, is it possible that the premium isn't always necessary? Could we just certify a producer like Kvarøy and validate their compliance with our rigorous standards around wages, benefits, workplace health and safety, and worker treatment—without giving the company or their workers any extra economic reward?

Premiums have, in many ways, been our key differentiator, setting us apart from other ethical sourcing models. Producers working with other labels, such as Rainforest Alliance and Fair for Life, are often able to negotiate a relatively small, market-based price premium for their certified coffee, cocoa, and other products. Fair Trade, by contrast, has pre-established, mandatory premiums for each product category, and we audit those payments to ensure that the producer benefit is met. It is one of the unique features of Fair Trade certification, historically. It's been part of our core philosophy and theory of change. We believe that producers who make the enormous effort to put our stringent social and environmental standards into practice deserve—and need—to be compensated by the market. Our premium is both the reward and the incentive for these better practices.

That said, perhaps there are producers, like Kvarøy Arctic, who would be better served by a more flexible approach to economic rewards. Perhaps we should consider allowing producers to reduce or even waive the premium they charge for their products in any given year. One could argue that greater flexibility on this issue may actually be more consistent with our philosophy of producer empowerment and self-determination. And it would implicitly recognize that much of the impact of Fair Trade derives from the implementation of our rigorous standards—not just the premium.

Being curious and willing to question even the most cherished elements of our model has, and will continue to be, crucial to our success as we seek to grow in new industries and markets. No topic should be taboo. Innovation and evolution must remain in our DNA, along with a permanent appetite for testing, exploring, learning, and continuously improving.

A sad epilogue to the Kvarøy Arctic story: in October 2023, faced with our unwillingness to grant them permission to waive the Fair Trade premium, Kvarøy informed us that they would be dropping their certification in 2024. "Unfortunately," they said, "we do not believe that the model as it stands works for a company like Kvarøy Arctic." Needless to say, the internal debate rages on: Are premiums a sacred tenet of our model or an area ripe for innovation?

LESSONS LEARNED FROM FAIR TRADE DAIRY

WHEN WE ANNOUNCED OUR PARTNERSHIP WITH CHOBANI IN 2019 to develop the world's first Fair Trade dairy standard, there was much fanfare in the business world. The move was featured in the *New York Times* and *Forbes* magazine—and for good reason. Not only was our entrance into the dairy industry an interesting and perhaps unlikely twist in the ethical sourcing plot, but partnering with Chobani's founder, Hamdi Ulukaya, gave instant credibility to the effort.

Hamdi, who has since become a close friend and brother, was raised in a nomadic community of sheep and goat herders in the mountains of Turkey and is considered by many to be the instigator of our modern love affair with Greek yogurt. Since founding Chobani in an abandoned Kraft yogurt factory in upstate New York in 2005, Hamdi has grown the company into a global giant (Cam, 2021). Chobani's value has increased to well over $1 billion and in 2022 represented roughly 20 percent of the US yogurt market (Trainer, 2022). To supply this growing market, they have expanded their operations significantly, with over 2,700 employees across their two manufacturing facilities in central New York and southern Idaho (Cam, 2021).

Alongside his business success, Hamdi is respected for his passion and commitment to various social causes, including job training and placement for immigrants and refugees. The quintessential conscious capitalist, Hamdi said during his 2019 TED Talk, "If you are right with your people, if you are right with your community, if you are right with your product, you will be more profitable, you will be more innovative, you will have more passionate people working for you and a community that supports you" (Pompliano, 2020).

As an immigrant himself, Hamdi has always been sympathetic to the plight of refugees and migrant workers, including those who work in the dairy industry. According to a 2021 article in *Forbes*,

"He was inspired to raise the standards at farms across the U.S. after one of his visits to Idaho, where Chobani has a 900-employee plant. He heard about the plight of undocumented workers, who make up an estimated 50% of the dairy workforce in the U.S. Many of these workers dread daily tasks, such as traveling to a supermarket to buy groceries, out of their fear of deportation" (Cam, 2021). Others feel that because of their immigration status, they are unable to seek the protections of the law when facing wage theft, sexual harassment, or workplace accidents. "[Undocumented farm workers] have no rights: How do they get paid? What are the conditions they live in? What kind of safety measures do they have [at work]?" Hamdi said in his *Forbes* interview. "So we asked Fair Trade USA if they could help us implement these standards in the farming community" (Cam, 2021).

With increased awareness from consumers and activists, the dairy industry has come under more and more public scrutiny for a combination of reasons, including worker treatment, environmental concerns, and animal welfare. In 2019, a Coca-Cola-owned dairy brand, Fairlife, was widely criticized after an undercover video surfaced of workers brutally beating calves in one of their operations (Corkery, 2019). While the biggest issue in that instance was animal cruelty, it also shone a light on the tough working conditions in the industry.

Our partnership with Chobani began in 2019 when we worked with them to launch a pilot program called "Milk Matters," a supply chain auditing process focused on worker well-being, environmental stewardship, and animal welfare. The goal of this partnership was to see if our already established Agricultural Production Standards could be modified to fit the unique needs of the dairy industry. Between 2019 and 2020, we worked with Chobani and used learnings from the "Milk Matters" initiative to inform the development of our dairy standards—including field research, stakeholder consultation, benchmarking of other approaches, prototyping the initial standards, piloting, farmer and worker training, and monitoring and evaluation. The standards established a premium of $0.45 per 100 pounds of milk, to be distributed to the farmers and workers within the milk supply chain—a cost that Chobani absorbed without passing it on to consumers (Cam, 2021). In a departure from our typical procedure, one-third of these dairy premiums went to farm owners to be invested in operational improvements and compliance with the standards, while the other two-thirds went directly to the workers. We normally require that 100 percent of the premiums go directly to workers but chose to adapt the standards in the case of dairy in order to give struggling farm owners much needed support. After a two-year journey of developing and testing the new program, Chobani launched the first line of Fair Trade Certified yogurts in their thirty-two-ounce multi-serving tubs in 2021.

It was a big moment for both Fair Trade and Chobani. As Hamdi said in a public statement at the time, "Fair Trade USA's certification—the first ever in the U.S. dairy industry—will help our dairy farmers build on their hard work to raise farming standards, take care of their workers—many of whom they consider family—[and] ensure the well-being of their animals and their land, while giving consumers greater peace of mind that the dairy they buy demonstrates a commitment to positive economic, environmental and social pillars" (Dairy Foods, 2021). For us, we were excited not only to be partnering with such a well-known brand as Chobani but also about what their participation might inspire in the industry as a whole. We hoped Chobani would serve as a lighthouse to the rest of the industry, as prAna and Patagonia had in our apparel initiative, and we believed their leadership would inspire other dairy brands to sign up as well.

Without a doubt, Hamdi's vision for Fair Trade was to transform the dairy industry as a whole, raising the bar and improving the lives of dairy farmers and farmworkers. Even though Chobani funded much of our work behind developing the program, there was no exclusivity to the partnership. On the contrary, both organizations were eager to build momentum in the industry. Hamdi and I even did a bit of a roadshow together in 2019 and 2020, speaking together about the initiative at the Consumer Goods Forum, the Conscious Capitalism CEO Summit, and other venues. The more time we spent together, the more I came to see Hamdi in the same light as I did so many other leaders in the ethical sourcing movement that I'd had the privilege of learning from over the years—pioneers like Bob Stiller, John Mackey, Ryan Gellert, Libby Wadle, Ben Cohen, Jerry Greenfield, Nancy Green, and Doug McMillon. It felt like we were writing a whole new chapter of capitalism together.

On the ground, our pilot dairy program was starting to generate real change. One of the biggest farms to benefit from the program was an operation called Si-Ellen Dairy located in the small Idaho town of Jerome. Si-Ellen is a third-generation farm operated by Mike Roth, whose parents were Swiss immigrants who started the dairy in 1921 in Vancouver, Washington, with only 100 cows (Schemmel, 2020). The Roths decided to shift their operation 500 miles to the east in the 1990s when they saw an advertisement in a dairy industry magazine encouraging farmers to set up shop in Idaho. The move paid off for the Roths. Si-Ellen has grown to include over 8,000 cows and more than 150 employees, many of whom have been with the company for over twenty years (Ehresman, 2021).

Like other dairy farmers, the Roths—and their workers—still stood to benefit from a program like Fair Trade. The dairy industry has extremely thin margins and doesn't tend to pay workers very high wages. The Roths had always tried to invest in the well-being of their workforce and the surrounding community. They offered a comprehensive benefits package to their mostly immigrant workers and had donated significant amounts of money over the years to the local women's shelter and suicide-prevention programs. Still, they felt that more was needed.

That's where the Fair Trade premiums came into play. "I was amazed at how excited the workers were about the program," Mike shared with me a few years into the program. "I remember hearing about the first Fair Trade committee meeting. There was this group of seven workers sitting in a conference room trying to figure out how to spend the hundreds of thousands of dollars from their premiums. These were all immigrants with no more than an eighth-grade education. They were humble and intelligent, and they took a lot of pride in their responsibilities." Based on the community-needs survey they conducted with the entire workforce, the committee decided to distribute their premiums in the form of gift cards to local stores that workers and their families could use to pay for groceries, gas, and clothing. This went a long way toward helping their families cover their basic living expenses.

For Mike, the benefits went beyond just the premiums. "It took a lot of effort to implement all the Fair Trade protocols, but it ended up being well worth it," he told me. "Going through the process of certification and all the inspections helped make the farm safer and more organized. It made us do what we were already doing, only better."

Hearing stories like Mike's has been encouraging. At the end of the day, we care deeply about the success of the program not just for workers but also for the farm owners themselves. To work effectively, ethical sourcing must be a win-win solution for all the key stakeholders. We were optimistic that the early benefits farmers and farmworkers were seeing would continue to grow as the program scaled. Our hope was, if we could show early impact, more businesses would sign on to the Fair Trade dairy program. Unfortunately, that has yet to become a reality. Since we launched the dairy initiative in 2021, we have pitched the program to dozens of other milk, yogurt, ice cream, and cheese companies, but so far none have chosen to come on board. The domino effect we hoped Chobani would create just didn't materialize.

In mid-2022, I got the call that no one ever wants to get. Hamdi himself called up to inform me that Chobani would be discontinuing its Fair Trade program at the end of the year. It was one of the hardest conversations I've ever had, not only because of the enormous setback to our dairy program but also because of how fond I was of Hamdi as a friend. Of course, it wasn't personal, and Hamdi and I are good friends to this day. Chobani continues to prioritize responsible sourcing, following the FARM Animal Care Program standards and advocating for improvement in labor standards through their own Dairy Worker Well-Being Program. But from where things stand as of this writing, our first experiment with dairy, while impactful for the grower and farmworkers, was a failure from a market perspective. Our bet that the dairy industry would find Fair Trade to be in their "enlightened self-interest" has not, as of yet, been a winning one.

Why didn't our first foray into dairy succeed? First, our timing wasn't great. We happened to launch the Fair Trade dairy initiative during a particularly difficult moment in the dairy market. Milk prices were at an all-time high when we attempted to recruit businesses to the program, due to supply chain disruptions from the Covid-19 pandemic. I suspect that absorbing the additional cost of the Fair Trade premium on top of the already elevated milk prices may have made our certification economically unfeasible for many companies. This speaks to the issue of "right-sizing" premium levels that we examined in the case of Kvarøy Arctic salmon.

A second hurdle facing the adoption of the dairy program may have been a miscalculation of the perceived relevance of Fair Trade and worker well-being in the dairy industry and among consumers.

Marc De Schutter is the chief cycles and procurement officer for Danone North America, a company that, as a B Corp, exhibits many of the values and priorities of conscious capitalism. Danone North America has not yet joined the Fair Trade dairy program, and Marc feels that one of the primary reasons the Fair Trade Certified label has yet to have an impact in dairy revolves around storytelling. As he says, "We need to shift the Fair Trade story from a push to a pull. That requires you to tell consumers why Fair Trade is important for dairy so they know what they are paying for and start to ask for it."

From Marc's view, the best way to do that is by connecting the social sustainability that Fair Trade represents with environmental sustainability, which has historically had more traction with dairy consumers. Danone North America tries to blend these dimensions of sustainability together. "Our message is that our products are better sourced for the consumer, the farmer, and the planet." He may be onto something. People's concerns over the health and environmental impacts of milk production have driven the demand for products like organic and grassfed dairy. Danone North America has put a lot of effort into aligning their sourcing practices with the non-GMO and regenerative agriculture movements, and they've reported positive results.

When we launched our Fair Trade dairy program, we made the difficult but conscious decision not to incorporate additional environmental or animal welfare standards. While Fair Trade does have a significant number of environmental stewardship criteria in our standards that farmers must meet to pass our audits, we have historically put greater emphasis on the social side of sustainability, on the people. We've chosen to let other programs and certifiers cover additional environmental and animal welfare issues, while we've stuck to our strength: social impact. But as we'll explore in more detail in Chapter 8, we may have done so at the risk of rendering ourselves less relevant to an increasingly environmentally conscious consumer.

As Marc suggests, in the future we will likely need to do a better job of connecting the well-being of the farmers and farmworkers to a healthier environment.

Third, stakeholder pushback may have been an important issue that deterred the dairy industry from joining us. From the activist side, a group of thirty-five small labor-rights organizations, led by Migrant Justice, the Fair World Project, and various unions, penned an open letter to me in 2021, attacking our dairy program. These organizations believed that our dairy standards were biased toward our corporate partners and hadn't taken into account the voices and needs of the workers. They were also unhappy that our dairy standards didn't require unionization. As such, they characterized Fair Trade dairy as a form of greenwashing rather than an effective protection for workers (Fair World Project, 2020). Of additional concern to the activist groups was the fact that some of the protections in our standards didn't apply to smaller farms with fewer than six workers. They contended that workers on these farms are at just as high risk as those on larger operations and so should be held to the same standard.

While I understand the sentiment behind their arguments, we chose to take a more pragmatic approach with our dairy standards. First, while Fair Trade standards, US law, and the International Labor Organization all protect workers' rights to freedom of association, we do not believe in requiring unionization. Quite simply, we believe this is a decision that workers must make for themselves, not one that Fair Trade or outside activists have the right to impose. Of course, if our auditors discover that employers are union busting or trying to undermine the workers' right to organize, we will always enforce our standards. In some cases, when workers or local activists have brought such violations to our attention, we've investigated and decertified the farms.

As for the issue of farm size, just as small farmers are exempt from certain labor laws in the United States, our standards lighten the burden of implementation on small family farms that often don't have the resources to implement every one of our requirements initially. Instead, we offer a more flexible on-ramp to smaller producers so they can get involved in the program and improve their worker benefits over time. That's one reason we allow some of the premiums generated from dairy sales to go back to the farm owners (not just the workers), giving small dairies the resources they need to improve conditions for their employees.

On the opposite end of the political spectrum sits another influential stakeholder in the dairy industry, the Dairy Farmers of America (DFA), which is a powerful, 10,000-member dairy cooperative and processor with revenue of $24.5 billion in 2022 (Berk, 2023). DFA represented most of the farmers in our pilot, so we needed their active support and collaboration. Unfortunately, their leadership and team never really seemed to buy in to the idea of Fair Trade certification on their farms and were uncomfortable with us having direct access to their farmers and farmworkers. Perhaps they viewed us with certain suspicion, as outsiders to the industry. Perhaps they feared that we might inadvertently upset the delicate labor-management equilibrium on the pilot farms. I have no idea what was happening behind the scenes between DFA, the brands, and the farm owners. But DFA's evident lack of enthusiasm for the pilot was certainly a challenge for us.

I believe the strongest ethical sourcing programs are those anchored in multi-stakeholder consultation and alignment. This is how we develop our standards and programs at Fair Trade USA: we consult with all of the relevant stakeholders—from farmers and workers to activists, brands, cooperatives, and consumer groups—and listen deeply to their diverse perspectives. Then we take all that input and try to engineer our standards, programs, and policies to enjoy the broad support of as many stakeholders as possible, recognizing that not everyone will be completely satisfied all the time. To be successful, a multi-stakeholder movement like ours requires the art of compromise. Such movements will grow if they can build empathy, curiosity, trust, solidarity, and pragmatism among their protagonists.

In spite of Chobani's decision to stop the program, I consider our foray into dairy valuable for the lessons learned. Speaking with participating farmers and workers has made clear that our program succeeded in generating positive impact for both. We will continue to assess and learn about that impact through our ongoing conversations and surveys of the participants. While we certainly faced some macroeconomic, programmatic, and stakeholder challenges, the experience raises interesting questions about how, together with our stakeholder supporters, we can more successfully manage such challenges in the future across our different product categories.

While the loss of Chobani was indeed discouraging, we're not ready to give up on dairy yet. As Hamdi said when he called me up to share his hard news, "Fair Trade dairy is an idea ahead of its time, brother." I suspect he may be right, given the particular politics and economics of the US dairy industry right now. While our dairy program is currently on the back burner, we'll continue to engage producers and brands with curiosity about what it will take to eventually bring Fair Trade back into the world of dairy. As always, we believe that real social change is a long-term struggle.

THE FUTURE OF DOMESTIC FAIR TRADE

DESPITE SOME SETBACKS, I'M STILL BULLISH ON DOMESTIC FAIR Trade for several key reasons. On one hand, it's clear to me that the social side of the ethical sourcing movement needs to expand its focus to include producers in wealthier countries like the United States. Today, only a handful of other nonprofit certifiers, such as the Equitable Food Initiative and the Fair Food Program, are work-ing in US agriculture. Farmers and workers across many industries in the United States deserve our support just as much as producers in Guatemala, Bangladesh, or Ghana. The US companies that choose to do right by their producers should be rewarded economically for those efforts. Fair Trade stands to play a key role in making that happen.

On the market side, I believe we're just getting started. Our cer-tification footprint is still very small in the United States, but we've seen preliminary growth in fresh produce. Some of our apparel and home goods partners are now asking us to certify their US factories as well. And in 2022, my friend and former chief operating offi-cer Todd Stark conducted an insightful feasibility study regarding domestic Fair Trade expansion into the Midwest, which has given me more confidence in the potential for our impact to grow here in the United States. The study focused on an emerging category of farmers, whom Todd refers to as "high-road producers" (HRPs), defined as farmers who "invest in better wages and conditions for their workforce and more sustainable, climate-friendly agricultural practices." The thesis of the study was that Fair Trade certification could support the HRPs by giving them access to more stable buyers and premiums, thereby offsetting their increased production costs, which "are often higher than those of lower-cost producers who show less care for their farmworkers and the environment." Our cer-tification could thus help reward and motivate the producers who are making the effort to do the right thing.

The findings of this study were promising. It included a wide range of discussions with the many stakeholders involved, including HRP growers, buyers from supermarket chains, produce distribu-tors, food service providers, local consumer advocates, and national brands. The study also included extensive consumer research that explored the potential for midwestern shoppers to buy products that were both Fair Trade Certified and identified as locally sourced from the region. The conclusion from these stakeholder perspectives was clear: there is significant interest in expanding Fair Trade certification into the midwestern US market, certifying the region's producers and activating its companies and consumers. But the success of such an initiative would depend on a significant investment of resources on both the supply and demand sides of the equation, including farmer training and certification, consumer education, stakeholder engagement, and extensive industry outreach.

Of course, our plans to expand domestic Fair Trade go far beyond the Midwest. But this study is, to me, evidence that there's huge need and growth potential for ethical sourcing in relatively wealthier countries like ours. Our collective success in that endeavor will be defined, as it always has been, by how deeply we are able to engage all the stakeholders involved, how quickly we can learn from our successes and failures, and how creatively we can continuously improve the shared value for all the participants in the system.

7

CREATING VALUE ALONG THE SUPPLY CHAIN

EXPANDING THE CIRCLE OF INFLUENCE

SINCE LAUNCHING FAIR TRADE USA, I'VE BEEN INVITED TO ATTEND and speak at the World Economic Forum, Clinton Global Initiative, Skoll World Forum, Conscious Capitalism CEO Summit, and various conferences and trade shows. Usually I find the greatest value at gatherings like these between the scheduled sessions. During the breaks I get to meet and learn from leaders and practitioners across many industries and initiatives. Whether over a presession coffee or a happy hour cocktail, these informal conversations help me to find new ideas and inspiration and to take the pulse of the changemaker community.

Over the last twenty-six years, I've noticed an interesting shift in the tone of my conversations. Historically, when the CEOs I spoke with talked about making their businesses more sustainable, they were usually referring to the things that happen within the four walls of their companies. This took the form of things like Whole Foods' commitment to employee empowerment in their retail stores or Walmart's dedication to increasing the energy-efficiency of their stores. They were essentially focusing on improving what they perceived to be the part of their organization they had direct responsibility for, and this has led to a lot of important positive change.

But over the last few decades, I've noticed a growing interest, and sense of urgency, around the sustainability of global supply chains over which buyers have only limited control. More and more business leaders are beginning to look outside their organizations and focus on the social and environmental impacts they are having across the intricate web of suppliers they depend on to keep their businesses running. The business world is waking up to the fact that their upstream supply chains (their raw materials suppliers) make up a significant portion of their overall impact—economically, socially, and environmentally.

Soren Bjorn, CEO of Driscoll's Berries, recently summed up this shift as "expanding the circle of influence." He explained his thinking:

> As we've grown bigger and bigger as a company, and expanded into more and more places around the world, we've begun to realize that our circle of influence is much larger than just our employees. For example, we probably have more than 100,000 people just picking our berries this year—and they're not all local people. A lot of them are migrant workers who are moving around to follow the jobs, often across borders. The impact we can have on small communities across a wide geographic area is significant. So the circle we draw around our business has expanded.

Supply chains have, of course, always been crucial to global business, but there has been a marked increase in concern about their reliability. There are lots of reasons for this. The Covid-19 pandemic proved to be one of modern history's most dramatic disruptions to global supply chains. As a result, more attention than ever was given—by consumers and businesspeople alike—to just how vulnerable the world's mostly invisible supply networks truly are and how they can so easily disrupt our daily lives.

Similarly, the impacts of climate change have accelerated a movement toward net-zero carbon emissions across many sectors. As companies make bold commitments to going carbon neutral, they are starting to pay closer attention to the total climate impact of their business models, including their suppliers—and their suppliers' suppliers. With the global proliferation of smartphones and social media over the last decade, there is more transparency than ever into the real impacts that consumer and business decisions can have on the people, communities, and ecosystems at the other ends of supply chains.

As a result of all this, companies are seeing a big opportunity to advance both their business and their sustainability efforts through improved supply chain transparency, management, and performance. A 2022 study by Ernst & Young surveyed over 500 large companies across a variety of industries about their supply chain practices and found that, on average, 50 to 70 percent of operating costs are associated with supply chains. Accordingly, they found that "eight in ten supply chain executives are increasing their efforts toward sustainable supply chain operations" (Alves et al., 2022). These efforts look different in every industry, of course, and are motivated by different risks, concerns, and opportunities.

Specialty coffee companies of all sizes must pay attention to the well-being of the farming communities and ecological health of the regions they source their coffee from, at least in part because it helps them secure their access to high-quality coffee into the future. Companies also have concerns about the reputational risk of something like a child-labor scandal popping up in one of their suppliers. Similarly, apparel companies need to have visibility into the practices of the factories that sew their garments in order to make sure they don't end up with an unanticipated media crisis over poor labor practices, safety concerns, or another Rana Plaza disaster. Additionally, companies need their supply chains to be reliable, and this may be the biggest motivation for wanting greater transparency and more stable relationships with suppliers.

I see the rising importance of supply chains as both an opportunity and a challenge for Fair Trade and the ethical sourcing movement as a whole. We have helped stakeholders build transparent, responsible supply chains and sourcing relationships from the very beginning. We have always focused on the farmers and workers at the beginning of the production cycle to make sure they are treated justly and compensated fairly for their work. Our approach helps consumers and companies invest in the economic and ecological stability of the communities where their goods are produced. We also provide consumers and companies with a high level of transparency into the impact of their purchasing decisions. Our job has quite literally been to help expand company leaders' understanding of their own circles of influence. So one might conclude that existing models of ethical sourcing like Fair Trade are now in the right place at the right time, poised to meet the growing industry demand for greater transparency, traceability, and sustainability.

Historically, I believe we've done a solid job of helping our partner companies make their supply chains more sustainable and reliable. But I don't believe we have effectively tracked and measured the concrete business value of that impact. We haven't yet defined or quantified more precisely what a reliable supply chain looks like and the financial value of that increased reliability. And we are not alone. The 2022 Ernst & Young survey mentioned earlier found that "33% of companies lack a business case for sustainable supply chains and nearly half of respondents said their companies are struggling to measure the return on sustainable supply chain activities" (Alves et al., 2022). I believe this is one of the most crucial next steps for Fair Trade and the broader ethical sourcing movement. We need to help companies create the fact base to prove (to themselves and their shareholders) that making their supply chains more responsible will create real value for the firm. I'm convinced that making this case will help take models of ethical sourcing like ours to the next level and show that doing good really is good business.

In this chapter we'll explore this future through initiatives that we are already incubating with various industry partners. Specifically, we'll discuss what I see as three key components of the business case for supply chain sustainability: transparency, reliability, and storytelling.

HAPPY WORKERS ARE MORE PRODUCTIVE WORKERS

Ask just about any manager, CEO, or entrepreneur in any industry what the most important aspects of their business are, and a majority will likely include the productivity and engagement of their workforce in their answer. Indeed, the people who work in your factory, on your farm, or in your office are usually the key to the success of your operation. Much has been written about the importance of people and culture for organizational success. As legendary management consultant and writer Peter Drucker is credited with saying, "Culture eats strategy for breakfast."

In my conversations over the years with business leaders and producers we've partnered with, most refer to the importance of worker retention and morale to their success. Our certified farm and factory owners often speak about how the investments Fair Trade helped them make in their workforce created better retention rates, higher productivity, and better overall relationships between management and employees. The culture of dignity, respect, and collaborative problem solving that Fair Trade standards encourage is frequently cited as a significant contributor to employee engagement.

Take Wholesum, for example, run by my friend and board chair Ricardo Crisantes and his family. When I asked him about whether Fair Trade helped make his operations more stable, his answer was unequivocally affirmative.

> In the produce business, the work requires a lot of skill. Workers have to know how to de-leaf, prune, and pick our tomatoes, cucumbers, and peppers at the optimal ripeness. We invest a lot of time and money to give them the training they need. If you have a lot of worker turnover from year to year, it takes a lot of effort to train-up the new crew. So as we began to invest in the infrastructure of our worker community, we had less turnover. Our workers were better trained and happier and they did better work. It's had a big impact on our profitability.

In the produce industry, a majority of workers are migrants, and worker retention can be difficult. While Ricardo's farms are located in northern Mexico and just across the border in Arizona, a large percentage of his employees come from Mexico's southern and central provinces of Oaxaca and Guerrero, over a thousand miles away. Like other farms in the region, Wholesum's workforce used to have pretty high turnover. For years, Ricardo would see them leave after the harvest was over and head back to their families in the south—and he wouldn't see many of them ever again. In some cases, workers were choosing to stay home rather than make the long journey north, or they were choosing to take better-paying jobs at the maquiladoras, or factories, in the area.

But as Wholesum's workers began to invest in the infrastructure of their community using Fair Trade premiums, Ricardo began to see more familiar faces come back year after year. As discussed in Chapter 6, they funded computer centers, daycare centers, medical programs, and even soccer fields in the communities surrounding the farms. In addition to their wages, which are competitive with entry-level positions at the factories in the region, workers get all these other benefits they don't get elsewhere. And they work in a place where respect, dignity, and worker voice are the expectation. This makes working for Wholesum more attractive for their families. Many workers from the south even began to relocate their entire families to the north so they could benefit from the thriving communities that were growing up around Wholesum's farms.

The culture of care and collaboration that Ricardo and his family have created there has helped them achieve a level of stability in their workforce that improves their bottom line. They've created jobs that people want to keep. For every worker they're able to bring back each year, they save on training costs. They don't have to pay labor recruiters to find new workers. They have a more skilled, engaged, and stable workforce. That's just good for business.

While it might seem obvious that workers who are more satisfied with their work will perform better, it's shocking to me how often the cold calculus of many companies overlooks this truth. This hasn't been the case for Driscoll's, which has invested millions of dollars in the infrastructure of the communities in Mexico where so many of their berry pickers live. According to Soren Bjorn, this has had a big impact on worker productivity. "In the berry industry, we work with a highly perishable set of products. So any time you have employees that are generally happier, they tend to do better work," he explained to me. "We do regular employee surveys, and we've seen a night and day improvement in the satisfaction rate since we certified some of our farms as Fair Trade. We know that the happiness of our employees also has an impact on the quality of the product, even though it's sometimes difficult for us to measure."

For Driscoll's, one of the biggest improvements they've seen is in the quality of their management along the supply chain. Implementing Fair Trade standards has encouraged the company to be much more conscientious about the in-field managers who supervise field-workers on a daily basis. As Soren explained to me,

> Our supervisors are now much more conscious about what they're doing. They are operating with greater empathy. This has created an environment that's just better to work in. Think about it. The number one reason anyone leaves their job is because they don't like the person they're working for. But if management is doing a better job of supervising, employees feel better about the people they're working for, and they're more likely to stay. So our retention rates are much higher. There's no doubt about that. We have a lot fewer complaints than we did before.

IMPROVING WORKER ENGAGEMENT

ONE OF THE MOST IMPORTANT WAYS THAT FAIR TRADE HAS helped many of our partners make their supply chains more stable is by improving worker-management relationships. In many industries, worker relations are a big hot spot and lead to all kinds of disruptions, from labor strikes to low retention. Historically, unions have been one mechanism through which workers sought to achieve better pay or protections and negotiate with management. But in many regions of the world, unionization is either not possible, due to severe repression against organizers, or simply not attractive to workers. This is where we can help.

According to Vivien Alan, who has been a leader on our Producer Services team since 2010, "The Fair Trade model is a creative way of promoting worker empowerment." Vivien is a true veteran of the ethical sourcing movement. Born and raised in Costa Rica, she was hired by her country's first Fair Trade coffee cooperative, Coocafe, in the late 1980s, where she worked directly with farmers in technical assistance programs. Later she was a Fair Trade auditor and trainer for FLOCERT, the European Fair Trade auditing firm. Since Vivien joined our team, she has focused much of her efforts on helping workers take a more active and empowered role on certified farms, including educating them about their rights and helping them manage Fair Trade funds—all within a framework of mutual respect and collaboration with management.

Vivien shared a bit about the reality she encounters on most farms when they enter the Fair Trade system. "At first, farm owners can be suspicious of Fair Trade committees, which are democratically elected by the workers, because they tend to be generally suspicious of organized labor. But they put up with them because their function is ostensibly to decide how their premiums are invested and distributed." Our Fair Trade premiums are a safe topic because everyone—farmers, workers, retailers, and consumers—knows about them and generally likes them. As Vivien points out, "Fair Trade certification helps the owners get used to the idea of workers organizing themselves. They gather together for meetings, elect representatives, discuss needs and project ideas freely, and decide democratically on how to deploy significant amounts of resources toward the projects of their own choosing."

This kind of engagement is a significant departure from the top-down, paternalistic charity that many owners historically bestowed on the people who worked for them. In these scenarios, owners would provide services or aid to the worker communities, but these benefits were completely controlled by management. Because the Fair Trade committee has authority over the premium projects, a different kind of interaction emerges in which workers and managers are forced to set aside the traditional workplace hierarchy and collaborate as partners toward a common goal. In fact, we often hear managers express surprise and a newfound respect for workers' capabilities through their interactions with the committee. By allowing their workers to organize within the framework of Fair Trade certification, owners are relaxing some of the control they're used to having over their workers. In doing so, they are allowing the seeds of worker engagement to be planted. Eventually, the worker experience with Fair Trade almost invariably evolves into a deeper collaboration between workers and management.

We've added another important new tool for worker empowerment in the latest version of our Fair Trade agricultural standard. All certified farm owners are now required to allow their workers to create what we call social engagement teams (SETs). Members of the SETs are democratically elected and have a mandate to tackle workplace issues that arise, including worker grievances and health and safety concerns. SET members get training from our staff about their rights and responsibilities under the Fair Trade standard, as well as about how to raise issues and problem-solve collaboratively with management. We also train management on how to work productively with the SETs. Between the Fair Trade committees and the SETs, workers gain a voice within the farm or factory that they wouldn't otherwise have. The spirit of collaboration and mutual benefit they try to embrace is in stark contrast to the conflict and distrust that characterizes much of the relationship between workers and management historically.

The dynamic is similar in the apparel industry, where labor strife has been all too common over the years. Over decades of struggle, the union movement played a critical role in improving conditions in so-called sweatshops around the world. But today, there are very few unions left in the apparel industry. According to Cara Chacon, Patagonia's former vice president of social and environmental responsibility, "When we first set up the Fair Trade committees, most of our factories didn't have anything like it. There weren't any mechanisms for managers and workers to talk about their problems and how to solve them together. The committees helped management understand the real issues that workers worried about like childcare, transportation to work, health and hygiene, financial literacy, access to computers, etc. These were challenges beyond the normal stuff they thought they wanted or heard complaints about that could improve their work experience."

Of course, I don't mean to suggest that unions aren't important and don't have a role to play across the industries where we're involved. One critique of Fair Trade over the years has come from some sectors of the union movement. They've suggested that because Fair Trade doesn't mandate unionization, our model isn't directly addressing the management-worker power dynamic. As a result, they feel we are undermining the union movement. That is certainly not our intention; nor does it accurately reflect the reality on the ground. Roughly 35 percent of all the large farms and factories we've certified already had, and continue to have, unions. Moreover, local union representatives are often quite active on the Fair Trade committees and SETs. So the notion that Fair Trade undermines unions is, in my view, simply not true.

Union activists also argue that as long as management has sole power over the decision to become Fair Trade Certified or drop that certification, the worker engagement our model brings can be easily taken away. They're right. Ours is a voluntary model that depends on mutual benefit between owners and workers. The kinds of owners who gravitate to Fair Trade and other ethical sourcing models tend to be more enlightened and collaborative. They tend to already have a more harmonious relationship with labor and understand the business value of those relationships. In all these years of certification, we've rarely had a farm or factory owner get certified, try the model on for size, and then withdraw because they didn't like our worker-engagement criteria. Of course, this could always happen in the future as we continue to grow. But for now, we're confident that the shared value generated by our model outweighs the discomfort that owners might feel over having a more engaged and vocal workforce.

So, yes, our standards absolutely defend the right to freedom of association. We believe that workers have the right to organize themselves into unions if they choose. But we also believe, based on our own experience, that there are other, equally viable approaches to advancing worker rights, agency, and dignity in the workplace. As Cara put it, "I absolutely support unions, but they aren't always an option in every factory setting or region. This is a challenge for brands and their human rights practitioners aiming to improve factory conditions across the globe in every factory and every situation. So in the absence of that option, Fair Trade is a wonderful way to open up the lines of communication between owners and workers." I agree completely.

The improved relationship between workers and management has been a big part of how Fair Trade helps make supply chains more stable and secure for the brands we work with. Over and over, we hear that the more harmony there is between a supplier's workers and management, the more stable and reliable that supplier is considered. Typically, there's less worker turnover and higher productivity. Employees are happier, more engaged, and aligned with the goals of their company. They become more invested in the success of the enterprise and are able to share in that success. As Ricardo Crisantes says of his vegetable crews, "They know that the more tomatoes and eggplants we are able to grow, the more we'll be able to sell. When we sell more produce, they get more Fair Trade premiums." It's a unique kind of worker empowerment and well-being that comes from collaboration rather than confrontation.

Of course, we live in a time where there are still many unscrupulous farm and factory owners who make profits by cutting corners and exploiting their workers. Clearly, there is a dark side of business. Not all owners are enlightened or ready to embrace partnership with their workers. In such situations, workers have every reason to organize and fight for their rights. But in this gradual transition from extractive and exploitative capitalism to regenerative, conscious capitalism, this new kind of worker engagement modeled by the more enlightened businesses we've certified creates a kind of demonstration effect that I believe is beginning to ignite change within the industry.

YOU, MY FRIEND, GET ONLY OUR BEST

I've heard many companies' stories about the benefits of developing stronger relationships with their suppliers. In the case of Green Mountain Coffee Roasters (GMCR), it improved the quality of their coffee. T.J. Whalen, who worked with GMCR during the early years, shared an interesting story about a visit to one of the cooperatives in Guatemala where they were sourcing. "I was talking to some farmers on a drying patio, where there were rows and rows of coffee beans spread out in front of us, drying in the sun. I asked them about the difference between the rows, and the cooperative leader proceeded to walk me through the spectrum of different beans. The rows on the left were lower-grade coffees, sold at or below the market rate. Next were the middle-grade beans to be sold at the market average. Next were the premium beans for their specialty partners. Then the last row was for us."

> The moment was illuminating for T.J. He realized that they were saving their best quality for GMCR, in part because of the premiums they would receive for selling it as Fair Trade. Just as importantly, they had saved the absolute top-quality beans for GMCR because they had built such strong relationships with them over the years and felt such a deep sense of loyalty and shared interest. This is how it works in the coffee industry and many others. When the buyer treats the seller well, the seller will, in turn, want to give that buyer everything they're looking for. They want them to succeed.

BACKING IT UP WITH DATA

WHEN WE BEGAN DISCUSSIONS WITH WALMART IN 2019 ABOUT piloting a Fair Trade tomato program, we were thrilled. We were, of course, happy to expand our business with the retail giant and bring the benefits of our model to the farmers they work with. But what really intrigued us about the conversation was the potential to create major ripple effects within the tomato industry as a whole.

It may come as a shock to some that, in recent years, Walmart has been a kind of influencer in the ethical sourcing movement. In fact, many credit the company for bringing organic food into the mainstream. Starting in the early 2000s, Walmart started selling organic products at their stores, appealing to a higher-end clientele. Then, in 2014, they launched an initiative aimed at bringing organics to a broader audience by pricing them only slightly higher than their conventional counterparts, which was at least 25 percent lower than other organic retailers at the time (Wohl, 2014). It worked. By 2017, Walmart had grown to become the largest seller of organic products in the world—a distinction they've maintained ever since.

At the time, some criticized Walmart's push into organics, suggesting that their low-price model was undercutting many competitors and putting a squeeze on suppliers (Sustainable Business, 2014). But it's hard to argue against the impact they've had on helping bring the organic industry to a whole new level. That's the power of a big player like Walmart. Their supply chains run broad and deep, and they tend to have a big influence on whatever industry in which they choose to put their energy. We were hoping that our tomato program with them would eventually give us major momentum in the produce industry.

So in 2021, we kicked off the pilot, certifying a small but meaningful percentage of Walmart's tomatoes. The program was similar to our other produce programs in that we required all farms to be audited and certified against our social and environmental standards. Walmart paid our standard premium of around five cents per pound (it varied, depending on the variety), which was distributed to the workers on the participating farms. In addition, Walmart asked that we track a series of other performance indicators, such as sales figures, on-farm worker retention, and farm productivity. They wanted real data to assess the success of the pilot and inform their eventual decision to discontinue or expand.

This level of tracking was new for us. And frankly, I'm impressed and grateful that Walmart took such a rigorous approach. The initial results helped build a concrete business case for the program. According to worker surveys at the end of our first year, 89 percent of the workers on their Fair Trade Certified farms stated their intention to return the following season, significantly above normal industry retention levels. Some 94 percent of the workers said they would recommend working on these farms to someone else. In that first year, Walmart tomato sales generated $1.2 million in Fair Trade premiums, impacting the lives of over 11,000 tomato workers in Mexico with projects from education and health to housing improvements

(*The Packer*, 2022). As a bonus, Walmart reported to us that their sales of Fair Trade tomatoes in the first year grew faster than sales of non–Fair Trade tomatoes, which was also considered a win.

As a result of this measurable, positive performance, Walmart decided in early 2023 to declare the pilot a success and made it an official program. Now, in 2024, conversations are in the works to significantly scale up their Fair Trade produce program, which we believe could have tremendous impact on farmworkers and communities as well as a powerful ripple effect in the industry.

Interestingly, the ripple effect has already begun. One of Walmart's largest tomato suppliers is a company called NatureSweet, which sells unique snacking tomatoes in a distinctive volcano-shaped container that now adorns most supermarket produce sections across the country. NatureSweet has long prided itself on worker well-being and environmental stewardship. In 2023, it became one of the largest agricultural companies to achieve B Corp certification (Business Wire, 2023). So perhaps it wasn't surprising when NatureSweet eagerly embraced Walmart's request that it join the Fair Trade pilot. Led by Chilean-born visionary Rodolfo Spielmann, NatureSweet soon decided to certify all its farms and go 100 percent Fair Trade on its branded snacking tomatoes, benefiting over 6,000 greenhouse farmworkers and making headlines in produce industry publications. As my friend Rodolfo said, "The reason we're doing Fair Trade . . . is to hold us accountable to the highest possible bar, making sure we are not missing anything on treating our workers with the dignity they deserve. . . . We invite all growers to join the movement" (International Fresh Produce Association, 2023).

Equally significant is that NatureSweet is going to bake the premium into their overall product pricing with retailers like Walmart, Safeway, and Kroger. That means that they won't be giving retailers a choice between a more expensive Fair Trade product and a cheaper, non–Fair Trade alternative. Going forward, Fair Trade will be an integral part of their brand strategy, something still quite rare among our growers and brand partners in the produce industry, where margins are razor thin. A move like this from one of the world's leading snacking tomato suppliers could help to set a new ethical standard in the industry.

Our experience with Walmart and NatureSweet reflects what I believe is a new chapter in the ethical sourcing movement. Up until now, we've been able to grow our partner network in large part based on companies embracing Fair Trade for sales or branding benefits— or because their leadership thought it was simply the right thing to do. On the supply chain side, we've gathered and reported a lot of compelling anecdotal evidence from our suppliers about benefits like increased worker retention. These stories are certainly compelling and have led many brands to value the supply chain security that Fair Trade helps deliver.

But if we are going to move Fair Trade and other ethical sourcing models into the mainstream, we must generate more measurable proof that it's good for business, like the kind we've begun to gather for Walmart. If we want to grow Walmart's Fair Trade tomato program from a fraction of sales to 100 percent—a move that would likely transform the tomato industry forever—we'll need to show, with cold, hard data, how it benefits their suppliers, the farmworkers, and Walmart itself. In the near future, I believe delivering impact and supplier-performance data on demand must become the new normal for Fair Trade and the broader ethical sourcing movement.

THERE'S NO SUCH THING AS PLAUSIBLE DENIABILITY ANYMORE

ON APRIL 24, 2013, THE APPAREL INDUSTRY RECEIVED A WAKE-UP call. An eight-story building called Rana Plaza in the suburbs of Bangladesh's capital city, Dhaka, collapsed. The structure housed five different garment factories in addition to a bank and some retail stores. Investigators eventually discovered that the factory owners knew the building was unsafe, yet pressured workers to continue working. More than 1,100 people were killed in this horrific tragedy, which quickly grew into an international scandal.

In many ways, Rana Plaza served as a kind of awakening for consumers and companies about the need for more transparency in the supply chains that keep the global fashion industry booming. Bangladesh is home to the world's second-largest garment industry, and many major international brands were connected to the factories involved in the accident (Koenig and Poncet, 2022). Yet, up until the incident, many apparel brands weren't really aware of exactly where their clothes were being sourced. In fact, it wasn't until investigators combed through what was left of the building and found labels on the various garments amid the rubble that anyone knew for sure what brands were being manufactured in the building (Westerman, 2017).

The lack of transparency was shocking. It led labor and human rights groups worldwide to demand more accountability from companies for the safety and security of the workers at the distant, often obscure ends of their supply chains. A group of organizations drafted a transparency pledge for big apparel brands to sign that included a commitment to disclose all the sites that manufacture their products. Companies like Patagonia and Nike were among the seventeen different companies to sign the pledge (Westerman, 2017). While conditions didn't change overnight, the worldwide response to Rana Plaza marked the beginning of a significant shift in the apparel industry and beyond.

Before Rana Plaza, many companies tried to claim "plausible deniability" for poor conditions and worker rights abuses occurring in their supply chain because they didn't directly own the factories or farms where their goods were produced. The traditional thinking was that those suppliers were independent operators and therefore outside the purview of the brands that sourced from them. Companies could take more of a "cover your ass" approach: as long as their suppliers had passed a basic level of compliance with local regulations, these companies could essentially say they had done their due diligence. If and when something bad happened, they were off the hook.

But Rana Plaza began to change all that. Over the past decade, I've noticed that companies have—slowly but steadily—begun to take a more proactive approach to safety and worker well-being in their supply chains. Rather than sit back and wait for a crisis to occur, more and more companies have begun to get involved in vetting and auditing their suppliers, hoping to avoid the "next Rana Plaza." This horrific human disaster taught us that brands are co-responsible and perhaps even complicit in what is happening within their supply chains, whether they know about it or not.

We live in the smartphone era, after all, where supply chain issues are more visible than ever before. Consumers, especially Millennials and Gen Z, are more engaged and have higher expectations. As Patagonia CEO Ryan Gellert recently told me, "The pervasiveness of social media has forced a higher level of transparency from companies with their customers, their employees, and others." The public's expectation today is that you will have a clean supply chain, full stop. It's not enough for companies to simply know who their suppliers are. They now need to know what's happening within those farms and factories and be able to provide assurances. Their circle of awareness and accountability has to be wider. This is true beyond the apparel industry as well.

THE VALUE OF VISIBILITY

It's probably not a coincidence that our apparel certification program grew faster in the wake of Rana Plaza. While no one officially said their motives for partnering with us were related to the incident, the timing suggests that there was a connection. Much like the coffee crisis of the early 2000s, which brought big companies like Starbucks and Proctor & Gamble to our doorstep, Rana Plaza forced apparel companies to seek new ways to mitigate their moral and reputational risk. Sure, most brands already had some kind of code of conduct and social compliance audit program in place in their suppliers' facilities. But the rigor of many of those audits was clearly lacking. So demand has grown for the kind of high-quality audit and verification that a mission-driven, nonprofit certification body like Fair Trade USA can ensure.

Not surprisingly, in the ensuing years, our factory auditors have gone in and uncovered issues and violations that the brands' auditors didn't detect—leading to swift corrective action by factory management. In part, it's because we require rigorous auditor training at the auditing firms with whom we've partnered (SCS Global, Elevate, and Control Union). Our auditors typically spend more days on-site and go deeper on critical issues such as health and safety. They conduct worker interviews during each visit to capture their input on conditions and compliance. We also conduct "shadow audits" for quality control. And we have highly trained field staff in the countries where we work who regularly visit the factories to train workers and collect information about the premium impact in each facility. This on-the-ground presence gives our program greater depth of assurance for participating brands.

Our certification and label definitely help apparel companies tell their customers a more credible story about worker well-being in their supply chains, but we're doing more than just improving public perception. We give brands a much deeper level of transparency into what is actually going on with their suppliers, all in the spirit of collaborative problem solving. This, I believe, is one of the most important benefits of ethical sourcing models like Fair Trade. Not only do we give companies a stamp of approval in the eyes of an increasingly conscious and demanding consumer base, but we also give them an unprecedented level of visibility into actual farm and factory conditions, which enables greater accountability and quicker progress.

The business community is hungry for more supply chain transparency across industries. The 2022 Ernst & Young study cited earlier in this chapter found that supply chain visibility was the top priority for the supply chain executives surveyed. This was up from being a top-two priority in 2021 and 2019. Yet, in spite of this growing interest, only 37 percent have seen an actual increase (Alves et al., 2022).

This gap between intention and action is likely due to the fact that most companies continue to have little understanding of exactly where their products are coming from beyond their most immediate suppliers, who are often brokers or distributors two layers removed from the actual farm or factory. A 2022 report from McKinsey & Company found that under half of supply chain executives surveyed understood the location of their most direct (aka "first-tier") suppliers and "the key risks those suppliers face." The survey found that "only 2 percent could make the same claim about suppliers in the third tier and beyond." This means that the vast majority of the companies studied know little if anything about their supplier's suppliers. And this is a big deal "because most disruptions originate in these deeper supply chain tiers" (Henrich, Li, and Perez, 2022).

In fact, a 2020 study by the *Harvard Business Review* found that even companies considered to be "sustainability leaders" are having difficulty understanding the furthest links in their supply chains. The study investigated the effectiveness of sustainability initiatives within three different multinational corporations (MNCs) operating across Mexico, China, Taiwan, and the United States. They focused on the MNCs that had established significant sustainability standards for their suppliers to adhere to and hoped this would have a positive lift up the supply chain. Unfortunately, the study found that many of the "lower-tier" suppliers were "violating the standards that the MNCs expected them to adhere to." So the "hoped-for cascade effect was seldom occurring."

This, to me, presents a significant opportunity for third-party certifiers like us to get involved and add value to the supply chain initiatives of companies. In fact, I believe it is one of the next frontiers in the ethical sourcing movement. Collectively, we need to do a better job of highlighting the power of ethical sourcing models to shine a light up and down the supply chains and help make them more sustainable. We want companies to come on board as much for the supply chain visibility and reliability we can bring them as for the positive impact to their brands. Ethical sourcing needs to show that we're not just about sustainability; we're about sustainable business models.

TRANSPARENCY = COLLABORATION = PROBLEM SOLVING

ONE OF THE BIGGEST BENEFITS OF HAVING TRANSPARENCY UP AND down the supply chain is that it creates opportunities for creative problem solving that wouldn't otherwise be available. Take, for example, an issue we encountered with one of our Fair Trade Certified furniture factories in Vietnam. I can't share the name of the factory or the companies they supply for confidentiality reasons, but the story is a fascinating example of the supply chain challenges that many companies face.

Through our auditing process, we discovered that the factory met our conditions in all but one area: their workers were frequently putting in eighty-hour workweeks, especially during peak selling seasons. This was not only a violation of our Fair Trade standards, which cap the workweek at sixty hours, but also of Vietnamese labor laws. In a typical "pass-fail" auditing system, the factory would have been found out of compliance and given some kind of penalty, or they would have simply failed and not received certification. Given the gravity of the excessive overtime violation, our certification team discussed and considered decertifying the factory and walking away. But then we decided to take a different approach.

Because we had good relationships with all the stakeholders in the supply chain—the workers, the factory owners, and the companies that sourced their furniture there—we were able to bring everyone to the table to figure out why employees were being asked to work so much overtime. More importantly, we hoped to come up with a solution that would benefit everyone involved.

It would have been easy to simply assume that the factory was greedy and unscrupulous. We could have concluded that they were putting profits above people and simply punished them with decertification. But we chose to start by assuming that the parties had generally good intentions and a willingness to look for practical, mutually beneficial solutions. We're glad we did. It turns out that the excessive overtime issue was rooted, to a significant degree, in "buyer behavior." Essentially, the furniture retailers who were buying from the factory would often make large orders at the last minute, based on seasonal demand fluctuations, and weren't giving the factory much notice. In these instances, the factory had to mobilize their labor force to work long extra hours to fulfill the late orders.

Compounding the "rush order" issue was the fact that the factory had only short-term contracts with their retail partners. Because of this, the factory couldn't count on their business in the long term and therefore didn't feel they could make the investments in technology and new equipment needed to raise their productivity. They weren't willing to go to the bank and get a loan to invest in modern infrastructure that would help them handle demand fluctuations without overtaxing their workers, because they couldn't be sure they would be able to secure the business long enough to pay back the loans. It's not common for factories like this one to push back on buyers and not accept their late purchase orders—after all, they needed the business. So they didn't. And their workers paid the consequences by having to work excessively long hours.

Through several meetings with the factory and the buyers where we pored over spreadsheets and purchase orders, we identified the root of the problem and then started brainstorming how to solve it. It was in everyone's best interests to find a solution, with or without Fair Trade certification, so the discussions were remarkably frank, collegial, and productive.

In the end, we came up with a strategy that met everyone's needs. First off, the retailers committed to being more proactive in their ordering practices. They agreed to give the factory as much advance notice as possible when a big order was coming, even if the exact details of the order had yet to be solidified, so the factory could prepare to scale up. Perhaps more importantly, the retailers agreed to make long-term commitments to the factory so the owners could have the confidence in future business they needed to invest in improving the productivity and efficiency of their operations—without having to rely on excessive overtime to meet the production schedules. Over the following year, we collectively tracked overtime and saw it come down steadily. At the same time, the owners were able to actually raise their workers' wages due to the increased productivity, and the factory came into full compliance with our standard.

The lesson for us, which is also relevant for other approaches to social compliance and ethical sourcing, is that supply chain transparency opens the door to better collaboration between stakeholders. When you have better collaboration between stakeholders, you can find new and creative solutions you might not otherwise discover. These solutions can lead to better results for the factory and the brands and improved working conditions for the factory workers. In this case, we found a win-win-win solution, made possible by transparency and trust. I believe this is the future of supply chain management.

CONNECTING PEOPLE AT OPPOSITE ENDS OF THE SUPPLY CHAIN

IN THE SPRING OF 2022, AS THE DEADLY GRIP OF THE COVID-19 pandemic was starting to loosen, I revived one of my favorite rituals: visiting my local bookstore. On this particular occasion, I went to the iconic Powell's Books, located in Portland, Oregon—not my city of residence, but one where I am a frequent visitor. Powell's is a kind of palace for book lovers, occupying a full city block in downtown Portland. Its three stories are sectioned off into a loosely organized series of rooms, color-coded by topic, filled with sprawling stacks so high as to require ladders to reach the books on the uppermost shelves. The atmosphere feels like a Disneyland for books, where you can drift between genre-defined worlds in search of your next good read. Powell's is the kind of place you don't just go for a specific title. It's best experienced by allowing yourself the time to get lost.

I had given myself a good chunk of a Saturday morning to explore, and midway through my journey, I decided to recharge with a quick coffee break at the in-house café. As I waited in line to place my order, I noticed a sign sitting atop the large glass pastry case separating the patrons from the baristas with the title "Ask Me About How Our Coffee Impacts Farmers." My curiosity was naturally piqued, so I read further. The sign said, "We all need to pay more for coffee because it costs more than we think it does" and then explained how the café ensured that all of their coffee beans were grown by farmers who were fairly compensated for their labor.

By the time I finished reading the sign, they were ready for me to order, so I asked the friendly, tattooed young man behind the counter for an Americano. While I waited for the barista to prepare my drink, I couldn't help but eavesdrop on a conversation between a man and woman behind me in line who were both focused intently on the informational sign. "Oh, that's what Fair Trade means," said the man to the woman, who nodded in agreement. "No one's ever explained it to me before."

Listening to their Fair Trade epiphany, I felt an odd mixture of emotions—one that I've become familiar with over the years. On one hand I was happy to hear the Fair Trade brand that my colleagues and I have worked so hard to popularize over the decades being casually mentioned by a random coffee shop customer (even though the phrase "Fair Trade" didn't actually appear anywhere on the informational sign). On the other hand, I was frustrated that this was the first time they'd really understood what it means—indicating that the precise meaning of Fair Trade probably still remains elusive to many people.

In the early years of Fair Trade, I did a lot of media appearances, especially in response to how our model was helping to address the global coffee crisis of the early 2000s. I would use the same phrase in all my interviews to describe what we were doing: connecting consumers to the farmer and the family at the bottom of their coffee cup. That has always been the consumer-activation strategy of Fair Trade: humanize the product. Bring the producer to life. Build empathy and care for those who make our products possible. Yet we can only do that if we succeed in making transparent the long, complex, and opaque supply chains that bring products from field and factory to our kitchen table and closet. Twenty-six years later, I still don't think we've effectively delivered on that strategy.

Never has the Fair Trade movement in general been so successful in our efforts to awaken the public to the social and environmental impacts of their everyday purchases. More than ever before, everyday consumers *do* understand that every purchase matters. Yet, despite this progress, far too many people are like the couple in line at Powell's and don't really understand what Fair Trade truly represents. They know that, like other sustainability labels, it's generally a good thing. They have a vague notion that Fair Trade Certified items are produced in a way where those who work to grow and manufacture them receive a better deal. But they don't necessarily have an emotional connection to the real impact their purchases are making. Our label, for most consumers, is just a badge.

I'm convinced that in order for ethical sourcing to grow in consumer popularity, we have to get better at telling stories. The question is which stories to tell and how to tell them. Do consumers want "impact data" about how Fair Trade is changing each industry we're engaged in, with statistics on outcomes like farmer income, health and education indicators, and workplace safety? Do they want colorful personal stories about the real people who benefit from ethically sourced products every day? What do consumers need to become more emotionally invested in Fair Trade and other models of ethical sourcing, to feel more empowered and engaged? This is an ongoing inquiry for us. While we're still testing the technology and systems required to capture more robust data and content from the field, we can draw inspiration from a lot of interesting experimentation going on in the ethical sourcing industry as a whole.

A CHICKEN WATCH PARTY

When it comes to connecting consumers with the source of their food, an outstanding example is Vital Farms. The company isn't a Fair Trade partner—we haven't entered the egg business yet—but they are a true pioneer in the ethical sourcing movement and a B Corp to boot. Vital Farms, founded in 2007 by my friend and scuba-diving buddy Matt O'Hayer, has since grown into one of the most successful ethical food companies in the United States. Their eggs have become synonymous with the "pasture-raised" moniker they've helped to popularize over the last decade. They are also some of the best-tasting, most nutritious eggs available. In fact, I eat them virtually every morning for breakfast when I'm at home.

While cooking breakfast recently I had a vision of what Fair Trade's storytelling could become. I was scrambling a few of Vital Farms' eggs on the stove and had their colorful, recycled cardboard carton open in front of me on the counter. On it I noticed the words "See a farm where these eggs were laid." Below was a white space stamped with the name of a farm and a date. Upon further examination I found instructions to go to a section of the Vital Farms website and enter the name of the farm in order to see a video with a 360-degree view of the actual hens whose eggs I was about to eat (or at least their farm-level peers). I whipped out my phone, and a few clicks later I was watching a video of hens grazing in a forest on Boone Creek farm in Missouri with no cages in sight.

I was amazed. The level of transparency into Vital Farms' egg supply chain was remarkable. From my own vantage as a consumer, the story was quite compelling. Even though I was already a regular buyer of Vital Farms' eggs, it made me even more passionate about their brand and their mission. It made me appreciate their pasture-raised promise even more because I could see the hens grazing happily right there in front of me. It made me want to keep buying their eggs, regardless of their premium price tag, and then tell all my friends to do the same. They were truly delivering on their company's original tagline: "Honest food, ethically produced, no bullsh*t."

To be honest, I also felt a little envious. I was a thirty-five-year veteran of the ethical sourcing movement and had built my organization on the promise of connecting consumers with the source of their products; yet my friend's company was kicking my butt on the storytelling front. I wanted to talk to Matt about how they did it, so we scheduled a time to talk over Zoom.

He told me that figuring out a way to track their eggs from the over 300 family farms they source from all the way to the cartons people buy at the grocery store was a monumental task. Matt lit up as he described the technology they installed for their traceability program at their award-winning egg-washing and -packing plant, Egg Central Station, in Springfield, Missouri. "We've built these massive conveyor systems. They're 50,000 square feet of stainless-steel machinery equipped with robots that weigh all the eggs, assess their quality, and then sort them. Then they go down what look like bowling lanes. There are dozens of them feeding eggs into different cartons that get special codes printed connecting them to their farm of origin."

An operation like this obviously required a significant investment of time and money to build, and I wanted to know if making all this effort to give customers this level of transparency and connection to the story had been worth it. Matt's answer was simple. "Of course it has. All that effort pays for itself by building customer loyalty." This makes sense to me, of course, because I experienced it firsthand. Having that visual experience of engaging with a product and seeing the authenticity of its claims makes you want to keep buying it.

For Matt, it's also about making their product stand out in a very competitive marketplace. "It helps distinguish us from all the other egg brands. There are so many sustainability labels right now. It's gotten really crowded in that scene, and many companies are making a lot of claims—cruelty free, cage-free, etc. This has led to a lot of consumer confusion and a loss of trust around sustainability claims. But that hasn't been the case for us."

It's true. Vital Farms is considered to be the unofficial "godfather" of pasture-raised eggs. When Matt started the Austin-based company in 2007, they made a lot of effort to distinguish the pasture-raised label, which requires 108 square feet of pasture per hen, from other labels. Cage-free, for example, simply means the chickens aren't locked up in cages, and free-range requires only twenty square feet per hen. Their efforts have paid off. When they launched the company, pasture-raised eggs represented only a tiny fraction (0.7 percent) of the $5 billion egg industry. By 2016, the percentage had grown to 2.7 percent, with Vital Farms representing roughly 73 percent of that share (Sorvino, 2018). As of 2023, they were the number two overall egg brand in the United States and accounted for 93 percent of the pasture-raised market (Vital Farms, 2023).

Matt attributes a big part of their success to the trust they've built with customers through their unwavering commitment to supply chain transparency and traceability. As Matt told me, "We've hired companies to do anonymous studies for us where they follow consumers around in grocery stores. They watch what people buy and then ask if they can interview them. They ask questions about why they buy our eggs. What we've been told over and over is that customers simply like a brand they can trust. Once they find it, they keep buying it. But in order to build that trust, your brand has to be honest all the time."

THE FUTURE IS TRANSPARENT

I BELIEVE THAT VITAL FARMS' APPROACH TO HONEST, TRANSPARent storytelling represents the future of the ethical sourcing movement. For Fair Trade specifically, we need to invest in technology and the kind of supply chain data collection and storytelling connection that Vital Farms has done with their suppliers. Right now, our consumer experience is relatively two-dimensional. It's essentially just the Fair Trade Certified label on a package. There's no visual story attached to it. It lacks humanity, which is ironic, given our mission and extraordinary impact. As Keurig Dr Pepper chief sustainability officer Monique Oxender pointed out to me in our recent conversation, "I think the evolution we're seeing in the consumer marketplace is that they want to see more than just a smiling farmer. They want to understand what's behind the smile. They want to have real clarity on the real impact their purchases are making."

This is something I believe Fair Trade USA can develop in the next couple of years. We already collect a significant amount of data from our auditing processes. We have an amazing producer support team in the field—our boots on the ground in factories, farms, and producer communities all around the world. These "manual" data-collection opportunities are uniquely valuable to collect rich data and insights from producers on their compliance with the standard and its impact. We also need to develop our capabilities to capture and process data remotely using smartphone worker surveys, satellite imagery, sensors, artificial intelligence, block chain, and other emerging tools. Ultimately, if we want to capture the imagination of consumers and move them to action, we need to be able to turn all this producer data and content into meaningful storytelling. I believe that stories that elevate the humanity in our daily products and give us a sense of the power of our purchases will ultimately be decisive in the mainstreaming of Fair Trade and ethical sourcing.

The trend toward transparency and traceability up and down the supply chain is only going to grow over the coming years. Technological innovation will continue to make this easier and cheaper over time. Companies won't have any excuse for not knowing where their products come from and the conditions under which they are sourced. Plausible deniability with regard to bad practices will be a thing of the past. With greater visibility and a deeper understanding of their supply chains, the most successful companies will be those that have found ways to create value by making their supply chains more secure, reliable, and resilient. A partnership mentality between brands and suppliers, based on reciprocal benefit, will become more common. And the leap from supply chain transparency and reliability to supply chain sustainability will follow. This is precisely the promise of ethical sourcing. It not only protects companies from threats and risk but also holds the potential for creating significant new value for the firm, enabling its future success.

For us, the consuming public, things will also change as Gen Z comes of age. As we face the global threat of climate change and become more and more connected to each other through smartphones and social media, the reality of our mutual interdependence as a human family is only getting clearer. I believe that consumers will increasingly reward those companies that deliver sustainability through their products, which includes the sustainability of their supply chains. Today's consumers, and tomorrow's, are too savvy for hollow claims. They want more authenticity and more accountability.

8

FOR PEOPLE
AND PLANET

THE EXISTENTIAL ISSUE OF OUR TIME

IN THE FALL OF 2020, AS THE WORLD WAS STILL REELING FROM THE Covid-19 pandemic, the harsh realities of climate change hit close to home for me and my Fair Trade colleagues. During the first half of November, two massive Atlantic hurricanes moved through Central America only weeks apart. Eta and Iota, as they were called, reached categories four and five, respectively, and wreaked havoc across the region. The torrential rainfall, high winds, storm surges, and persistent flooding caused significant damage to the people and infrastructure of the region. Mountain streams and rivers overflowed their banks, flooding fields. Excessive rainfall led to landslides that wiped out entire farms, homes, and infrastructure. As my friend Rodolfo Peñalba, head of Comsa, a coffee cooperative in the central highlands of Honduras, told me at the time, "We lost harvested coffee, warehouses, vehicles, and roads. Two co-op members were killed. It was devastating."

Much of the damage was focused in some of Central America's most impoverished areas. These regions had already been devastated by the Covid-19 pandemic combined with a perpetually unstable agro-export economy. The double impact of Eta and Iota turned out to be the proverbial straw that broke the camel's back. Approximately 7.5 million people across Central America were affected. Farms and businesses were destroyed. Hundreds were killed. Thousands were displaced. The storms caused approximately $8.3 billion in total damage and accelerated the mass immigration north that was already underway in the region (International Federation of Red Cross and Red Crescent Societies [IFRC], 2021).

Nicaragua, Honduras, and Guatemala were hardest hit. According to the Economic Commission for Latin America and the Caribbean (ECLAC), roughly 80 percent of Honduras's agricultural sector was impacted. Damages in that country reached approximately $1.86 billion (IFRC, 2021). These nations are home to many of the farmers who produce Fair Trade coffee, cocoa, bananas, sugar, and pineapples. While we don't have exact data for the percentage of our producers affected, it was significant. It broke my heart to see the overnight devastation in some of the communities we had worked so hard to assist. The situation really drove home the central importance of climate change to all of us on the planet, and particularly to the marginalized populations that Fair Trade has always sought to support.

It wasn't as if 2020 was the first time I had recognized the profound existential threat posed by climate change. Environmental sustainability has been a core value for the Fair Trade mission since the beginning. For many of us, the plights of people and the planet have always been intertwined. But something about the devastation of Eta and Iota made it really sink in. According to ECLAC, it was the heaviest hurricane season in recorded history. There were thirty named storms that year, thirteen of which became hurricanes. It was also the fifth year in a row with above-average storm activity globally (IFRC, 2021). It was becoming obvious to many of us that the devastating impacts of climate change weren't something we needed to prepare for in the future—they were already here.

A LIFELONG ENVIRONMENTALIST

Protecting the environment has always been important to me. I developed a deep appreciation for nature during the childhood camping trips I took with my family in the Texas hill country and Colorado Rockies. As a teenager, I was an avid rock climber and backpacker and would frequently go on wilderness treks with my buddies. One of my first social causes was the "Save the Whales" movement in the 1970s. I still have the T-shirt to prove it! During my eleven years in Nicaragua, I loved working with coffee farmers up in the forested highlands, waking up to the song of exotic birds and the smell of rain-soaked volcanic soil. We lived close to the land, always tied to the natural rhythm of the seasons. After I started the coffee co-op PRODECOOP in 1990, we launched the country's first certified organic coffee program as a way of supporting farmers who wanted to preserve the natural habitat in and around their farms. This program also allowed us to get our farmers additional revenue in the form of organic premiums. That was

> when I fully realized that my love of nature and my pas-
> sion for improving people's lives were deeply connected.
> In the sustainability movement, people and planet are
> inseparable.

PUTTING A STAKE IN THE GROUND

IN SEPTEMBER 2020, THOUSANDS OF MILES AWAY FROM THE HURRI-
cane devastation in Central America, Walmart CEO Doug
McMillon delivered a speech at the company's virtual Sustainability Milestone Summit that I believe history will eventually deem
a watershed moment in the conscious capitalism movement. Videos and transcripts of the talk quickly made their way through the
business community. McMillon, who has become a well-known
advocate for sustainability over his decadelong tenure at the helm
of Walmart, used the speech to make a bold declaration. Walmart
would become a "regenerative company," he said, "one dedicated to
placing nature and humanity at the center of [its] business practices."

While Walmart has not always received public recognition for
its dedication to sustainability, their track record under McMillon
has actually been quite impressive. At the time of the speech, their
entire global operations were being powered with 29 percent renewable energy, and they had diverted 80 percent of their waste away
from landfills and incineration. They'd also raised their minimum
wage 50 percent since 2015. But as McMillon pointed out, what
Walmart had accomplished up until that point just wasn't enough,
given the severity of the climate crisis and the company's outsized
role in the consumer economy. As he said in the speech,

> Worldwide, environmental losses are cascading. What was once
> called climate change is now a climate crisis. Ice sheets are collapsing,

extreme weather events are increasing, catastrophic fires are occurring, oceans are acidifying and biodiversity is decreasing. Our natural systems are changing, and what they're telling us is we're not doing enough. We're actually doing irreversible damage to our planet. Nature sustains life, let alone the products our customers rely on. We must reverse nature loss before we reach a tipping point from which ecosystems will not recover.

Such words could be expected from the leaders of Greenpeace and Conservation International. The fact that they came from the CEO of the world's largest company was truly remarkable.

McMillon's characterization of the climate crisis was indeed eloquent. Becoming a "regenerative company" sounded very cutting-edge. But his speech wasn't just lip service. McMillon backed up his declarations with real public commitments. The company set a goal of achieving zero carbon emissions by 2040, without using carbon offsets. They made a commitment to "protect, manage and/or restore at least 50 million acres of land and one million square miles of ocean by 2030 related to ecosystems that produce food and other consumer products." They also committed to transforming their own operations in the United States, United Kingdom, Japan, and Canada to zero waste by 2025. And all this came on top of earlier sustainability pledges around renewable energy, zero waste, and the implementation of responsible sourcing practices with their top twenty commodities by 2025 (Walmart, 2024).

The commitments McMillon laid out in his "regenerative company" speech represented bold action, especially for a global giant like Walmart. Seeing such a mainstream company take climate change this seriously was an indication that the business community was shifting, and we had an opportunity to be a part of this shift. The environmental side of sustainability had always accompanied the social side in Fair Trade USA's mission, but as McMillon pointed out in his speech, we needed to do more.

As we look into the next phase of Fair Trade's evolution, it's clear to me that the issue of climate change will need to become more central to our mission. Similarly, I believe the ethical sourcing movement will be more successful to the extent that it can hold social, labor, and environmental goals in balance. In Fair Trade, we will need to make a bolder case for climate justice and show how hard the climate crisis is already impacting the most marginalized people on earth, like our friends at Comsa. Perhaps more importantly, we'll need to show how addressing living wage, worker well-being, human rights, and community development through programs like Fair Trade can directly help to protect nature and combat climate change. We want consumers and companies to know that by choosing Fair Trade, they are also protecting the planet. In order to do all of this, we need to find more and better ways to bake environmental sustainability into our standards and programs.

That's what I will explore in the chapter ahead: how Fair Trade has, up until now, worked to benefit both people and the environment and how we envision becoming even more effective and impactful in the future.

CLIMATE CHANGE ISN'T AN EQUAL OPPORTUNITY ISSUE

WHEN I WANTED TO SPEAK WITH SOMEONE ABOUT THE RELATION-ship between climate change and social sustainability, I couldn't imagine a better person than my old friend Tristan Lecomte. Tristan, as you may recall from earlier in the book, is the founder of one of the world's pioneering Fair Trade companies, Alter Eco, in Paris. After leaving Alter Eco, Tristan founded a company called Pur Projet that helps brands offset their carbon emissions through "carbon insetting" reforestation projects in their supply chains. I spoke to Tristan, a French native, from his current home in Chiang Mai, Thailand. He was particularly alarmed and passionate about the disproportionate impact that climate change is already having on marginalized farmers around the world.

"We tend to forget that poor people and poor countries are the most affected by climate change. Extreme climate events, for example, are much more present and visible in tropical areas than in the US or Europe. These countries are also the least equipped to deal with them. They have ailing governments. They don't have as many subsidies to invest in building climate resilience or adaptations." For Tristan, there is a disturbing irony in the situation.

Many of the poorer countries most affected by climate change are also the least responsible for causing it, because their carbon footprints are much smaller. The average Ethiopian person, for example, has a carbon footprint of roughly 400 pounds of CO_2 per person per year, whereas the average American has a footprint of twenty tons (40,000 pounds). That's 100 times more. When you look at CO_2 emissions over the last fifty years, what we call "developed countries" represent 92 percent of the global total. So climate change is really unfair to these small-scale farmers in Africa and the rest of the developing world.

The devastation we saw to the agricultural populations of Honduras, Nicaragua, and Guatemala resulting from Eta and Iota were a tragic reminder of climate change's disproportionate impact on rural communities in the tropics. But the less headline-worthy impacts are also important to consider. As Tristan points out, prolonged periods of hot weather are becoming more common everywhere in the world, especially in coffee-producing regions. "When there's a heat wave during the coffee flowering season, the flowers on coffee trees are 'burned,' which dramatically reduces their harvest. Most of these coffee farmers are heavily dependent on one crop for their income, and so they can essentially lose everything."

The threat climate change poses for the coffee industry, in particular, is on the radar of every major coffee company today. As Green Mountain Coffee Roasters founder Bob Stiller told me, "Pardon the pun, but the coffee industry is in hot water." Monique Oxender, who serves as chief sustainability officer for Keurig Dr Pepper, filled out the picture for me. "We've known that coffee has been under threat in very tangible, visible ways for a couple of decades now. As the climate warms and lands have been depleted, farmers have had to move to higher and higher altitudes searching for better conditions. But there's only so high up you can go, and you eventually run out of mountain." Coffee and virtually every other agricultural product worldwide is struggling to adapt to our changing climate, and smaller farmers—with fewer resources and little margin for error—are the most vulnerable.

The impacts of climate change are more obvious for an agricultural commodity like coffee, but they're also being felt by workers in other industries. Cara Chacon (Patagonia's former vice president of social and environmental responsibility) told me that the apparel industry is starting to pay more attention to the impact of climate change on their workers. "There are finally studies coming out on the effects of climate change on workers in the apparel supply chain and the hardships they're creating. And these studies match the impacts I've seen over the past two decades."

Cara also talked about the impact of heat waves on worker well-being and productivity. A July 2023 article in the *New York Times* cited some groundbreaking new research about the economic impact of hotter working environments, especially in factories (Davenport, 2023). According to one study published in the *International Journal of Biometeorology* in 2021, worker productivity drops by 25 percent when the temperature is over 90 degrees; when it reaches 100 degrees, productivity drops by 75 percent (Foster et al., 2021). Another study published by *Environmental Research Communications* found that the impact of heat was greater on workers in poorer countries, where the average worker loses approximately 5 percent of their wages on each hot day due to exhaustion and dehydration. In wealthier countries, losses are only 1 percent on average (Behrer, 2021).

Cara says that over the past five years the apparel industry has been waking up to the rise in climate-related worker hardships and displacement due to issues like food scarcity, extreme weather, and even rising sea levels.

We are looking at the very real possibility that the climate impacts will force workers in many supply chain sourcing hubs to move because they literally can't live in that area anymore. One easy way anyone can research the issue is to explore the National Oceanic and Atmospheric Administration (NOAA) website and use their Sea Level Rise Viewer to project how global coastlines will change over the next 20–30 years. For example, NOAA projects that much of Ho Chi Minh City in Vietnam will be underwater by 2050. This is one of the biggest apparel manufacturing hubs in the world. If NOAA's projections are accurate—and we assume they are as we are seeing the impacts play out in real time—there could be millions of people worldwide who are going to be displaced within a few decades. (NOAA Office for Coastal Management, 2024)

The link between environmental disasters and social problems is increasingly clear. But the effect also runs both ways. There is a growing understanding in sustainability circles that when we invest in the socioeconomic stability of producer communities, people are better able to contribute to protecting the natural environment. It turns out that, in many cases, the best stewards of the natural environment are those who directly depend on it for their sustenance.

FROM SUSTAINABLE TO REGENERATIVE

In recent years, you may have heard the term "regenerative agriculture" used in everything from nonprofit mission statements to Netflix documentaries. Indeed, the concept has become quite popular in sustainability circles and beyond. Since 2020, many large companies, including Unilever, PepsiCo, General Mills, Nestlé, and Walmart, have built regenerative agriculture into their sustainability commitments. While there is no universally accepted definition of the term, it includes practices centered around some core principles: minimizing soil disturbance, using cover crops, reducing chemical inputs, diversifying crops and intercropping, conserving water, and integrating livestock.

On the surface, regenerative agriculture may seem simply like a rebranding of the term "sustainable agriculture," which has been widely used for decades to describe food systems that do less harm and seek to sustain the natural environment. But the shift in terminology also represents a shift in mentality. To sustain something means to protect what's there. Advocates of regenerative agriculture argue that conventional farming has already done so much damage to our ecosystems—depleting soil, reducing biodiversity—that we shouldn't just aim to "sustain." The agriculture of the future should regenerate, restore, and replenish the natural resources upon which it depends.

STEWARDS OF THE LAND

ON A COOL, MISTY OCTOBER MORNING, SANTIAGO RIVERA LEADS me and my group of coffee buyers on a tour of his farm. Santiago, you may remember, was an early member of the Fair Trade cooperative I started in Nicaragua in 1990. There's a certain pep to his step that comes with days like this, when he gets to proudly lead a bunch of gringos on an educational tour of his farm and tell us his story. As we try to keep up, pushing our way past the thick, leafy foliage adorning the long rows of coffee bushes, Santiago is in "nature mode."

He points out the avocado trees he planted among the coffee plants in one quadrant of the farm. He explains how, in addition to generating food for his family, they also provide important shade for his cash crop below and protect the valuable soil from erosion on the steep slopes. He motions upward toward the taller canopy trees—species like caoba, kapok, and inga—and asks if we can hear the migratory songbirds singing. He recounts a time in his life when coffee prices were so low, and he was so poor and desperate, that he had to cut down many trees on the property to sell as firewood just to feed his family.

At one point, Santiago stops and picks a coffee cherry off one of his trees, motioning for us to gather round and take a look. He smashes the bright red cherry to reveal a small, white larva—a coffee berry borer, he explains. A dead coffee berry borer, to be more specific. Santiago tells us how the tiny insect met its end by ingesting a fungus called *Beauveria bassiana*, which he has sprayed throughout the farm. It's an alternative to pesticides he learned about from his co-op's integrated pest management (IPM) program, a protocol for reducing pesticide use within agricultural systems worldwide. Because the fungus is nontoxic to humans, he's been able to keep the borers under control without endangering the health of his family or his water supply. Santiago is proud of the fact that, like most Fair Trade farmers, his shade-grown coffee is also certified organic.

At one point on our walk, I glanced up at the faces of the buyers for whom Santiago's tour was intended. They represented some of our most important importers, like Royal Coffee and Sustainable Harvest, and were no strangers to small coffee farms. Yet I could see how impressed they were by Santiago's level of environmental knowledge and sophistication. With no high school degree (much less a college diploma), Santiago has learned the art and science of agroecology on his small plot of forested land through hands-on experience and some training from his local co-op. It's a familiar drill for him now. Through the co-op's "farmer-to-farmer" training program, Santiago now hosts his peers and teaches them about his approach and results, creating a powerful demonstration effect for others in the region.

Like so many farmers, Santiago knows his livelihood depends on the land he cultivates. He and his family know the damaging effects water pollution can have on their health. He's intuitively aware of the natural cycles on the farm and how he must be a careful steward of its delicate ecology in order to sustain healthy production into the future. Santiago has even started to feel the impacts of climate change through rising annual temperatures and prolonged periods of drought, which threaten to reduce his yields. He does his part by protecting the trees on his farm and planting more. He feels motivated and proud to care for his little slice of mountainside—the water, soil, and forest ecology—for the sake of his family's economic future.

Tristan Lecomte sees a huge opportunity to empower farmers like Santiago to become even better stewards of their local ecosystems. In Tristan's experience, when farmers are able to access both the resources and the training, they adopt farming techniques that are much more ecologically friendly. "Traditionally, small farmers have a diversity of crops, as opposed to a monocrop, and are more resilient.

They have better soil, they're better adapted to climate change, and they can store more carbon."

For example, much of the coffee grown by small farmers falls under the category of "shade grown." If you've paid attention to coffee labels, you've likely seen this term. It essentially means that the coffee was grown under the shade of taller trees that make up the forest canopy. Forests, in fact, are coffee's natural habitat. The wild coffee plants from which modern varieties were developed all grow in the shade. Most of the coffee grown in the world was shade grown until the 1970s and 1980s, when governments in coffee regions made a concerted effort to plant new "full-sun" varieties. These varieties were more productive but required more chemical inputs in the form of fertilizers and pesticides. They also required farmers to cut down the forests that provided shade for their coffee, eliminating a valuable carbon sink and habitat for wildlife.

Today, much of the world's coffee is "full sun," but roughly 25 percent is still shade grown, and that percentage is much higher on small coffee farms (Jha et al., 2014). So there's an environmental advantage to preserving smaller, family run, shade-grown operations. In many cases, when small farmers go belly up, they sell their land to larger estates, which tend to be more chemical intensive and reliant on predominantly sun-grown varieties of coffee. The land is essentially converted from a more diverse agroforestry ecosystem to a more chemical-intensive, full-sun monocrop. This releases carbon, degrades soil, reduces wildlife habitat, and increases vulnerability to the changing climate. In other cases, small farmers end up selling to large cattle ranchers who cut down the forest to plant pasture. This often leads to contamination of water sources and a public health crisis in rural communities. Similar dynamics are at play in other agricultural industries as well.

Tristan believes that small farmers like Santiago could be some of the biggest allies in the fight against climate change.

There are approximately 500 million small-scale farmers in the world. Yet only a small fraction have adopted agroforestry practices or regenerative agriculture practices or climate friendly agricultural practices so far. I believe we should focus our efforts on helping these people. They are the most affected by climate change, but if we can get them the resources and the training, they can also help to fight it. If we get them a decent price for their product, we can help them to adapt to the changing climate and directly contribute to climate action by planting trees or implementing regenerative practices.

In our work with small farmers like Santiago, I've seen this causal connection between social investment and environmental sustainability time and time again. To borrow a concept from psychology 101, there's a kind of Maslow's hierarchy of needs at play. As people are able to rise above the poverty level, they have greater capacity to consider and test new, more environmentally sustainable farming methods. When they're not worried about feeding their families, they are better able to invest in the long-term stewardship of the land that supports them. When they know they will be able to stay on their land, they will more naturally begin to think about future generations.

It's in their best interest to do so. They live on the land where they farm, and so do their families. Farmers and workers in developing countries often don't have the kinds of buffers between themselves and their natural environment that many of us in richer countries tend to have. They don't have the ability to disconnect from the natural world. They drink the water that could be contaminated by their own use of agrochemicals. They rely on the long-term health of the soil they cultivate on a daily basis and plan to leave to their kids. Many farmers are increasingly seeing how their farming choices affect the climate where they're trying to grow their crops, for instance, impacting rainfall patterns and rising temperatures. If they can access the proper training and support to make their production more ecologically sustainable, most of the farmers I know will enthusiastically implement what they learn.

GREEN HALO EFFECT

When I think about the public perception of Fair Trade, I tend to think that we need to do more to educate consumers about the positive environmental impact of our model. But when I talked to Adam Werbach about this issue, he had a different take. Adam is a seasoned veteran in the sustainability movement and a bit of a genius. He was the youngest president of the Sierra Club at age twenty-three and has since had an impressive career as founder and CEO of Act Now Productions and chief sustainability officer for Saatchi & Saatchi, where he helped Fortune 500 clients develop strategic sustainability initiatives.

Adam was later at Amazon as their global lead of sustainable shopping. In that role, he helped launch Amazon's Climate Pledge Friendly initiative, which helps customers find products on Amazon that have a net-positive impact on the environment. In his work with Amazon, Adam was privy to an extraordinary amount of data about consumer behavior. In a recent chat, he had an interesting insight to share with me. "We found that customers essentially see environmental and social sustainability as one. With Fair Trade, specifically, we found that consumers attribute environmental benefits

> to the brands that have Fair Trade certification. It's
> the way the consumer's mind works. They believe that
> because it's good, socially, it must be environmentally
> good as well."

OUR APPROACH TO THE ENVIRONMENT

SUSTAINABLE AGRICULTURE AND ENVIRONMENTAL CONSERVATION
have been requirements of our Fair Trade standards from the very
beginning. In fact, roughly one-third of the compliance criteria in
our standards are environmental—and this is especially true in our
requirements for farms and fisheries.

Our Agricultural Production Standard, for example, requires
farms to implement practices that protect soil, water, and forest
resources. But our biggest focus has been on agricultural chemicals.
The sad reality of global agriculture is that despite decades of research
showing the harmful impacts of chemical pesticides, fungicides,
herbicides, and fertilizers, these agricultural inputs remain common.
Organizations like the Environmental Working Group, the Pesticide Action Network, and the UN Environment Programme have
created extensive lists of the most harmful agricultural chemicals in
use worldwide. These include cancer-causing agrochemicals that are
banned in the United States but still manufactured and exported by
US companies to many countries around the world.

In response to this reality, we created our own list of banned
chemicals for all Fair Trade farms. While it's not at the level of an
organic certification, which doesn't allow any chemical inputs, I'm
proud of how extensive our banned chemicals list truly is. It's based
on those developed by many leading environmental organizations,
but we've gone a step further than most. For example, we no longer allow the use of Monsanto's Roundup, one of the world's most

popular herbicides, on Fair Trade farms. This created quite a stir among our coffee farmers in some countries, where Roundup was used extensively to control weeds between rows of coffee trees. As my friend Carlos Vargas, former CEO of Costa Rica's largest coffee cooperative, told me, "When the Fair Trade restriction on Roundup was first implemented, our farmers were pretty upset. But with technical assistance and support from the co-op, we helped them develop other means of weed control, such as planting nitrogen-fixing cover crops between rows to suppress weeds. This approach added fertility to the soil and helped them save money. In the end, the farmers came around."

Integrated pest management (IPM) is also a cornerstone of our agricultural standards. While not as stringent as organic, IPM is an ecosystem-based strategy for controlling crop-damaging insects on the farm. It does allow for the use of some pesticides, but only after other measures have been taken, such as using biological controls (like Santiago's use of *Beauveria bassiana* to fight the berry borer), planting pest-resistant varieties, or implementing mechanical or environmental barriers to pests. When used, chemical pesticides must be applied more sparingly and strategically than in conventional agriculture. Among its benefits, IPM reduces production costs and exposure risks for farmers and helps protect bees, which are vital for crop pollination. Interestingly, Walmart and other retailers have announced plans to source their produce exclusively from farms that implement IPM practices in the future.

Beyond IPM, most Fair Trade co-ops provide extensive training and technical assistance to their members in support of sustainable-agriculture practices that go beyond the requirements of the standard, such as organic composting and fertilization. These simple practices can generate the multiple benefits of reducing cost, boosting farm yields and farmer income, and protecting or restoring the natural environment.

Our Capture Fisheries Standard also has significant environmental requirements. Many of our criteria build on the Marine Stewardship Council's environmental standards and focus primarily on decreasing overfishing and "bycatch." To control overfishing, we require our certified fishermen to use a variety of different methods to give the marine life populations they depend on a chance to regenerate. In some instances, certified fisheries are required to use a "quadrant" system. The ocean is essentially mapped with GPS into distinct areas, and fishermen are required to rotate through them systematically, allowing enough time for the ecosystem to recover before returning to a specific location.

Bycatch is another big issue, particularly in the tuna industry where we have begun to certify. Traditionally, large tuna boats have used big nets that they drag across the ocean, scooping up the fish below. In addition to capturing tuna, the nets also end up capturing many other species, including dolphins. Our standards require all certified tuna operations to either switch to pole-and-line fishing or, if using nets, to modify them to include an escape route for dolphins, which helps ensure that Fair Trade tuna is also "dolphin safe."

Even our Factory Production Standard has environmental requirements, which are mostly focused on energy and pollution. We require all facilities to have plans in place to reduce energy consumption. We also ban the use of all toxic chemicals on the American Apparel and Footwear Association's Restricted Substances List (American Apparel and Footwear Association, 2023). Water pollution is a big issue in the apparel industry, so we have strict requirements for the treatment of wastewater before it leaves factories and makes its way into waterways. This is particularly important for denim, where the "blue water" leaving factories is saturated with toxic dyes used to give blue jeans their classic hue. Rivers and streams around many factories are literally dyed blue, and the chemicals cause significant damage to both people and the aquatic ecosystem (Warren, 2021).

I'm proud of the level of environmental protection we've built into our standards. It's helped us to deliver on our promise to consumers that when they buy a product with our label on it, they're not just supporting producers; they're also investing in a cleaner environment. But in addition to enforcing environmental regulations among our producers, we also provide incentives for those who make the extra effort to protect and regenerate the natural environment—namely, in the form of our organic premiums.

FAIR AND ORGANIC

THE NEXT TIME YOU'RE WALKING THROUGH A GROCERY STORE, TRY surveying the various products bearing our Fair Trade Certified label—bananas, tea, chocolate, coffee. If you pay attention, you may notice a trend. On most products, alongside our little green and black label, you're likely to see a US Department of Agriculture organic seal as well. In fact, roughly 70 percent of Fair Trade food products today are also certified organic. The two sustainability labels are, in many ways, the perfect complement for each other—one representing ecological and the other representing social sustainability. As my Spanish-speaking friends would say, Fair Trade and organic are *amigos inseparables*.

There are many reasons for this interconnection. Part of it has to do with the target audience for both products. The same conscientious shoppers who care about Fair Trade also tend to care about organic products, health, wellness, and the environment—and they are usually willing to pay a bit more. For this reason, many of the companies we work with combine the two labels (often adding others). They are essentially supercharging their brand's sustainability reputation.

The connection between the two movements isn't just in the mind of the consumer. It also represents some very concrete commitments that our industry partners have made to health, wellness, and environmental sustainability. Companies committed to organics were the first to join us and ask if we could certify their farms, combining the two labels. They were philosophically predisposed to support farmers. They also knew consumers would pay more for organics, which gave them a way to cover the extra cost of Fair Trade at a time when consumer demand for our products was still untested.

But perhaps the biggest way that we have rewarded sustainable agriculture and organic cultivation, historically, is through the extra price premiums we offer our farmers in many of our categories for going organic. Most significantly, with coffee our standards guarantee an additional price premium of $0.30 per pound for all coffee beans that are also organically certified. That's in addition to the guaranteed price minimum of $1.40 per pound and our $0.20 per pound community development or impact premium.

Our established organic premiums are particularly important for producers because they can't get them anywhere else. Outside Fair Trade, consumers will generally pay a higher price for organic products, and some of this trickles down to the farmers. But organic certification alone doesn't guarantee farmers a premium. The prices organic farmers are able to fetch on the open market fluctuate dramatically. So our established premiums provide a significant incentive for farmers to go organic. It's an incentive that many of the producers we've worked with have responded to.

I'm confident that our commitment to organic agriculture will continue to play an important role in Fair Trade's approach to battling climate change in the future. Organic production, it turns out, is better for the climate. Studies by the Rodale Institute's Farm Trial program have shown that organic food production uses 45 percent less energy and emits 40 percent less carbon than nonorganic production. So the more of our farmers we can motivate to go organic, the lighter their carbon impact will be.

INVESTING IN CLEAN WATER

The environmental impact of Fair Trade doesn't only come from organic price premiums and ecological standards. Many of our communities around the world have used the funds from their community development premiums to fund nature-positive projects within their communities.

One example of how premiums have addressed both an environmental and a public health issue comes from the Aprocassi cooperative in Peru. In this community, as in many coffee-growing regions around the world, small farmers historically "washed" their coffee harvest in small washing stations, or processing mills. This involved removing the outer pulp of the beans and mucilage and then resting the inner "parchment" coffee in a water tank for twelve to eighteen hours to allow for flavor-enhancing fermentation. Traditionally this process required a lot of water, which was typically diverted from nearby streams. The runoff created by these activities was then diverted back into the nearest stream. This led to severe water pollution, destruction of fish and other wildlife habitat, and serious human health problems for communities living downstream who often bathe and wash dishes in the streams.

To address the issue, Aprocassi invested their community development funds to support their farmers in switching pulping and fermentation systems to modern Colombian machines, reducing water usage by 92 percent. They also helped farmers dig evaporation ponds where the wastewater could settle, keeping the runoff

> out of the streams. Within three years, every member of the co-op had implemented the new system. After that, regular water testing conducted by the co-op helped communities verify the reduction and eventual removal of the harmful bacteria and other contaminants they had previously battled. According to Abdias Ortiz, the co-op's general manager, "This had a tremendous positive impact on the ecological health of the streams. Our fish stock gradually came back, and we saw a significant reduction in gastrointestinal disease in the downstream communities."

WE NEED TO DO MORE

I'M PROUD OF OUR EFFORTS TO BUILD ENVIRONMENTAL SUSTAINability into our model. As we've discussed thus far in this chapter, there's a direct correlation between improving the social and economic stability of producers and the health of the environment in their communities. Between the environmental components of our standards and our organic premiums, ecological sustainability is already a big part of our impact. Yet, as Doug McMillon conveyed in his 2020 speech, we all need to do more. Marginal improvements are no longer enough. Climate change is too consequential an issue for us not to be dedicating even more of our time, energy, and resources to it. We need to "green" the Fair Trade movement.

These are discussions we've begun to pursue in earnest at Fair Trade USA and in the ethical sourcing movement. We're conducting research into ways we can do a better job of contributing to the climate cause. We're having a lot of conversations with the experts who can help us think about this topic in deeper and more innovative ways. We are making connections with other environmental groups and climate-smart organizations like Tristan Lecomte's Pur Projet to generate ideas and partnerships. Like so many aspects of our model, this is an evolving opportunity for innovation, and we're right in the middle of it.

One of the most obvious ways we can address climate change within Fair Trade would be to add more "climate-smart" agricultural requirements, training, technical assistance, and incentives to our standards and programs. Even though roughly one-third of our criteria are already environmental, few focus explicitly on climate change mitigation and resilience. Similarly, we offer financial incentives for organic certification but nothing related to climate-positive measures such as regenerative agriculture. It may be time to expand our focus from supporting organic agriculture to also supporting nonorganic regenerative and climate-smart agriculture.

There are many climate-friendly practices we could build into the model. They all revolve around increasing the amount of carbon that any given agricultural system preserves by reducing carbon outputs and increasing carbon absorption. At the core of these climate-smart practices is soil management, and for good reason. Soil is the foundation of our food system, and the more we can protect it, the more we can contribute to the long-term health of agricultural ecosystems. Soil is also the biggest carbon sink on the planet. In fact, the world's soil contains almost twice as much carbon as all the plants and animals and atmosphere combined (Ontl and Schulte, 2012). According to a study by Colorado State University's Natural Resource Ecology Lab, applying a variety of soil conservation measures could help soil absorb and store another four gigatons of carbon annually (Paustian et al., 2019).

Soil-friendly, carbon-farming methods are broadly applicable to any scale of agriculture. For example, by applying compost to soil, planting legumes as cover crops, or integrating livestock into crop systems, farms can generate their own fertility and become less dependent on carbon-intensive chemical fertilizers (Paustian et al., 2019). No-till farming is another way to reduce the amount of carbon loss from the agricultural system. When plowed or tilled, the soil releases carbon into the atmosphere, and the delicate soil ecosystem is damaged. We are exploring ways that we can address these different dimensions of soil conservation by updating our standards and farmer-training programs.

Another idea we're exploring is adding a carbon-sequestration premium to the model. Currently, of the approximately 1 million farmers we work with, roughly 600,000 are practicing agroforestry on their land. Many of them are coffee or cocoa farmers who, like Santiago, have integrated trees into their agricultural system, and collectively they represent a significant carbon sink. Yet most of them have no way to monetize the "ecological service" they're providing to the planet. There may be ways for us to get these farmers credit in the form of premiums, like we do with organic certification, for planting and preserving trees on their farms or implementing regenerative soil practices. Not only would this bring more income to our existing farmers and reward their current practices, but it could also incentivize more farmers to transition to carbon sequestration in their operations.

When I asked Tristan about ideas for how we can improve our climate impact, he talked about a process called carbon "insetting," which is at the core of Pur Projet's mission. Carbon insetting enables companies to offset their carbon emissions by planting trees within their own supply chains. Normally, carbon offsetting occurs when a polluting company buys a "carbon credit" to make up for the greenhouse gases it has emitted. Those credits typically fund environmental projects around the world that aim to reduce future emissions, such as reforestation and renewable energy projects. Insetting is similar, except it entails a more directed investment in environmental projects within the supply chain of the company purchasing the offset. Instead of supporting a random project somewhere in the world, insetting allows a company to both offset emissions and strengthen its own supply chain.

Pur Projet provides insetting services and "nature-based impact projects" to companies like Nespresso, Mars, and General Mills by helping them invest in improving the carbon-smart agricultural practices of their farmers. Agroforestry is a big focus. In Colombia, for example, they are helping coffee and cocoa farmers integrate more native tree species into their farms. Not only do these trees help rebuild native plant and animal habitats, but they also sequester carbon. In many cases, these farmers are then trained in ecological logging practices and sustainably harvest wood that they can sell for extra income. Through their insetting projects, Pur Projet is able to provide meaningful carbon reductions for its client companies, improve ecosystem health, and provide better livelihoods for their farmers. It's a win-win-win scenario.

Insetting is fast becoming an alternative to traditional offsetting as more and more companies begin to make net-zero commitments. In fact, it's a big part of the Net-Zero Standard, launched by the Science Based Targets initiative (SBTi) in 2021. According to SBTi co-founder Alberto Carillo Pineda, the standard "offers companies robust certification to demonstrate to consumers, investors and regulators that their net-zero targets are reducing emissions at the pace and scale required to keep global warming to 1.5°C" (Science Based Targets, 2021).

Tristan sees a golden opportunity for Fair Trade and other ethical sourcing programs to promote insetting in global supply chains. Given our years of friendship, he is quick to give me a hard time when he thinks we're moving too slowly. "You're already in there auditing and working with everyone in the supply chain, and you've built a lot of trust. You could simply add another layer to your existing infrastructure," he told me with a look of playful reproach. "You could help your farmers develop and sell insetting as a new service in the form of planting trees, conserving forest, or protecting the soil. What are you waiting for?"

This is, of course, a fantastic idea. Companies already work with us, in part, to showcase to their customers that they're committed to sustainability on the social side. Helping them to offset their carbon footprint and then communicate that in a compelling way to consumers could be a huge opportunity for everyone.

As we consider how to implement climate-centered improvements to our model, we have several different options—and limited resources. First, we could define the producer practices we'd like to support, then codify them into our standards. This could include, for example, a requirement that all farms get a certain percentage of their fertility from compost or cover crops to reduce their use of carbon-heavy chemical fertilizers. If we went in this direction, we wouldn't be able to make these changes mandatory overnight. Rather, we would have to gradually integrate them so that our existing certified producers would have time to adapt their methods. And I'm skeptical about how much farmer support we would get in the multi-stakeholder consultation that we would need to conduct before implementing such significant changes to our agricultural standard—unless, of course, significant philanthropic funding was available to support the transition. Clearly, more farm research is needed to demonstrate how regenerative agriculture ultimately benefits farmers by boosting soil fertility, improving yields, and reducing production costs. The adoption of new practices would accelerate if farmers could see them as in their own best interest.

Alternatively, we could make these added carbon standards optional, almost like extra credit for farmers who meet the core Fair Trade standard. Then farmers could choose to implement them and take advantage of the annual Fair Trade audit to verify their fulfillment. As a result, they would gain an extra level of certification—akin to a climate-friendly merit badge—which they could use to negotiate better prices for their products from buyers interested in paying to reduce or offset their carbon emissions. Perhaps we could even develop an added premium with this extra climate designation, like we do with organic certification. So if producers choose to go above and beyond our base standards and get verified as having fulfilled climate-friendly criteria, they could potentially obtain a climate premium from our industry partners.

If we're going to successfully implement climate programs in our model in the future, we will need better tools to measure impact. Technology will be a big enabler in this regard. We are now preparing to geolocate and map all our farms around the world so that we can use satellite imaging and remote sensor data to monitor and measure their progress over time with, say, forest conservation. Having rich, real-time geospatial data will help us to verify and support the real impact of our programs. Further, translating these practices into simple metrics, like tons of carbon sequestered from the atmosphere, will help farmers monetize their practices by selling to companies who want to reduce or offset their emissions. I believe that with more meaningful data, we can make quicker progress toward getting climate-smart farmers the financial support they deserve.

OUR KIDS ARE EXPECTING IT

I RECENTLY HAD A CONVERSATION ABOUT CLIMATE CHANGE WITH Bryant Ison, a former collaborator, that had a big impact on my perspective. I first met Bryant in 2014 when he was a marketing director for PepsiCo. We partnered with PepsiCo to certify the cane sugar for a new line of craft soda they were launching called Caleb's Kola, hoping to appeal to the more socially conscious Millennial generation of soda drinkers. PepsiCo later discontinued Caleb's due to poor sales, but I remain impressed with Bryant's insight and grateful for his commitment to our partnership.

When I asked Bryant to share his thoughts about the importance of climate change to the Fair Trade movement, his answer was simple. If we want to remain relevant to younger generations, Fair Trade has to make climate a priority. "The eco anxiety of Gen Z is through the roof," he said. "They're constantly on social media and being fed an unprecedented level of catastrophic messages related to climate change. By contrast, they also see that the governments of the world are not willing to do anything about it. As a result, it creates a tremendous sense of anxiety."

Bryant has three sons, ages twelve, sixteen, and twenty-three, so he's experienced this general mentality directly.

My youngest son recently went on an ecological field trip for school, and I got a chance to sit through their reports. All the kids were talking doom and gloom. They essentially all think that humanity is done for. The earth is sick and dying, and we're all toast. We have this whole generation of kids who essentially see disaster on the horizon and don't know what to do. So if there's a way that Fair Trade can make the connection to climate, it can at least give them something they can do. It won't, of course, solve the ecological catastrophe all by itself. But what if buying Fair Trade could be a simple act of helping both people and the planet? It would help address the anxiety of their generation.

Bryant's experience reflects mine as well. My son, Emiliano, is currently thirty-three, and my daughter, Camila, is twenty-five. They are both well informed and concerned about the state of the world. In their own ways, they're both social justice activists too. But they struggle with their generation's general sense of hopelessness every day. Many consider them and their cohorts to be the digital generation, but I also think of them as the climate generation. They've been raised their whole lives hearing about the catastrophic impacts of climate change, and that's been stressful. But it's also created a profound expectation. They expect companies and governments to do something about the climate. They're the ones who will be in the prime of their lives in 2050, when many of the more shocking predictions of climate collapse may occur. It's their future we have in our hands, and I believe we all have to do more to protect it.

So as we move into the next chapter of the Fair Trade and ethical sourcing movements, it's crucial that we embrace the climate challenge with greater intention and creativity. We also have to do a better job of communicating this connection between social well-being and environmental sustainability to the increasingly concerned citizen-consumers of the world. We have to make the case—and back it up—that investing in a more equitable global economy will also bring a more environmentally sustainable one.

9

WHO PAYS FOR THE COST OF SUSTAINABILITY?

HOW MUCH WILL YOU PAY FOR YOUR BANANAS?

When you walk into a grocery store, what's the first thing you see beyond the automatic sliding doors and the shopping carts? Think about it for a moment. Of course, the answers will vary based on what store you're shopping at and which entrance you're using. But it's likely that one of the first things you'll see is a big pile of beautiful, greenish-yellow bananas with a large sign over it listing the price. In 2024, the average retail price in the United States was somewhere around $0.58 per pound.

You probably haven't given the price of bananas much thought, but this often-taken-for-granted number is critical in the wonky world of supermarket psychology. For many in the grocery business, it's a well-known fact that customers often choose where to shop, consciously or unconsciously, based on the price of bananas. The tropical fruit is what's called a "known value item" (KVI), like bread or milk. So supermarkets compete with each other to offer the lowest prices possible, and they make sure to showcase them in the prime real estate within the store.

Grocery stores are so obsessed with the price of bananas that they often discount them at the expense of their margins. In a typical produce department, for example, the average markup across all fruits and vegetables is roughly 35 percent. For bananas, the average is more like 10 to 15 percent. When stores run price promotions, which they frequently do for KVIs, they're often only breaking even. The fruit ends up being a kind of loss leader for retailers anxious to satisfy a banana-hungry public and keep them coming back for more.

Bananas have long been a staple in the US diet. The United States is the world's largest importer of bananas, consuming one-quarter of the global total; 75 percent of US consumers eat the fruit regularly (*National Geographic*, 2017), and on average we each consume twenty-seven pounds of bananas per year (Dorfner, 2017). They are the world's biggest fruit export, accounting for roughly $7 billion annually, and the fourth-largest agricultural commodity on earth behind wheat, rice, and corn. We consume more bananas than apples and oranges combined, and their comparatively lower prices reflect that (Koeppel, 2008).

Yet, as Joe Fassler points out in his 2019 article for the *Counter*, the low price of bananas has created a strange kind of ignorance about their true cost. "Low cost tends to lend products an air of invisibility. It's only when a purchase really costs us that we start to look more closely, asking larger questions. And the singularly low cost of bananas has thrust them into a unique position in our lives. They're both ubiquitous and completely unexamined. We rely on them completely, and yet we know nothing about them" (Fassler, 2019).

When you start to examine the low price of bananas, a bizarre irony emerges. As Fassler writes, "Strangely, we pay less for bananas than we do for durable, easy-to-transport items of produce that come from much closer to home. Considering that the delicate and intensely perishable fruit lives no more than two weeks once chopped from the tree, and is shipped from thousands of miles away in chilled containers, it's unthinkable that it costs less than white potatoes, or carrots—which both go for about 70 cents a pound at retail."

These artificially deflated prices come at a significant cost. Bananas are considered one of the most environmentally and socially damaging agricultural commodities on earth. Starting in the late nineteenth century, when the world's two biggest fruit companies, Chiquita and Dole, were formed under the names United Fruit and Standard Fruit, respectively, the endeavor to grow, transport, and sell this highly perishable fruit has wreaked havoc on the ecology and communities of the tropical nations where bananas are sourced. Governments of nations derisively dubbed "banana republics" have been toppled. Rainforests have been burned down to clear land for banana plantations. Water sources have been poisoned, and hundreds of thousands of workers have been put to work in conditions akin to slave labor. All of this in the name of cheap bananas (Koeppel, 2008).

Of course, the banana industry today has come a long way and isn't as damaging as it used to be, thanks to improved regulations and a much more conscious public and industry. Dole, Fyffes, and Chiquita, in particular, have begun to rectify some of their past agricultural misdeeds by developing partnerships with Fair Trade USA, Rainforest Alliance, Fairtrade International (FLO), and various organic certifiers. But banana production remains one of the most environmentally harmful and socially disruptive agricultural industries in the world. Much of the ecological damage stems from the fact that bananas are an extreme monoculture. Nearly all of the world's banana exports are from one specific variety, the Cavendish. This makes them extremely ecologically fragile and susceptible to a wide variety of diseases. As a result, banana cultivation is highly dependent on chemical inputs. In fact, the banana export industry uses more petrochemicals than any other crop besides cotton (Koeppel, 2008).

Most of the world's commercial bananas are still grown on large plantations, thousands of acres in size and staffed by thousands of workers who often live in company towns. I've visited some of these plantations across Latin America. Workers are often subjected to dismal working and living conditions. In some countries, they still sleep in crowded bunkhouses situated in or next to the fields where they work. They work long hours and are often exposed to toxic insecticides, herbicides, and fungicides, which are sprayed by crop dusting planes while workers are still in the fields or adjacent villages (Calabria, 2017). As in most agricultural industries, these workers aren't paid well for their efforts. In fact, workers collectively receive only 4 percent of the price you pay for a supermarket banana (*National Geographic*, 2017).

The disparity between what a banana costs a consumer and the true cost of production and distribution along the supply chain perfectly illustrates a core question in the world of sustainable business: Who bears the cost of the externalities? Economists define externalities as "the environmental and social costs of production that are not reflected in the price of a product" (Edmonds, 2012). But someone has to pay these costs. Often, externalities such as pollution and its public health impact have been borne by society or addressed through government-sponsored cleanup campaigns paid for ultimately by our tax dollars. In agriculture, many of the direct and immediate externalities caused by destructive production practices are felt by the workers and communities where the products are grown. As Dan Koeppel eloquently sums up in his 2008 book *Banana: The Fate of the Fruit That Changed the World*, "For a hundred years, we have allowed whatever risk there is in bananas to be borne elsewhere: in the town squares of Colombia, along railroad lines in Costa Rica, by the blue-skinned sprayers of Bordeaux mixture in Guatemala" (Koeppel, 2008).

In 2018, Fairtrade International (FLO) conducted a study attempting to quantify the externalities of banana production. They surveyed banana farms across the Dominican Republic, Colombia, Peru, and Ecuador to see if the average price consumers pay could fully account for the true social and environmental costs associated with bananas. The results were illuminating but not surprising. FLO found that the average wholesale box of forty pounds of bananas was priced $6.70 lower than it should be, which translates to roughly $0.17 per pound too cheap. Some 60 percent of these externalized costs were deemed to be socioeconomic, including insufficient wages and social security for farmers and workers. The other 40 percent were environmental costs and included things like water depletion and climate change (Fairtrade International, 2018).

The same study also surveyed Fair Trade banana farms to see if the externalities in these operations were less. They were. The study found that under typical pricing and with our premium, Fair Trade bananas had only $3.65 per box of externalities, which translates into $0.09 per pound—half the deficit of conventional bananas. Of particular interest to me was the fact that in Fair Trade production, most of the remaining externalized costs were environmental as opposed to social. This is because Fair Trade farmers and workers receive so much financial benefit from our programs.

On the other hand, it is interesting and a bit uncomfortable to note that, according to this study, not all externalities were absorbed by Fair Trade banana standards, practices, and premiums. This reflects the delicate balance faced in the ethical sourcing movement every day between cost and impact. It also explains our emphasis on continuous improvement over time, recognizing that market realities don't allow quick fixes to the challenges of externalities without public policy interventions and legislation.

This all makes sense, of course. Fair Trade is designed in part to help bring as many externalities as possible back into the economic equation, especially on the socioeconomic side. In bananas, for example, our biggest partner is Dole. They came on board with us in 2009, when one of their big accounts, Whole Foods, asked them to certify their organic bananas as Fair Trade. Dole pays a premium of two cents per pound for their Fair Trade organic bananas, which goes directly back to their producer communities in Costa Rica, Colombia, Ecuador, and Peru. Dole passes this premium on to retailers, who pay a little more to sell bananas with the Fair Trade Certified label on them. In this way, both companies and consumers are helping to account for costs that have traditionally been externalized.

The Fair Trade bananas program has been effective at helping improve the livelihoods of certified farmers and plantation workers over the past decade. Between 2013 and 2022, we've certified 824 million pounds of bananas, mostly organic fruit sold at Whole Foods. Through those sales, we've generated over $16 million in premiums for farmers and workers, which is great news. Those producers have invested their premiums in better housing, daycare, education, health care, and other vital services. As Mabel Obregon, president of her Fair Trade committee, told me on my last visit to the Dole farm where she works in Costa Rica, "The premiums and our community projects have changed our lives. Forever."

On the other hand, the Fair Trade banana market has not grown at the rate we hoped, and we have yet to penetrate the mainstream of the market. Whole Foods remains our biggest retail partner for bananas, accounting for over 90 percent of the total volume. Despite significant progress with Costco and Walmart in other fresh produce items like peppers, grapes, tomatoes, and berries, we haven't been able to generate any significant banana volume with other retailers beyond Whole Foods.

Moreover, our banana program has had some serious fits and starts since we first launched the fruit, with much fanfare and a front-page feature article in *USA Today*, in 2004. Our first breakthrough came in 2007 when Sam's Club began sourcing Fair Trade bananas from our producers in Colombia for many of its club stores. Even though the Sam's Club program was never national, it still moved significant volume at a reasonable price point for the consumer, thanks in part to the fact that the fruit was conventional (not organic) and was only sold in three-pound bags. The result: tremendous impact in post-conflict areas of Colombia where plantation owners, farmworkers, and unions all came together in collaboration around a new approach to labor relations that brought benefits to all. I had a chance to visit many of these farms and see the projects firsthand—new housing for workers, daycare centers, and scholarship programs were their main priorities. The difference was massive. Most importantly, the respect from and harmony with management that the workers reported feeling were like spiritual medicine for a region desperately in need of peace.

Yet, despite these inspiring accomplishments on the ground, Sam's Club reported that the bananas weren't meeting their margin or sales expectations, and the three-pound bag presented too many logistical challenges. Responding to pushback from club store managers, the head produce buyer eventually decided to pull the plug on the program in 2016. We have not yet been able to resuscitate conventional bananas in the US market.

It seems clear that the biggest impediment to the growth of our Fair Trade bananas program has been price sensitivity—among both retailers and their consumers. According to Rudy Amador,

Dole's vice president of corporate responsibility and sustainability, getting retailers to agree to pay more for the Fair Trade Certified label is particularly difficult for a commodity like bananas. "We're a high-volume, low-margin business, and the structure of the industry doesn't help," he told me over coffee during my recent visit to one of their farms in Costa Rica. "When you're selling a commodity to supermarkets, they hold all the power. The largest supermarket in the world, for example, is fifty to sixty times bigger than Dole in terms of sales. So when they negotiate with us on price, they hold all the leverage. They point to the fact that bananas are a staple and the prices need to be low in order to pull customers in to buy other things."

I agree with Rudy that it will be difficult for Fair Trade bananas to grow, given the heightened price sensitivity in the market. This raises some hard questions. Are consumers willing to pay the extra two cents per pound—especially in an inflationary economy—to care for the farmworkers and the environment? If not, can companies absorb that extra cost and reduce their already slim margins in return for the kind of brand distinction and supply chain stability a label like Fair Trade Certified can bring them?

While the question of price is particularly difficult for bananas, it's an issue we face to some degree across all our products. In fact, I think it's one of the biggest issues facing the ethical sourcing movement as a whole, especially if we want to scale in any meaningful way. If we are going to create a new kind of capitalism that can internalize the direct social and environmental externalities that have historically been unaccounted for by business, who should shoulder the financial burden? In other words, who should pay for the cost of sustainability?

The answers to this question are quite complex. If we put all the onus on consumers, the price of ethically sourced products will remain higher and less accessible. Fair Trade bananas, for example, may continue to be a product only available at places like Whole Foods. But if sustainable products are priced at a level that the average, cost-conscious consumer can afford, who will foot the bill for the extra cost needed to produce these items more sustainably?

These are critical questions as we look toward the future of ethical sourcing. As part of my research for this book, I posed the "Who should pay?" question to almost everyone I interviewed. Unsurprisingly, there was no consensus. Some felt it was on the consumer to pay for sustainability. Others felt the costs could easily be absorbed by businesses. Others felt they should be shared. I think they're all correct. The calculus is different for every company and product category.

MULTIDIMENSIONAL POVERTY INDEX

In recent years, the Dole Fruit Company has begun to approach their supply chains with a more holistic view. In fact, they have recently begun to adopt a sophisticated new method of measuring the overall well-being of the communities where they work. As Dole's Rudy Amador told me,

In 2010, some people at Oxford University developed a method of measuring poverty called the Multidimensional Poverty Index (MPI). It measures a particular country's poverty not just on income but on other factors like access to education, health care, internet, and other criteria. Countries like Costa Rica, where I am based, have used the MPI to identify specific needs and tailor their social programs to address them.

In 2019, our president of fresh fruit products, Renato Acuña, heard about the MPI being adapted by a Costa Rican NGO to be applied at the business level and immediately called me up. We decided to take the business MPI concept and apply it in agriculture for the first time, starting with our Costa Rican operations. We interviewed more than 8,000 employees about their lives and overall well-being and got an 86 percent response rate. The results were illuminating. I never knew so much about our workers and their families. We found a lot of unexpected gaps in the communities where we operate. We're now developing social initiatives within Dole and working on alliances to address them, and we plan to extend the business MPI survey to our operations in Ecuador, Guatemala, and Honduras.

WILL CONSUMERS PAY FOR SOCIALLY SUSTAINABLE PRODUCTS?

On a recent visit to Austin, Texas, I had a chance to spend a day hanging out with my buddy John Mackey, co-founder of Whole Foods. Between biking around beautiful Barton Creek and playing some fiercely competitive rounds of backgammon, we had a chance to chat about the world—and the world of sustainability. When I asked John who he thinks should pay the extra costs associated with sustainability, his answer was characteristically quick and unequivocal. "Ultimately, it's the consumers who have to pay. I think products that are certified organic or Fair Trade should cost more. Consumers should pay a premium for them."

John's response didn't surprise me, especially given his track record in the sustainability movement. He built Whole Foods into the retail giant it is today based on his bet that conscious consumers would be willing to pay more for higher-quality, healthy, and sustainable products. "There's a kind of pay-for-what-you-get dynamic at play with sustainable products," he told me. "When they cost more, the benefits are clearer to the customer. People feel more virtuous when they're paying the premium. They feel like they're making a sacrifice, but they're doing it because they believe in the values. That's true for organic and I think it's true for Fair Trade."

I agree with John's take on the consumers' willingness to pay a premium for sustainability, at least in some segments. There's a lot of data to back it up. For example, a 2021 study by the Wharton School's Baker Retailing Center found that two-thirds of those surveyed said they would pay more for sustainable products (First Insight, 2021). Our own Fair Trade consumer research has shown similar results. Consumers, when asked, tend to say they'll pay more for products with the Fair Trade Certified label on them. As cited in Chapter 3, dozens of studies like these show similar consumer willingness to pay more for products that carry social or environmental attributes.

But when I see data like this, I wonder why our movement hasn't grown more quickly. If such a large percentage of consumers really are willing to pay more for sustainable products, as they say in surveys, then why do Fair Trade products still make up less than 1 percent of what US consumers spend on goods? Even organic products, which have become widely available across nearly every category of food, only account for 6 percent of US retail food sales (Organic Trade Association, 2023). I asked Greg Spragg, who helped us launch our line of Fair Trade coffee with Sam's Club in 2005, about this disappointing phenomenon. "I tell people this all the time. What consumers say on a survey and what they actually do are two different things. If you survey a lot of younger people especially, the majority say they are willing to pay more. But when they go into the supermarket or shop online, they only have so much money to spend. They may change their mind. When budget gets in the way, they often make another choice."

Greg articulated what has come to be known in consumer research circles as the "intention gap." While a tremendous amount of data shows that many consumers would prefer to buy sustainable and ethical products and are willing to pay more for them, there's some skepticism among the experts and in the industry about how much these good intentions translate into actual shopper behavior and growth in sales. Like Greg, many have suggested that plenty of people will say they prefer products that are sustainably produced, but that doesn't necessarily mean they will actually buy them when given the choice, especially if the retail price is higher.

On the other hand, an encouraging body of research shows that the gap between consumer intention and purchase behavior is beginning to shrink. In the spring of 2023, for example, McKinsey & Company and NielsenIQ published a joint study exploring the different rates of sales growth for products with and without sustainability claims. The expressed intent of the study was to look "beyond the self-reported intentions of US consumers and examine their actual spending behavior—tracking dollars instead of sentiment." The study was conducted over a five-year period (2017–2022) and included 44,000 brands across thirty-two food, beverage, personal-care, and household categories. The findings were fascinating. Over that five-year period, holding prices constant, the actual sales growth of products making environmental, social, and governance (ESG) claims (6.4 percent growth) outpaced those that didn't (4.7 percent growth). The average cumulative growth over that period among ESG products was 28 percent compared to only 20 percent for non-ESG products. This trend is likely to continue, the study concludes (Frey et al., 2023).

Studies like these suggest that the gap between consumers' intentions to buy sustainable products and their actual purchasing behavior is starting to close. Spending habits are shifting toward more sustainable products, and conscious consumers are beginning to put more of their money where their mouths are. As we've already examined earlier in the book, Millennial and Gen Z consumers are particularly demanding in their expectations of companies' social and environmental responsibility—suggesting that conscious consumerism is a macrotrend. But the research has yet to explore whether consumers are also willing to pay more for sustainable products—or, more precisely, it has yet to ascertain how many consumers and how much more.

While the research on this topic has been limited, Harvard government professor Michael Hiscox has done a handful of significant studies showing that consumers are willing to pay more for Fair Trade Certified products. In a 2015 study published by Stanford University, Hiscox and his colleagues Jens Hainmueller and Sandra Sequeira explored customer behavior across multiple locations at a large US grocery store chain. They found that sales of two popular coffee brands rose by 10 percent when carrying the Fair Trade label. Even more significantly, they found that those sales increases remained steady with an up to 8 percent price bump (Hainmueller, Hiscox, and Sequeira, 2015). Michael, who I've known and admired for many years, says these results are promising and show that many consumers will indeed pay more. But further research is needed.

In the meantime, I remain optimistic about the consumer's role in helping build a more sustainable model of capitalism. In fact, I do believe that the "intention gap" will continue to shrink, especially as Millennials and Gen Z get older and have more discretionary income. Companies will continue to study these consumer trends and respond to them, expanding the assortment, availability, and convenience of sustainable products. We *are* making progress. But what about the pace of change? What needs to be true for us to truly democratize the ethical sourcing movement and make sustainable products affordable and attractive to the mainstream?

From John Mackey's vantage point, responsible purchasing may never be a mainstream movement. At least not anytime soon. He believes that "conscious consumerism is partly an epiphenomenon of increased prosperity. As people have more disposable income, they're willing to invest it in sustainable products. So you could say Fair Trade is kind of a luxury good. The people who are really struggling to pay their mortgages, put clothing on their kids, and pay their medical bills may be a lot less concerned about Fair Trade. People who have higher income can basically afford to be more conscious."

It's difficult to argue with John's logic, looking through the lens of this current moment in time, especially in light of inflation. The segment of the population that can "afford to be conscious"—that is able and willing to pay more for sustainability—may be a minority of shoppers for the foreseeable future. But as John points out, "That doesn't mean it can't be a very big niche, and it doesn't mean it can't continue to grow." Others, like Walmart's Doug McMillon, would argue that products can be both sustainable and affordable if the scale is there. While it's difficult to say exactly what percentage of the population has the awareness, interest, and means to buy sustainable products today, that segment is significant—and it's clearly growing.

While not all consumers are able or willing to pay more for sustainability, I believe that enough of them are to make a critical difference. Let's say, for example, that roughly 25 percent of US consumers are regularly buying sustainable products today, which I believe is a pretty conservative estimate if you examine the studies I've cited in this book (GreenPrint, 2021). But getting even half of that audience to buy Fair Trade products loyally and consistently, even if they cost a bit more, would enable a dramatic leap from the 1 to 5 percent of market share we currently account for in our various categories. This, in turn, would unleash dramatically greater impact for farmers, workers, and their families. So there is a huge opportunity for growth, even within the limits of the current conscious consumer segment.

How fast will that growth be? I believe the pace of change will be driven not only by shifting consumer trends but also by the competitive dynamic between companies that are already battling for the lucrative conscious consumer segment. This dynamic will lead to innovation, and consumer prices for products that are ethically sourced should come down over time.

CLOSING THE INTENTION GAP

SO HOW DO WE CLOSE THE INTENTION GAP? HOW DO WE DEMOCRA-tize sustainable products, making them accessible to everyone and moving from niche to norm? How do we more powerfully activate the consumer in order to scale our impact on the world? This is and will remain the quest of my life. It's why I wrote this book.

Many of the people I interviewed for this book spoke about the importance of storytelling. Specifically, brands and retailers need to do a better job of communicating the benefits of sustainability. US consumers are a sleeping giant, powerful to effect change but not yet fully aware of their own strength. Many of my colleagues in the movement believe that good storytelling is the key to awakening the sleeping giant.

According to former prAna CEO Scott Kerslake, the story you tell your customer will directly affect how much extra they're willing to spend on sustainability. "There's a certain amount of price elasticity around any given customer's willingness to pay more. Many consumers will pay a higher price for a product if it's going to support their values. But they won't do it if you don't tell the story." Scott and his team at prAna did this by creating a series of beautiful videos during visits to the factories where their apparel was made. They built the production budget right into their business model, and it worked. "We were able to pass on the extra premiums associated with Fair Trade to our consumers, and they were happy to pay," Scott says. "But we couldn't have done that without telling the story properly."

For some brands, communicating the benefits of Fair Trade has to do with connecting it to consumers' self-interest, particularly around quality. According to T.J. Whalen, who was instrumental in launching the Fair Trade program for Green Mountain Coffee Roasters (GMCR) in the early 2000s, "There needs to be a 'me' proposition in all this. You need to convince consumers that Fair Trade equals better taste. If the farmer gets paid more, they can invest in their crops, and that leads to a higher-quality product. A lot of people can get on board with something like that."

For T.J. and GMCR, finding the right way to communicate the value of Fair Trade took some trial and error. In the early years, they tried to appeal to the conscience of consumers by emphasizing the negative consequences of buying unsustainable coffee. But that didn't work very well. As T.J. recalls, "I remember being in focus groups and hearing consumers say things like, 'Hey, man, you're putting a lot of weight on my shoulders. I'm not personally responsible for the destitute poverty in equatorial coffee-growing regions. Frankly, I just want something that's going to energize me in the morning and make me feel good. So stop making me feel bad.'"

The negative feedback GMCR received for their more guilt-laden approach to storytelling inspired them to shift toward a more positive tone. Eventually, they came up with the "Better Coffee for a Better World" slogan, and it really took off. "It was a message of optimism and positivity that's tied into quality," T.J. recalls. "That was really the breakthrough that allowed consumers to engage with our brand and get behind it."

While there are plenty of successful examples of our partners communicating the value of Fair Trade to consumers, we still have a lot further to go. Rudy Amador from Dole shared an interesting story with me about a recent trip he made to the United States to visit some of the stores where Dole's bananas were sold.

> I was invited by Whole Foods for a new store opening, which is something I've never done before. I was there to field questions from the customers about the pineapples and bananas they were selling in the produce section. I was struck by how little consumers knew about what organic was. It was even worse with Fair Trade. These were highly educated, relatively affluent people, and they knew very little about the true meaning of either label. So there's a lot of work to be done, and that's not easy to do. It's very difficult to get retailers at the store level to invest in educating their customers on these issues.

Rudy is right. Not only do we need to do a better job of communicating the value of Fair Trade in a general sense, but we also need brands and retailers to make the effort. Fair Trade USA is a relatively small nonprofit organization—our total budget in 2023 was only $22 million. So it's unlikely that we'll ever have the resources to run a Super Bowl ad on television. Sure, there are scrappy, low-budget ways to reach the public through celebrity endorsements, influencers, and social media. And we have our grassroots movement of supporters in Fair Trade colleges and towns around the country. But the biggest potential for consumer education and engagement is our network of 1,700 brands and retail partners. They have the resources and the vested interest, from a commercial perspective, to invest in awakening the consumer. They have the biggest platform, in store and online, to tell their consumers the Fair Trade story. By logic, the more they promote their Fair Trade products, the more they will sell. So why aren't companies doing more?

One issue is simply the complexity of execution when it comes to in-store signage and promotion. Smaller, independent brands and stores do a better job at this. The larger supermarket chains, unfortunately, are usually quite reluctant to do anything special in-store to promote Fair Trade because it's so hard for them to execute uniformly and successfully. Online promotion of sustainable products is certainly cheaper and easier, but even there we rarely see fantastic content. Amid so many competing priorities and resource constraints of their own, it seems that few brands and retailers have truly cracked the code on masterful storytelling around sustainability.

A notable exception was the natural grocery chain Wild Oats, which was an early partner and ally. In 2004, Wild Oats decided to convert 100 percent of its private-label coffee, which was roasted by GMCR, to Fair Trade. Shortly after launching their new program, which proudly displayed the Fair Trade Certified label on the front of every package, I had a chance to take GMCR's Bob Stiller and Wild Oats CEO Perry Odak to Mexico to visit some of the coffee farmers who were supplying the program. I remember standing in the yard of a farmer named Isidro Perez, listening to him tell his life story. As Isidro proudly told us about the impact of Fair Trade in his community, including enabling him to send all his kids to high school and three to college, I looked over at Perry and saw tears in his eyes. It turns out, Perry grew up on his father's small dairy farm in upstate New York. He knew all about milking cows and struggling to make ends meet. Perry connected so deeply with Isidro and his journey that day that he decided to do something extraordinary: when he flew back to the States, Perry had a huge Fair Trade label and our message painted on the wall of every Wild Oats store in the country. Literally.

Another fascinating (and frustrating) issue we face is that some companies we work with are reluctant to call too much attention to their own Fair Trade offerings for fear of casting a negative light on their "uncertified" products. This is more often the case with brands and retailers that sell a relatively small percentage of Fair Trade.

They're afraid that if they tell the Fair Trade story too visibly or too compellingly, their consumers might naturally start asking if the rest of the company's products, by definition, are "Unfair Trade." This concern has led to a certain explicit reluctance by some brands to promote their own Fair Trade lines.

My observation is that when brands reach a sort of critical mass in their Fair Trade program, which is often when they've converted around 20 to 30 percent of their total product line, we tend to see prouder and more proactive promotional efforts. At this level, there's more at stake, more of a vested interest in seeing that product succeed, and perhaps a greater belief among consumers in the authenticity of the company's commitment. For whatever reason, this is the level at which we tend to see many companies lean into storytelling.

These are some of the issues we need to tackle in the near future. If we want to further empower consumers to do their part in the sustainability effort, we need to do our best to help connect them to our incredible human impact story. The more we can do this, in collaboration with companies and other stakeholders in our movement, the more we can close the gap between the consumers who intend to shop sustainably and those who really do.

STARTING UP-MARKET

Whenever we go into a new product category, we typically start by recruiting companies that offer the highest-quality, sustainable products, which are generally also higher priced. These segments more readily fit with Fair Trade in terms of their pricing, brand reputation, and customer base. This is why we started with the specialty segments in coffee, tea, and chocolate.

In produce, we started with products that were already certified organic. In apparel we launched with higher-end brands like prAna and Patagonia. Starting at the top end makes it easier for our brand partners to cover the costs of Fair Trade. They can absorb our premiums through their own margins, which tend to be higher for specialty/gourmet brands. Or they can charge their customers more as they are already paying a premium for a specialty product and don't tend to balk at a few additional cents.

Once we've established a foothold within the top end of the market, we begin to work our way down to the mid-tier brands over time. In coffee, for example, we've begun to focus a lot of our efforts on growing our private-label business over the past decade. Today, private label—that is, a supermarket's own "house brand" of products—is the fastest-growing segment of Fair Trade coffee. Sam's Club's "Member's Mark" coffee, for example, is now 100 percent Fair Trade Certified. Target, Kroger, Safeway/Albertsons, Costco, Whole Foods, Trader Joe's, and many other retailers now have significant Fair Trade private-label coffee programs.

Similarly, in apparel, we launched Fair Trade denim initially in 2019 with Madewell, a premium brand that sells their stylish jeans for over $100. Three years later, we were able to expand the denim program through a partnership with Target, which now offers Universal Thread jeans with our label at a more moderate price point of $25 to $35. This evolution speaks directly to our dream of making Fair Trade products accessible and affordable to everyone.

SHOULD BUSINESSES FOOT THE SUSTAINABILITY BILL?

It might come as a surprise to many that a lot of our brand and retail partners don't pass the costs of Fair Trade on to their customers. Instead, they absorb them into their business models. In essence, these companies choose to pay the cost of social sustainability themselves. They do so for a variety of reasons: some for brand differentiation; some for the stability it brings to their supply chains; others because they believe it's just the right thing to do. Many companies choose to take on the costs of Fair Trade for all of these reasons. They see the cost of absorbing the Fair Trade premium as worth it for the benefits to their businesses.

Take e.l.f. Beauty, for example. When I asked CEO Tarang Amin whether or not sustainability and affordability are mutually exclusive, he just chuckled. If you're not familiar with e.l.f. (short for "eyes, lips, face"), they are one of the most popular—and profitable—beauty brands. They're also one of the most affordable. Starting in 2004, they built a loyal following based on the somewhat radical promise to provide premium-quality cosmetics at affordable prices. The company website touts their mission statement: "We make the best of beauty accessible to every eye, lip, face and skin concern."

But in addition to combining high quality and affordability into their brand, e.l.f. Beauty is even more unique in also being a deeply purpose-driven company. They publicly stand for inclusivity and positivity, they are double-certified as "cruelty free" (meaning no animal testing) by both People for the Ethical Treatment of Animals (PETA) and Leaping Bunny, they are vegan, and they don't use parabens (harmful chemicals) in any of their products. As of 2022, they have added the Fair Trade Certified label to their product line—making them the first ever beauty company to offer products manufactured under the Fair Trade factory standard.

I first met Tarang over a decade ago when he was an executive at Clorox. Warm, sincere, and as smart as they come, Tarang has become a friend, coach, and thought partner to me. In our many conversations over the years, Tarang has always been supportive of our mission and curious about how our impact works. So when we both found ourselves on work trips to Thailand at the same time in 2019, I invited him to come visit some Fair Trade factories with me. We visited an apparel and a surfboard factory, spoke with management and workers, and learned a lot about how Fair Trade was working for them.

"I could see the impact Fair Trade was making in the lives of these factory workers," Tarang recounted over lunch at our favorite Vietnamese restaurant in downtown Oakland, just a few blocks from his office. "Many of them were migrant workers from Cambodia, so a lot of the government services weren't accessible to them. The premiums helped them to set up their own training, schools, and health care. A light bulb really went off for me. I was like, 'Wait a minute, we have factories too.'" In 2022, we certified four of e.l.f.'s partners' manufacturing facilities in China, which produce roughly 80 percent of the company's products. By 2024, we'd certified a total of seven.

When you go to the cosmetics section at Target, Walmart, or your local drug store, there's a good chance you'll now find e.l.f. lipstick or eyeliner bearing the Fair Trade label. But you won't see a price difference between those certified products and any others. "I consider the Fair Trade premiums a cost of doing business," Tarang told me, "so we don't pass them on to the consumer." Like some of the companies we work with, e.l.f. has chosen to internalize the extra costs associated with working with us. "We do our research. We really look at our community to find out what is important to them. Our customers want premium quality at great prices; but they also want clean, cruelty-free, and sustainably sourced products. That's why, at least for us, Fair Trade should not be a premium we pass on to the consumer. It should be part of the overall value proposition. That's what makes us win in the market: our promise that you can have it all with prestige quality and great prices that are vegan, clean, cruelty-free, and Fair Trade Certified."

OFFSETTING THE COSTS OF SUSTAINABILITY

e.l.f. is not the only company to absorb their sustainability investments into their operating expenses without raising their consumer prices. Take Honest Tea, for example, which had been a longtime Fair Trade partner before their parent company, Coca-Cola, discontinued the brand in 2022. Their founder, Seth Goldman, has long been a kindred spirit and friend of mine. Seth recently told me, "One of our ambitions as a business was to democratize sustainability and make these products available to everyone, not just the wealthy." In 2015, the company decided to certify all their sugar as Fair Trade in addition to the tea that went into their beverages.

According to Seth, "The move to Fair Trade sugar increased our costs by about half a penny per drink, which was only a tiny fraction of our overall cost of goods. The glass bottle, by comparison, costs roughly ten cents. We used Coca-Cola's buying power to renegotiate the contract with our bottle supplier and saved roughly a penny. So we added value to the product by converting to Fair Trade sugar, and still improved our gross margin."

It's natural to wonder how the choice not to ask consumers to pay extra for their Fair Trade and other labels affects e.l.f.'s margins. Are they consciously choosing less profit in order to be certified by all these labels? When I asked Tarang this question, he lit up.

I think people often think too narrowly about the margin question. They approach it from what I call a "sourcing standpoint," which is a mentality that every penny matters—every extra penny spent is a margin hit. So they want to reduce costs no matter what. But I have a different proposition. Our margins are growing—and not by a little bit. They're growing by a lot. The reason behind this is simple. The number one driver of margin growth is growth. The more growth you have, the more you're spreading out costs against that growth. When people try to isolate these individual factors, they miss the bigger picture. Our brand proposition includes sustainability, and for us sustainability is very meaningful and compelling to consumers. It's driving our growth and ultimately helping our margins.

It's true. Thanks in no small part to their brand proposition, e.l.f. is the topmost-preferred cosmetics brand among teens in the US market (Piper Sandler, 2023). They recently passed CoverGirl, Revlon, and L'Oréal Paris to become the second-largest color cosmetics brand in the United States. They are one of only five publicly traded companies in the consumer goods world to deliver an average of 20 percent growth consistently over twenty consecutive quarters. "A lot of this growth is values driven," Tarang says. "Generation Z, in particular, cares about what we stand for as a company. They've rewarded us with the growth we've seen. I think people would be willing to pay a little bit more for it. But our stance is different. We don't want our community to pay more. We have to be what we stand for and what differentiates us."

Tarang is obviously passionate about the values-inspired growth they have experienced on the sales side of the margin equation. But he's equally convinced that it's also helped reduce their overall costs. "Conscious capitalism actually correlates well with better financial results," he told me. "The reason why I don't think investing in something like Fair Trade has to lead to a huge margin hit has to do with our supply chains. If we have more engaged workers at our suppliers, who are better taken care of, we're going to see savings in other ways—in creative ideas, in problem-solving, in overall productivity."

Tarang shared with me the example of how investing in their suppliers has had a dramatic bottom-line impact on their operations in China. "Our whole setup in the country is completely different than any other company. Walmart tells me this all the time. They don't understand how we are able to produce this level of quality at our prices. They have over 3,000 sourcing people in China compared to our 88, and they can't touch us when it comes to costs. I tell them that it's because they're so focused on getting the lowest price out of their suppliers."

Tarang tells me this story with an air of well-deserved pride in his voice. It's as if he's discovered a sustainable business secret that has given his company an edge but that he's more than willing to share with the world.

We approach each of the factories that manufacture our products as their long-term partner. We want all of our suppliers to be profitable. So we don't hammer them on costs. We want the best combination of cost, quality, and speed in the industry; and we can't get that if we're beating them up on price. They would have zero incentive to improve their quality. So we invest in our suppliers. We share our quality assurance practices with them. We help them to develop lean manufacturing techniques in their operations, and they end up being much more efficient as a result.

For Tarang, the partnership with Fair Trade is the natural out-growth of the progressive, collaborative relationships e.l.f. has been building with its workforce, both employees and third-party suppliers up the chain. According to Tarang, since their initial public offering in 2016, the company has granted over $150 million in equity to their employees, not including executive officers. That stock has dramatically increased in value. As Tarang told me, "That's real wealth creation for the community we serve. Fair Trade has helped us to extend that to the workers in the factories who are making our products."

Our program with e.l.f. is less than two years old as of this writing, but the early results with their customers are promising. They recently shared with me a consumer study they conducted, which found that 60 percent of those surveyed were aware of their partnership with us, and of those, 58 percent said Fair Trade certification was important to them. Further, eight in ten respondents said that our label makes them more likely to purchase the brand. Given e.l.f.'s dedication to serving the values of their customers, these results are a sign of good things to come.

We are thrilled about the potential of working with e.l.f. to bring Fair Trade deeper into the cosmetics industry. But perhaps even more exciting is the business case we're building with them for Fair Trade. If a company like e.l.f., with its firm commitment to affordability, is able to absorb the costs of Fair Trade into their business model without passing them on to the consumer and remain profitable, other companies will see that they can do the same. Of course, I'm not suggesting that all companies can or should completely cover the extra costs associated with sustainability. Not every company is as consumer-centric as e.l.f.; nor do they all have the same margin structure. I believe that consumers need to play their part as well.

But e.l.f.'s example highlights the opportunity that many companies have to absorb the cost of sustainability and remain profitable in the process. Perhaps in these early decades of the transformation of capitalism, e.l.f. offers a promising case study with important insights for others—and serves as a harbinger of things to come.

CREATING VALUE FOR INDUSTRY

THERE'S AN INDUSTRY PHRASE I OFTEN USE: "DISINTERMEDIATING the supply chain." It essentially means finding ways to shorten your supply chain and reduce middlemen so you can more directly connect suppliers to customers. Big companies like Walmart often speak about this topic. By cutting out the middlemen, you can send more money down the line to producers without having to increase the price to your consumers on the other end.

We've found that disintermediation is a big benefit of the kind of supply chain transparency that ethical sourcing models like ours make possible. The more intimately connected you are to your various stakeholders and the more trust you've built with them, the more opportunities you have to shorten the links in the chain—for the benefit of everyone involved. This reduces costs for the businesses we work with, which in turn helps them absorb the extra costs associated with ethical sourcing.

Walmart CEO Doug McMillon is a big believer in this approach. I met Doug in 2005 when he was CEO of Sam's Club and we were just starting our coffee program with them. Over the years, he's become a friend and thought partner. Every time I make the trip to Walmart's headquarters in Bentonville, Arkansas, Doug finds time to sit with me and catch up on family, business, and the state of the world. He is a great listener, always curious and eager to learn. And he's a big supporter of the Fair Trade program, although he would be the first to admit that Walmart can and should do more with us.

On a recent visit to Bentonville, Doug and I talked about this price/sustainability issue. "In our experience," he said, "customers are looking for value. It's our job to be creative and find ways for the more sustainable choice to also be a good choice from a value perspective. We work with suppliers and organizations such as Fair Trade to improve practices in the supply chain and use innovation to make merchandise affordable."

For example, Sam's Club (a wholly owned subsidiary of Walmart) chose an unconventional route with its Member's Mark private-brand Fair Trade Certified coffee. In a typical coffee supply chain, the biggest value add is in the roasting process, and that generally happens in countries where the coffee is ultimately sold. So in the United States, for example, most of the coffee you buy on the shelf is roasted and packaged by a company here in the United States. The beans themselves are grown in producer countries like Colombia and Brazil, where farmers and cooperatives sell their green coffee beans to exporters. These exporters often then sell them to importers, who in turn sell the beans to the roasters. Sometimes there are brokers along the way too. So in the typical coffee supply chain, there are essentially two or more layers of middlemen between the producers and the roasters.

Sam's Club found a way to shorten their supply chain by partnering with an outstanding coffee roaster based in Colombia called Colcafe. Colcafe, located in Medellín, sources all their coffee directly from co-ops and independent farmers in the region. They roast and package the beans in their world-class facilities and then ship them to Sam's Club's distribution centers in the United States. In doing so, they essentially bypass the middlemen who typically connect cooperatives with roasters, in the process saving money. As a result of this disintermediation, Sam's Club was able to cut enough costs to account for their Fair Trade premiums and didn't have to pass them on to their members.

Of course, disintermediating the supply chain isn't unique to Fair Trade specifically or ethical sourcing as a whole. But we have found that the kind of trust and transparency we foster generates more opportunities to make a more direct connection between opposite ends of the supply chain. When companies do this, they have the potential to generate more income for their producers while saving their customers money in the process.

THE ART AND SCIENCE OF THE PREMIUM

WHEN IT COMES TO THE ISSUE OF PAYING FOR FAIR TRADE, OUR premiums are central to the equation. We have other mechanisms in place for some products, like the guaranteed minimum prices for coffee and chocolate. But our mandatory, preset premiums are the bread and butter of the Fair Trade model, our unique selling point. We believe that when producers are more responsible and sustainable, the market should reward them. Moreover, if there's an attractive financial incentive in any ethical sourcing program, more producers will join, practices will improve, and lives will change.

In our approach, Fair Trade premiums are paid by the brands and go directly back to the producer communities. In 2024, we hit a major milestone: that year we passed the $1.2 billion mark in cumulative premiums that we've generated through our efforts here in the US market. Currently we're generating close to $100 million per year across all categories, with plans to expand that in the years to come. In our system, the premiums are both the primary measure of our impact and the price tag of sustainability.

Yet, in recent years, we've come to realize that our premiums are, in many cases, too high to achieve the kind of scale and impact we believe is possible. Companies like e.l.f., which is scaling toward certifying 100 percent of their products over the next three years, are so far the exception. Many of the companies we work with still only certify a small to moderate percentage overall of their products. The most common explanation we hear from our industry partners for why they aren't converting more of their product lines to Fair Trade is that the premium per pound is too high to scale. This has led us to explore how we might "right-size" our premiums for each industry in an effort to allow companies to dramatically increase their overall volume and, with it, the impact they generate for producer communities. Ultimately, it comes down to simple math.

In 2019, we conducted our first experiment with right-sizing premiums. We had just reviewed the results of a pilot we conducted with a produce brand that had brought Fair Trade certification to one of their farms to test and learn. After two years, their evaluation was positive on both the farm-level impact and the market acceptance. The premium, however, which they were taking out of their own margins, was prohibitively high for them to scale. Their proposal to us: if we reduced the premium to what they felt was an economically feasible level, they would expand their program to 100 percent of their farms in a key growing region of Mexico.

This presented us with a difficult decision. On one hand, a move like this could be seen as a watering down of the worker impact of the Fair Trade program. After all, weren't our premiums the heart of the model? If the brand paid less per pound, one could understandably conclude that the workers—at least the ones on that first farm—would be getting less money.

But the calculation wasn't that simple. First off, scaling the program, even at a somewhat lower premium, would generate a lot more financial benefit for a lot more workers because we would be able to certify all of the brand's farms in the region. The way the math worked out, by lowering the premiums by half, we could increase the volume tenfold. In absolute dollars, that meant growing the total premium from $150,000 per year to $750,000 per year. That would mean a lot more resources for the workers and their families throughout the region for daycare facilities, health-care services, water projects, and scholarships. Reducing the premium per pound and increasing the volume would have a much bigger impact on those communities overall.

Another important twist in the premium debate has to do with the fact that none of our certified farms are able to sell all of their harvest as Fair Trade. Invariably, they are forced to sell large portions at conventional market rates, and that doesn't generate any premiums. This means that the workers on those farms do the same amount of work but don't get premiums for much of their labor. This is true within many other industries as well. In coffee, for example, I earlier cited the Coffee Barometer's latest findings—that Fair Trade coffee farmers on average are only able to sell 25 percent of their harvest to a Fair Trade buyer. Technically, all of that coffee qualifies as Fair Trade Certified, but premiums are only paid on the amount that companies want to buy as certified. Our challenge, from a growth perspective, isn't supply; it's demand.

At the end of the day, if we want to stimulate industry demand, we have to be curious about the premium levels. Our strategic hypothesis, twenty-six years into this grand experiment: by right-sizing premiums to a more scalable level, we will be able to dramatically increase the volume of Fair Trade Certified products that companies want to buy. That, in turn, will allow producers to sell a higher percentage of their total production, and ideally all of it, as Fair Trade and receive a premium for it. Even at the lower rates, the total premiums should add up to a lot more overall income being channeled back to the workers and their communities.

Suffice it to say, after much deliberation, we decided to agree to this brand's request and we're glad we did. They now certify all of their produce from that region as Fair Trade, representing roughly ten times the initial volume certified in 2018 . . . and growing. As a result, they now generate over $1 million per year in premiums for over 4,000 farmworkers and their families. Without a doubt, the growth of this partnership and its impact would never have been possible if we hadn't been willing to collaboratively experiment with a more scalable premium. Unlike Kvarøy Salmon, which wanted to waive the premiums altogether, this brand embraced the value of the premiums but simply wanted to find the right level for scale.

"Right-sizing" our premiums, I believe, can also help us create ripple effects across an entire industry. This is something we are looking at right now with tomatoes. Our pilot program with Walmart has been a success, as we explored in Chapter 7. But we are still only certifying a small percentage of their overall volume. Based on the previous produce-premium right-sizing experiment, if we are able to right-size the tomato premium to a more scalable level, then maybe we can increase our tomato program with them and other retailers. Imagine if every tomato sold by the world's largest retailer wore our label? Needless to say, it would have a dramatic, perhaps transformative impact on the entire tomato industry, improving the lives of hundreds of thousands of farming families.

In bananas, our growth has stalled, and I believe that is due to the intense price sensitivity retailers have around the product. What if we were able to find the right premium level for a company like Dole so they could fully absorb the cost themselves? What if Dole could simply build Fair Trade into its brand proposition in the way that NatureSweet and e.l.f. have? If Dole were able to sell Fair Trade Certified bananas without increasing the price, they might be able to convince more mainstream supermarket chains to stock them. Doing so could change the banana industry as we know it and position Dole as a model of sustainable business.

In early 2023, we conducted a rapid stakeholder consultation in the produce industry around the issue of premiums. At the time, our produce premiums were complex and expensive, ranging from two cents to nine cents per pound, depending on the item. Whole Foods and Costco accounted for 80 percent of all Fair Trade produce sales in the United States. Over the course of twenty years, since we launched bananas in 2004, we had failed to break into any other major retailer in a significant way. We were profoundly grateful for Whole Foods' and Costco's leadership in sustainable produce and the impact they were having, but we believed we could do more.

Over a three-month listening tour, we met with the leading growers of Fair Trade produce in Mexico and throughout Latin America. Most were only selling 10 to 20 percent of their total harvests as Fair Trade, earning relatively small premiums for all their work. Almost without exception, the growers expressed support for a simplification and right-sizing of our premiums in hopes of boosting volume.

One of the producers we spoke with was Jaime Tamayo, a long-time friend who is chief operating officer of Divemex, a leading Mexican bell pepper farm. Over his farm's twelve years in Fair Trade, its premium programs have provided vital scholarships for workers' kids, funding for home improvements, supplemental health-care insurance, and even dental and eye care. Yet only 5 percent of Divemex's total harvest is purchased by Fair Trade buyers that pay the premium. "Imagine all the great things we could do for our workers if we could sell a higher percentage of our harvest as Fair Trade," Jaime told me. "The premium is too high for most retailers. We need to prioritize selling more volume."

Our key industry partners also supported the move. So in late 2023, at the annual Global Produce & Floral Show, we announced with a bit of a splash our latest experiment: we would reset all premiums in fresh produce to two cents per pound, embracing radical simplicity and pivoting from our historic high-premium, low-volume model to a right-sized-premium, high-volume model. We promised to transparently and publicly report the results of this new initiative, both from a volume and total premium-impact perspective. And we pledged to evaluate these results with the stakeholders themselves to make sure that we are all learning together as we innovate for a more scalable, high-impact Fair Trade model.

Personally, I believe this high-volume strategy will drive far more impact dollars for far more people over time. Again, it's simple math.

Within this shift, our aim is to maintain our standing as having the highest-impact premiums of any other certification. We want to remain the gold standard in terms of financial impact for producers.

The discussion around premiums has become particularly relevant in the coffee industry, our biggest area of focus, representing roughly 40 percent of Fair Trade sales volume in the United States. In the spring of 2023, our former partner Fairtrade International (FLO) announced that they would be dramatically increasing the prices their standards require that farmers be paid for their coffee. This move sought to respond to the farmers' growing production costs in recent years. Specifically, FLO raised the floor price by 29 percent and increased the extra organic premium by 33 percent. The price increase meant that when you include the Fair Trade premium, coffee companies wanting to buy Fair Trade organic beans with the FLO label had to start paying a minimum of $2.40 per pound, up from $1.90—a whopping 26 percent increase with only four months' advance notice.

Naturally, this created quite a bit of sticker shock in the coffee industry. Most of our 400 plus coffee industry partners were concerned that we would follow FLO's lead and increase our prices and premiums by the same amount. For many of them, such a large increase in costs in such a short period would simply make Fair Trade unfeasible for them, and they would have to look for other ethical sourcing solutions, of which there are many (all cheaper than ours). A cost increase like this would most certainly make our vision of scaling our impact with coffee farmers more difficult, if not impossible.

So in response to FLO's announcement, we hit pause, conducted our own three-month stakeholder consultation, and listened to the perspectives of both industry and producers. Our industry partners talked about having just survived three years of Covid-induced chaotic conditions in the global coffee trade that had bankrupted many companies and generated losses for almost everyone. In 2023, coffee companies just wanted some stability. Interestingly, it wasn't just the industry that asked for a reprieve from FLO's price and premium increase. Most co-op managers wanted the higher prices and premiums from a philosophical perspective, given rising production costs that farmers were facing. But privately many expressed concerns that the move would backfire. My colleague Ivania Rivera, senior coffee trader for the Aldea Global cooperative in Nicaragua, put it succinctly at the time: "FLO's move was too big, too abrupt, and could undermine the industry demand for Fair Trade coffee that we have all worked so hard to build over the years."

In July 2023, we shared the results of our consultation and announced our decision: we would be implementing a price-stabilization policy, essentially freezing our coffee prices and premiums for at least a year at our current level. At the same time, we would be exploring innovation opportunities and creating a learning lab in which to experiment with our coffee model over the next few years, focusing on generating extraordinary demand and driving impact through volume. Toward that end, we hired IDEO .org, a leading design and innovation consultancy, to support our efforts, and we assembled an esteemed multi-stakeholder advisory board to guide the process. In essence, we decided to explore ways to create more value in our model for both industry and producers through data, technology, transparency, climate resilience, and consumer activation. We believed this approach would give us a better chance of staying relevant and attractive to the coffee industry as a whole, with a view toward significant volume growth in the years ahead.

Through all of this, our goal remains the same. Ultimately, we want to maximize the net impact for farmers and workers in order to improve lives and protect the environment. FLO feels that the best way to do this is to mandate the highest premiums and prices possible. It's a view we shared historically as well. But now we've come to believe that the key to greater impact is volume. If we want to grow Fair Trade products beyond the nominal market share we've carved out over twenty-six years and achieve the associated impact, we need to have the courage and creativity to innovate the model.

EVERYBODY CAN WIN

THESE ARE CHALLENGING TOPICS, AND THEY REFLECT THE COM-plexity inherent in efforts to adequately internalize the externalities of our global capitalist system. They require difficult—and some-times controversial—decisions over who, exactly, should pay for the sustainable world that we all want. We're in a time of intense debate and exploration within my organization and with our many stake-holders. Parallel conversations and experimentation are happening all over the ethical sourcing movement. Stakeholders are co-creating new prototypes of sustainability, which they're testing, iterating, and growing based on what they've learned. These are exciting times.

I think of our Fair Trade movement as having three crucial stake-holders: the consumers, the producers, and the companies. Each is looking to the Fair Trade model for particular gains. Producers stand to benefit from premiums and the many benefits and protec-tions of our standards. Consumers stand to benefit by obtaining higher-quality products that align with their values. Companies stand to benefit from increased sales, bigger market share, and more efficient and stable supply chains.

In conventional market interactions, these stakeholders often seek to gain at the expense of the others. This is the fixed-pie mentality. But the emerging wisdom in business circles everywhere, reflected in Fair Trade and other models of ethical sourcing, seeks to create new value that is shared among the stakeholders. In this approach, everyone benefits. But it's not always obvious how to accomplish this win-win scenario. Often, it just takes time . . . time for experimenta-tion and learning.

This is my vision for the future: a model of capitalism where everybody wins. If ethical sourcing models like ours can create real, measurable value for the industry, then consumers can conceivably get a better, more sustainable product for an affordable price. And hardworking producers can make more money, improve their lives, and be rewarded for preserving their ecosystems.

One of the biggest challenges, in my view, is measuring this shared value. We don't have great tools yet that can quantify the real value that ethical sourcing models can have for a business's profit and loss. That said, the rise of environment, social, and governance (ESG) concerns is pushing the field to create ways to measure the value creation from more sustainable business practices. So I believe this measurement challenge will get solved in the next five to ten years. Despite the pushback against ESG that we've seen recently from some sectors, I believe ESG reporting will become as commonplace as financial reporting in the future. This is a challenge and an opportunity for everyone.

In the meantime, the pace of change from business as usual to ethical sourcing will be slower than we want. But change is happening. The question is how fast. Will we evolve in time, before it's too late for the planet and its people?

CONCLUSION

WILL CAPITALISM BEND TOWARD SUSTAINABILITY?

SOME MORNINGS, WHEN I'M MAKING MY COFFEE AND LISTENING to the news on NPR, I can't help but feel upset about the state of the planet. Last summer, for example, was the hottest season in recorded history. Wildfires are burning, hurricanes are brewing, and the polar ice caps are melting at alarming rates. Progress toward the United Nations' Sustainable Development Goals is slow. In fact, the latest UN poverty figures make me so sad—and mad. For me, these numbers aren't theoretical. I've spent much of my life living with the poor or working to support the poor. So poverty is personal to me. It often seems like the life of the planet is hanging in the balance. As Greta Thunberg said in her famous 2019 speech to the World Economic Forum in Davos, "Our house is on fire."

Yet the daily news about our dire situation doesn't depress me. It feels like both a call to action and a reminder that social change is a long-term struggle. What we've accomplished thus far gives me a sense of hope and optimism about the future. When I take a step back and look at the grand arc of history, I see a generally positive evolutionary trajectory toward a more inclusive, just, and conscious society.

Consider that just over 100 years ago, with the passage of the Nineteenth Amendment, women were given the right to vote in the United States for the first time. Prior to that landmark event, half of the adult population of the country had no official say in the political decisions affecting their day-to-day lives. While we still have a long way to go toward gender equality—in the United States and across the world—we've clearly made significant progress over the past century. Few, if any, of us could imagine a democratic society in which this fundamental political right was afforded only to half of us.

There's also the minimum wage, which shares one of the core objectives of Fair Trade. Many people, myself included, feel that it should be higher—in the United States and in most countries around the world. But prior to the passage of the 1938 Fair Labor Standards Act in the wake of the Great Depression, most people would have considered the idea of a minimum wage "radical." Prior to that, workers' wages were solely determined by the market and the employers. That left a lot of people unprotected and open to tremendous exploitation. Today, most of us take the concept of minimum wage for granted.

The same goes for protecting the environment. Prior to the 1960s—only sixty years ago—most people didn't even know what the "environment" was. We rarely thought about ourselves as members of a delicate global ecosystem. In fact, many credit the famous "Earth Rise" photo taken by the Apollo 8 astronauts in 1968 with providing the philosophical spark that launched the modern environmental movement. We now have the Environmental Protection

Agency, the Clean Air Act, and most recently the Inflation Reduction Act of 2022, which, in its promotion of clean energy production, is the most ambitious attempt to address the climate crisis in US history. We've had major climate treaties in 1992, 1997, and 2015. Each one was perhaps flawed; yet each one made a demonstrable difference. As we move deeper into the twenty-first century, it's almost impossible for most of us *not* to think of ourselves, at least to some degree, as part of an interconnected global community.

Historically speaking, these are all profound changes in a relatively short time.

I don't mean to sound naive. Obviously, humanity still confronts an enormous number of complex problems. Tackling these issues gets me out of bed in the morning. The evolution I see is squiggly, not straight; punctuated, not continuous. It's frustratingly slow and full of setbacks. But it's progress nonetheless. The fact that much of the progress we've made has been achieved collectively, as a human family, makes me hopeful. Our track record, to date, gives me confidence that we can successfully tackle what we're facing today and will face in the future.

I think the business community will play a huge role in manifesting this better future. As Marc De Schutter of Danone North America put it to me, "We need to get capitalists to understand that they will not be able to create more profits if they continue screwing up the earth. When that day comes, there will be a massive change. And I think we're not too far from it."

I agree with Marc's take. In fact, I believe that we are indeed headed toward some kind of tipping point in the conscious capitalism movement—one in which our global economic system does a more effective job of internalizing the social and environmental externalities it has, for centuries, ignored. I believe that, in the future, the vast majority of companies will have sustainability built into their business models—not only because public policy and consumer demand will drive them in that direction but also because they'll see it's just a better way of doing business. There may even come a day when third-party ethical sourcing certifications like ours won't be necessary because sustainability is the new normal. I hope so.

While I'm convinced that we're heading in this more just and sustainable direction, the big question in my mind is the timeline. When will enough companies and consumers get on board? Are we looking at 20 years, 50 years, 100 years? How long will it take to lift most of the world's poor out of poverty? How long will it take for sustainable agriculture to become the norm? The biggest question for the ethical sourcing movement is what we can do to support and accelerate this process. How can we help pick up the pace of change?

IT'S NOT JUST ONE THING

WHEN I THINK ABOUT THE ROLE THAT FAIR TRADE CAN PLAY IN the evolution of business and society as a whole, one of the biggest questions is where we should focus our efforts. On one hand, we have some partners saying the most important thing that Fair Trade USA and its allies could invest in is expanding consumer awareness of our certification label. They believe the consumer will ultimately determine the success of Fair Trade, and they have a point. It would be fair to argue that the growth of the ethical sourcing movement has been hugely supported by the rising consumer demand for sustainable products. Companies are increasingly competing with each other to appeal to this relatively enlightened consumer audience, which is growing rapidly. This competition will drive further sustainability innovation and adoption.

But as we've discussed at length in this book, there is also a strong argument that it will be the business community that leads the way. Many leaders feel skeptical about consumers' ability to drive this transition toward a more conscious capitalism. They think fundamental change will only come by convincing executives and shareholders that investing in ethical sourcing is good for business beyond just sales. As Peter Handy, CEO of Bristol Seafood, told me, "Businesses, irrespective of the label and the Fair Trade brand, will find themselves to be more successful and more profitable over the long term by behaving in a way that's consistent with Fair Trade certification." Peter's perspective applies far beyond Fair Trade. More and more companies are discovering the profound benefits of investing in transparency, traceability, and the sustainability of their supply chains.

Still others feel that government will have the biggest role in shaping the future of global capitalism. Take the recent European Union Deforestation Regulation, which goes into effect in 2025. The new law prevents companies from selling products in the EU market that are linked to deforestation. It includes seven different commodities—coffee, cattle, cocoa, soy, rubber, palm oil, and wood—and a variety of derivative products like leather, soy oil, and even printed paper books (European Commission, 2023). Companies that don't comply will pay fines of up to 4 percent of their annual EU sales. It's a significant piece of legislation that will no doubt have a huge impact on US and global companies selling products in the EU market. More "due diligence" legislation like this is coming to the European Union. This will force companies, including all major US companies with European sales, to provide assurances about their supply chains, accelerating the pace of positive change and corporate accountability.

So, as an ethical sourcing movement, what should be our emphasis: consumer education, corporate engagement, or public policy? Which will be the biggest driver of change? My sense is that it will be a combination of the many stakeholders involved, as it has always been. It's not just about consumers, or businesses, or governments, or activists, or farmers, or academics, or workers. Each stakeholder community has a shared responsibility to co-create a more sustainable future. And for each of us individually? We, too, all have a key role to play . . . starting with the care and intentionality that each and every one of us can bring to our everyday purchasing decisions. As Mahatma Gandhi put it, "Be the change that you wish to see in the world."

FROM RESPONSIBILITY TO OPPORTUNITY

AT THE HEART OF THIS MULTIDIMENSIONAL APPROACH TO SUStainability is the concept of shared value, which we explored in the early chapters of the book and to which I'd like to return to now. "Creating shared value" has become somewhat of a mantra for me and many of my colleagues in the sustainable business movement. In fact, I would say at least half of the people I interviewed for the book mentioned this concept at one point or another during our discussions.

One of my conversations was with Guillaume Le Cunff, the CEO of Nespresso, who presented a fresh take on shared value that I hadn't heard before. "Looking at sustainability through the lens of shared value converts responsibility into opportunity. Rather than simply trying to comply with [environmental, social, and governance] requirements or meet certain expectations from your shareholders, you're pursuing new opportunities to create value for your business. You're doing things that are good for everyone in your supply chain, and they're also good for your own business and customers."

I love framing this as an opportunity, because it is. We all obviously have a responsibility to do more—for the planet, for the people at the other end of our supply chains, for each other and our own communities. But it's not just about taking responsibility or "doing less harm." At the heart of the Fair Trade promise is a whole new way of doing business. It's one that benefits everyone. It's a win-win model rather than one in which one stakeholder benefits at the expense of the others. It's not perfect, and it's not perfectly equal, but when I see the progress that the ethical sourcing movement has made throughout my career, I am optimistic.

Companies can do the right thing while differentiating themselves in the market and making their supply chains more secure and resilient. They can create new, more sustainable products that consumers love to buy. Consumers can derive that significant feeling of doing something good for the world with their purchases and connecting with the source of the goods that sustain them on a daily basis. Producers can get more opportunity to improve their lives and invest in their communities. They can get support for implementing more sustainable practices that protect the environment. They can develop a greater voice and vote in their workplace and communities. As my friend Santiago Rivera told me, "Fair Trade helped us regain hope in the future."

As Walmart CEO Doug McMillon said in his 2020 regeneration speech,

> We are experiencing, firsthand, the strength of "shared value" or a multi-stakeholder approach to business. We have become convinced that if a company takes the long-term view, addressing the needs of customers, associates, suppliers, communities and the planet, more value is created for everyone, including shareholders. It's an "and" approach. Yes, we have experienced short-term trade-offs, such as when we raised wages significantly several years ago and saw our stock price decline sharply in response to the news. But those short-term trade-offs fade away over the longer term as we make high-quality decisions to build a stronger business for all of our stakeholders. (McMillon, 2024)

These are bold words. Even if you are skeptical about the company's ability or willingness to back them up, it's hard to dismiss their significance. This is the kind of thing most CEOs wouldn't have dared to say twenty or thirty years ago, and to me, it shows how far we've really come. When the leader of the world's largest retail company makes statements like that, it means the conversation is shifting. It means that business leaders are finally finding ways to overcome the trade-off mentality of the past—one that pitted profits against sustainability. It means that conscious capitalists are finally beginning to reshape the parameters of global business around something more than just short-term profits for shareholders. I believe we're seeing a paradigm shift in a system of global capitalism that has, historically, been stubborn to evolve.

WE HAVE TO KEEP EVOLVING

FAIR TRADE AND ETHICAL SOURCING NEED TO KEEP EVOLVING. IF we're going to continue to grow our positive impact on people and planet, we have to stay curious and be willing to experiment and learn. If we're going to reshape the mainstream market, we have to collaborate deeply with the companies, producers, and other stakeholders who can help us do so. That process has to be a give-and-take. At times, we must be willing to stand our ground, on principle. At other times, we will need to embrace the art of compromise and pragmatism, knowing that social change takes time. I believe it's all about creative problem solving and reengineering business models to deliver sustainability, profitability, and impact.

When you look at a label on a package, whether it be Fair Trade Certified, organic, cruelty-free, or Rainforest Alliance, it's easy to think of that label as something static. As a consumer, you're trusting that certification labels mean something solid and credible. For Fair Trade consumers, that meaning revolves around the knowledge that the people who worked to produce a certain good were treated and compensated fairly. That is true. Many aspects of our model have remained constant. Our core standards are essentially unchanged. We've always taken a multi-stakeholder approach to developing and implementing the model. Our auditing process remains deep and rigorous, even as we've updated our methods. Our premiums have always been a driver of our impact, even as we've experimented with the numbers. Producer voice and participatory community development are still firmly at the heart of the mission. Our dedication to providing producers with their fair share has been steadfast.

But it's important to understand that when you buy a Fair Trade product, you're also investing in a process. It's something more fluid and dynamic than you might imagine. As much as you're contributing a portion of your purchase to the people who helped make the product, you're also investing in a new way of doing business. You're showing everyone in the value chain that you support a business paradigm where people and planet are as important as profit. You're voting with your dollar for a better world. And every purchase matters.

As we move forward into the next phase of the conscious capitalism movement, it's imperative that we all strive to continue learning and evolving—and to do so in collaboration with each other. Capitalism can't change overnight, and it can't change without people from every corner of the world doing their part. It takes farmers like Santiago Rivera committing to more sustainable farming practices, trusting that the market will reward them for all their extra efforts. It takes CEOs like Tarang Amin holding firm in his conviction that doing right by his suppliers and their workers will, in the end, improve his company's success. It takes activists like Deborah James holding companies accountable for their actions (and inactions). It takes shoppers like you and me being willing to spend an extra nickel or two for our morning coffee—not out of guilt but out of the deep satisfaction and sense of connection that comes from making a difference in the world with something as simple as a cup of coffee.

It takes all of us. And with all of us on board, the more enlightened future that many of us yearn for could be closer than we think.

ACKNOWLEDGMENTS

The inspiration for this book emerged slowly over many years of movement building. Michael Shimkin, my dear friend and first board chairman, was a successful entrepreneur and executive in the publishing industry. Michael knew a good book concept when he saw one and urged me to write about the movement and its impact, sharing the lessons of my journey as founder and CEO of PRO-DECOOP, Nicaragua's first Fair Trade coffee cooperative. Later, after we launched TransFair USA (now Fair Trade USA) and started building the Fair Trade market in the United States, Michael and I often discussed the value that such a book could have in informing and elevating the ethical sourcing macrotrend. Michael always advocated for a storytelling approach that would give voice to the protagonists of the movement and allow them to share their journeys in their own words. While Michael did not live to see this book come to fruition, his vision and wisdom certainly inspired its birth.

My early understanding of the power of direct market linkage as a strategy for empowering marginalized farmers to improve their lives grew out of my experience with PRODECOOP in Nicaragua. Thanks to the tireless efforts of almost 2,500 small family farmers and their families, we built a successful social enterprise by selling high-quality, organic, Fair Trade coffee directly to the global market. For almost thirty-five years, I've enjoyed a front-row seat on one of the most successful, high-impact Fair Trade cooperatives in the world. To this day, PRODECOOP and its farmers, led by the brilliant Merling Preza, shine as a learning laboratory for the core tenets of ethical sourcing, market-based solutions, and sustainable development. Their vision, courage, and tenacity inspire me still.

Jonathan Rosenthal at Equal Exchange had a profound impact on our success when I was at PRODECOOP. Equal Exchange is the pioneer of Fair Trade coffee in the US market. Jonathan, one of its co-founders, not only bought PRODECOOP's coffee on more favorable terms but truly lived and embodied the values of the movement. In our first few years, Jonathan took me under his wing and taught me the basics of the global coffee trade. This multilayered commercial partnership helped me develop a deeper appreciation for a less transactional approach to global trade anchored in fairness, mutual benefit, and strong human relationships. I'm grateful for Jonathan's many contributions to the ethical sourcing movement and to our thirty-five-year friendship, through which I've learned so much.

I am grateful for Mark Ritchie and Michael Conroy, two visionaries who helped spark the early growth of the Fair Trade movement in the United States through their leadership and funding. Mark and the Institute for Food and Trade Policy had the foresight to incorporate TransFair USA in 1995, paving the way for me to publicly launch the organization in 1998. At the time, Michael was a program officer at the Ford Foundation and gave us our very first grant, with which I would open our start-up "headquarters" in a dilapidated one-room office in downtown Oakland, California. Michael would later join the Fair Trade USA Board of Directors and become our chairman. Early on, he envisioned the Fair Trade movement taking hold in the US market. His brilliance as a thought leader in the world of certification proved invaluable during the early years of our journey.

Since the launch of TransFair USA in 1998, our extraordinary impact has come from the hundreds of incredible team members—staff, leadership, board, and advisers—who have joined our cause and contributed so much to our mission. I am especially grateful to Steve

Sellers, Todd Stark, Heather Franzese, Maya Spaull Johnsen, Felipe Arango, and David Sherman for their partnership and love. Fair Trade USA leaders and team members embody such a special mix of head and heart. Their camaraderie, ingenuity, resilience, entrepreneurship, and passion for mission have been the key to our impact in the lives of so many people around the world. It has been an honor and a joy to serve alongside such beautiful, dedicated people.

The six chairmen who have served at Fair Trade USA over the last twenty-six years also deserve special recognition: Michael Shimkin, Tom Bullock, Michael Conroy, Ron Cordes, James White, and Ricardo Crisantes. These extraordinary leaders brought unique vision, expertise, and dedication to the organization. Each one, in his own way, mentored me with wisdom and humility, nudging me to grow as a leader and servant to our cause. Their partnership and friendship have been a tremendous blessing.

Philanthropy fueled our start-up years as a nonprofit social enterprise. I am deeply grateful for the many funders of our movement—individuals, foundations, and companies—who invested in an unproven idea and helped bring Fair Trade to life. The Ford Foundation, TransFair USA's first philanthropic supporter, was truly a visionary and pioneer. Over four years, the foundation donated over $1 million and granted a $2 million loan, or Program Related Investment, which gave us the vital resources we needed to build the market, prove the business case for Fair Trade, and eventually become financially self-sustaining through earned revenue. This early support was essential for our success.

My thinking on the evolution of global capitalism toward a more conscious, multi-stakeholder chapter has been shaped over the years by the visionary works of John Elkington, Michael Porter, and Joseph Stiglitz. Stephan Schmidheiny, John Mackey, and Pamela Hartigan also influenced my perspective on the power of business to elevate consciousness and drive sustainability. These were the pioneers who detected these macrotrends early on and helped us develop conceptual frameworks for understanding and advancing the transformation of capitalism. I am profoundly grateful for their ability to articulate an emerging paradigm where people, planet, and profit all thrive.

I feel such profound gratitude for the organizations that discovered, defined, and developed the global social entrepreneurship movement, which seeks innovative approaches to systems change and social progress. Bill Drayton and Ashoka were the pioneers that "discovered" me in 2000. The Skoll, Schwab, and Avina foundations, *Fast Company* magazine, the World Economic Forum, and the Clinton Global Initiative also recognized my work and supported our cause. The funding, credibility, and community of kindred spirits they generously offered were invaluable.

I'm grateful to the Haas School of Business at the University of California, Berkeley, for its years of support, both during my MBA program and since. Its defining leadership principles continue to challenge and inspire me.

A big shoutout to Noah Gorovitz for his research support on this project. Noah was previously a high school and college activist and a Fellow for Fair Trade Campaigns. He conducted research and found evidence that enriched many of the book's key lessons. He also brought a depth of knowledge of the movement that made him a good thought partner for sections of the book.

I am so grateful for Ben Conard, another important contributor to the book. As chief of staff of Fair Trade USA, Ben helped with research, fact-checking, photos, and logistics. His skillful sleuthing, dogged persistence, tireless work ethic, and ever-cheerful energy helped this project tremendously.

Joel Pitney was my primary collaborator on this book, and I couldn't have asked for a better partner. Joel is a gifted writer with a brilliant mind and natural instinct for storytelling. Joel and I connected deeply through our mutual passion for social justice and sustainable agriculture. As he puts it, Joel was born to work on this book. Joel helped me develop the original book proposal and find our legendary agent, Jim Levine. He then helped me develop the structure of the book, storyboard the chapters and stories, interview the protagonists, and write multiple drafts of the manuscript. With my busy day job as founder and CEO of Fair Trade USA, there is simply no way I could have done all this without Joel's beautiful partnership every step of the way. Joel's wisdom, calm, perseverance, and good humor were essential ingredients for our success. I am forever grateful.

Big thanks to my agent, Jim Levine, for securing our publisher, for his wise counsel and advocacy, and for always believing in this book. I want to thank Ben Adams, our acquiring editor at PublicAffairs, for his creative input and guidance.

I'm grateful for each of our wonderful interviewees who took precious time from their busy schedules to share their stories, insights, and vision for the future of Fair Trade and ethical sourcing. This includes Vivien Alan, Rudy Amador, Tarang Amin, Soren Bjorn, Liam Brody, Cara Chacon, Ricardo Crisantes, Brian Durkee, Heather Franzese, Ryan Gellert, Seth Goldman, Peter Handy, Bryant Ison, Deborah James, Scott Kerslake, Tristan Lecomte, Guillaume Le Cunff, Billy Linstead Goldsmith, John Mackey, Doug McMillon, Mark Muckerheide, Mabel Obregon, Matt O'Hayer, Abdias Ortiz, Monique Oxender, Rodolfo Penalba, Michael Pollan, Merling Preza, Darcie Renn, Ivania Rivera, Mike Roth, Marc de Schutter, Greg Spragg, Bob Stiller, Jaime Tamayo, Hamdi Ulukaya, Carlos Vargas, Libby Wadle, Adam Werbach, Cameron Westfall, and T.J. Whalen. These remarkable leaders and practitioners are the protagonists of the Fair Trade movement, and this book is their story, told largely in their words.

I want to thank all the stakeholders who make the Fair Trade movement possible: the farmers, workers, cooperatives, companies, consumers, activists, philanthropists, impact investors, academics, NGOs, and many others who contribute every day to the success of this remarkable approach to ethical sourcing. I have learned so much from them. Every day, they write another page in this fascinating new chapter of global capitalism, helping bend our collective future toward justice and sustainability. They continue to inspire and illuminate my lifelong commitment to making the world better.

I want to thank my amazing family for their unwavering support and unconditional love during this journey. My kids, Emiliano and Camila; my sisters, Sheri, Cindy, and Leah; their partners, John and Jim; my partner, Chelsa; and my late mother, Ruth, all give me so much encouragement, guidance, strength, and inspiration. I love you, Fam, with all my heart!

There are so many who have generously helped, guided, and coached me on this journey, many not mentioned here. I thank you all.

And, finally, a big thanks to everyone who picks up this book and starts to use the remarkable power we all have—as conscious consumers, businesspeople, and citizens—to change the world, one purchase at a time.

BIBLIOGRAPHY

INTRODUCTION

Driver, Michaela. "An Interview with Michael Porter: Social Entrepreneurship and the Transformation of Capitalism." *Academy of Management Learning & Education* 11, no. 3 (2012): 421–431.

Kavilanz, Parija. "Starbucks Sued for Alleged Deceptive Marketing of Its '100% Ethically' Sourced Coffee." CNN, January 10, 2024.

Organic Trade Association. "Organic Food Sales Break Through $60 Billion in 2022." Organic Trade Association, May 10, 2023.

CHAPTER 1: TRADE NOT AID

World Health Organization. "Drinking Water." World Health Organization, September 23, 2023. https://www.who.int/news-room/fact-sheets/detail /drinking-water.

CHAPTER 2: MAKING THE BUSINESS CASE

Cheesman, Gina-Marie. "Green Mountain Coffee Roasters Named Largest Purchaser of Fair Trade Coffee." TriplePundit, September 22, 2011.

Deans Beans. "About Dean." Deans Beans, accessed February 28, 2023. https://deansbeans.com/pages/about-dean.

Neville, Mary Grace. "Positive Deviance on the Ethical Continuum: Green Mountain Coffee as a Case Study in Conscientious Capitalism." *Business and Society Review* 113, no. 4 (2008): 555–576. https://www.southwestern .edu/live/files/830.

Porter, Michael, and Mark Kramer. "The Big Idea: Creating Shared Value: How to Reinvent Capitalism—and Unleash a Wave of Innovation and Growth." *Harvard Business Review* 89, no. 1–2 (January–February 2011): 62–77.

Qualtrics. "For Employees, Shared Values Matter More Than Policy Positions." Qualtrics, June 2, 2022. https://www.qualtrics.com/news/for -employees-shared-values-matter-more-than-policy-positions.

US Department of Labor. "2018 CLCCG Annual Report." US Department of Labor, 2018. https://www.dol.gov/sites/dolgov/files/ILAB/legacy/files/CLCCG2018AnnualReport.pdf.

Wageningen University and Research. "Living Income in Cocoa." Wageningen University and Research, November 17, 2021. www.wur.nl/news article/living-income-in-cocoa.htm.

Walker, Rob. "The Joys and Perils of Attack Marketing: What's a Small Coffee Company Doing Impugning the Business Ethics of the World's Most Handsome Popcorn and Salad-Dressing Pitchman?" *Inc.*, April 1, 2004. https://www.inc.com/magazine/20040401/paulnewman.html.

Whoriskey, Peter, and Rachel Siegel. "Cocoa's Child Laborers." *Washington Post*, June 5, 2019. https://www.washingtonpost.com/graphics/2019/business/hershey-nestle-mars-chocolate-child-labor-west-africa.

CHAPTER 3: DO CONSUMERS CARE?

Atens, Jason. "This Is Steve Jobs's Most Controversial Legacy. It Is Also His Most Brilliant: When You Should Listen to Your Customers." *Inc.*, January 19, 2021. https://www.inc.com/jason-aten/this-was-steve-jobs-most-controversial-legacy-it-was-also-his-most-brilliant.html.

Ballatt, John, and Penelope Campling. *Intelligent Kindness: Reforming the Culture of Healthcare.* London: RC Psych Publications, 2011.

Bregman, Rutger. *Humankind: A Hopeful History.* New York: Little, Brown and Company, 2021.

Daily Bruin. "Fair Trade Coffee Trial Makes Its UCLA Debut." *Daily Bruin*, February 19, 2001. https://dailybruin.com/2001/02/19/fair-trade-coffee-trial-makes.

Edwards, Carlyann. "What Is Greenwashing?" *Business News Daily*, January 12, 2024.

European Commission. "Screening of Websites for 'Greenwashing': Half of Green Claims Lack Evidence." European Commission, January 28, 2021.

European Parliament. "Corporate Due Diligence Agreed to Safeguard Human Rights and Environment." European Parliament, December 14, 2023.

Fernandes, Janet. "Global: Are Consumers Mistrustful of Brands' Green Claims?" YouGov, February 10, 2023.

Filkowski, Megan, R. Nick Cochran, and Brian Haas. "Altruistic Behavior: Mapping Responses in the Brain." *Neuroscience and Neuroeconomics* 5 (2016): 65–75.

GreenPrint. "Business of Sustainability Index." GreenPrint, March 2021. https://greenprint.eco/wp-content/uploads/2021/03/GreenPrint-Business-of-Sustainability-Index_3.2021.pdf.

Gundava, Raghava, and Anupam Singh. "What Motivates Consumers to Buy Organic Foods? Results of an Empirical Study in the United States." *PLOS One* 16, no. 9 (September 10, 2021). https://journals.plos.org/plosone /article?id=10.1371/journal.pone.0257288#sec014.

IBM Newsroom. "IBM Study: Purpose and Providence Drive Bigger Profits for Consumer Goods in 2020." IBM Newsroom, January 10, 2020. https:// newsroom.ibm.com/2020-01-10-IBM-Study-Purpose-and-Provenance -Drive-Bigger-Profits-for-Consumer-Goods-In-2020.

International Coffee Organization. "Gender Equality in the Coffee Sector: An Insight Report from the International Coffee Association." International Coffee Organization, September 2018. https://www.ico.org /documents/cy2017-18/icc-122-11e-gender-equality.pdf.

Ioannou, Ioannis, George Kassinis, and Giorgos Papagiannakis. "How Green-washing Affects the Bottom Line." *Harvard Business Review*, July 21, 2022.

Le Grand, Julian, Jonathan Roberts, and Gauri Chandra. "Buying for Good: Altruism, Ethical Consumerism, and Social Policy." *Social Policy and Administration* 55 (2021): 1342–1355.

Non-Profit Source. "The Ultimate List of Charitable Giving Statistics 2023." Non-Profit Source, accessed February 27, 2024.

Ramonas, Andrew. "BlackRock, United Join Growing Club Citing Green-washing Risks." *Bloomberg Law*, April 3, 2023.

Russo, Amanda, and Gayle Markovitz. "Nearly 9 in 10 People Globally Want a More Sustainable and Equitable World Post COVID-19." World Economic Forum, September 16, 2020. https://www.weforum.org /press/2020/09/nearly-9-in-10-people-globally-want-a-more-sustainable -and-equitable-world-post-covid-19.

Simon-Kucher Newsroom. "Sustainability Study 2022." Simon-Kucher News-room, October 24, 2022. https://www.simon-kucher.com/en/who-we-are /newsroom/sustainability-study-2022.

Stifel Institutional Group. "Sustainability Survey and Index Launch." Stifel Institutional Group, May 2021. https://www.stifel.com/Newsletters /InvestmentBanking/BAL/Marketing/StifelSays/2021/Sustainability %20Survey.pdf.

CHAPTER 4: FAIR TRADE FOR ALL

Browning, David. "How Many Coffee Farms Are There in the World?" International Coffee Organization Kenya, March 27, 2019. https://www.ico.org /documents/cy2018-19/Presentations/statistics-item-3-enveritas.pdf.

Driscoll's. "Fair Trade Certification Program." Driscoll's, accessed February 29, 2024. https://www.driscolls.com/about/thriving-workforce/fair -trade.

Goodyear, Dana. "How Driscoll's Reinvented the Strawberry." *New Yorker*, August 14, 2017. https://www.newyorker.com/magazine/2017/08/21/how -driscolls-reinvented-the-strawberry.

Modelo, Manel. "Paradox of Fair Trade." *Stanford Social Innovation Review*, winter 2014. https://ssir.org/articles/entry/the_paradox_of_fair_trade.

Rice, Paul. "What If Your Drinking Water Made You Ill?" Nespresso, accessed February 29, 2024. https://www.sustainability.nespresso.com/what -if-drinking-water-made-you-ill.

Sheridan, Michael, Fernando Rodríguez-Camayo, Mark Lundy, Anton Eitzinger, Carolina González, Andres Montenegro, and Julian Ramírez-Villegas. "Using Scientific Evidence to Link Private and Public Sectors in the Planning Process: Observations from Coffee Sector Engagement in Nariño, Colombia." Centro Internacional de Agricultura Tropical (CIAT), Policy Brief no. 23 (2015). https://core.ac.uk/download /pdf/132681126.pdf.

Sherman, Scott. "The Brawl over Fair Trade Coffee." *The Nation*, August 22, 2012.

TriplePundit. "First Fair Trade Coffee Estate Already Improving Lives." TriplePundit, July 31, 2012. https://www.triplepundit.com/story /2012/first-fair-trade-certified-coffee-estate-already-improving-lives /81801.

Yu Hsi Lee, Esther. "Berry Farmworkers Toil 12 Hours a Day for $6. Now They're Demanding a Raise." *ThinkProgress*, April 1, 2016. https:// thinkprogress.org/berry-farmworkers-toil-12-hours-a-day-for-6-now -theyre-demanding-a-raise-ea4f5800caf8.

CHAPTER 5: FROM FARMS TO FACTORIES TO FISH

Business & Human Rights Resource Centre. "Out of Sight: Modern Slavery in the Supply Chain of Canned Tuna." Business & Human Rights Resource Centre, June 2019. https://media.business-humanrights.org/media /documents/files/Out_of_Sight_Modern_Slavery_in_Pacific_Supply _Chains_of_Canned_Tuna_4.pdf.

Chouinard, Yvon. *Let My People Go Surfing: The Education of a Reluctant Businessman.* New York: Penguin Random House, 2005.

Greenhouse, Steven. "Factory Defies Sweatshop Label, but Can It Thrive?" *New York Times*, July 17, 2010. https://www.nytimes.com/2010/07/18 /business/global/18shirt.html.

J.Crew, "ESG Report." J.Crew, 2022. https://www.jcrew.com/brand _creative/2023/202308-Aug/deib/JCrew_ImpactReport_190723.pdf.

Jurgensmeyer, Kaleigh. "Fair Trade Certified Wild Blue Shrimp: What Does That Label Really Mean?" Crowd Cow, August 3, 2020. https:// www.crowdcow.com/blog/fair-trade-certified-wild-blue-shrimp.

Legrain, Milli. "Famed Garment Factory Paying a Living Wage Struggles to Stay Afloat." *The Guardian*, April 2, 2021. https://www.theguardian.com/world/2021/apr/02/alta-gracia-dominican-garment-factory-living-wage-pandemic.

Madewell. "How We Do Well." Madewell, accessed May 21, 2024. https://www.madewell.com/do-well/fair-trade.html.

Matin, Imran. "What 'Cash Plus' Programs Teach Us About Fighting Extreme Poverty." *Stanford Social Innovation Review*, January 5, 2022. https://ssir.org/articles/entry/what_cash_plus_programs_teach_us_about_fighting_extreme_poverty.

Panhuysen, Sjoerd, and Frederik de Vries. "Coffee Barometer 2023." Coffee Barometer, September 13, 2023. https://coffeebarometer.org/documents_resources/coffee_barometer_2023.pdf.

Patagonia. "Cotton for Change." Patagonia, accessed February 29, 2024. https://www.patagonia.com/our-footprint/cotton-for-change.html.

Patagonia. "1% for the Planet." Patagonia, accessed February 29, 2024. https://www.patagonia.com/one-percent-for-the-planet.html.

prAna. "How Fair Trade Changes Lives." prAna, accessed May 21, 2024. https://www.prana.com/sustainability/fair-trade-certified.html.

Rastovich, Dave. "Making Surf Gear at a Fair Trade Certified Patagonia Facility." *2017 Patagonia Surf Catalog*, April 4, 2017, 4–5. https://www.patagonia.com/stories/know-better-do-better/story-31556.html.

Tickler, David, Jessica Meeuwig, Katharine Bryant, Fiona David, John A. H. Forrest, Elise Gordon, Jacqueline Joudo, et al. "Modern Slavery and the Race to Fish." *Nature Communications* 9, no. 4643 (2018). https://doi.org/10.1038/s41467-018-07118-9.

UN Food and Agriculture Organization. "The State of the World Fisheries and Aquaculture 2022." Food and Agriculture Organization of the United Nations, 2022. https://www.fao.org/publications/sofia/2022/en.

CHAPTER 6: BRINGING ETHICAL SOURCING HOME

Berk, Brian. "Dairy Farmers of America Is Dairy Foods 2023 Processor of the Year." *Dairy Foods*, December 15, 2023. https://www.dairyfoods.com/articles/96918-dairy-farmers-of-america-is-dairy-foods-2023-processor-of-the-year.

Berkowitz, Deborah. "Workplace Safety & Health Enforcement Falls to Lowest Levels in Decades." National Employment Law Project, December 17, 2019.

Cam, Deniz. "Chobani Launches the First Fair Trade–Certified Dairy Product in the U.S." *Forbes*, May 6, 2021. https://www.forbes.com/sites/denizcam/2021/05/06/chobani-launches-the-first-fair-trade-certified-dairy-product-in-the-us.

Chavez Foundation. "About Cesar Chavez." Chavez Foundation, accessed May 21, 2024. https://chavezfoundation.org/about-cesar-chavez.

Corkery, Michael. "Chobani Turns to Fair-Trade Program to Help Struggling Dairy Industry." *New York Times*, July 2, 2019.

Dairy Foods. "Fair Trade USA, Chobani Launch Certification Program for U.S. Dairy Industry." Dairy Foods, May 6, 2021. https://www.dairyfoods .com/articles/95010-fair-trade-usa-chobani-launch-certification-program -for-us-dairy-industry.

Dreier, Hannah. "Alone and Exploited: Migrant Children Work Brutal Jobs Across the U.S." *New York Times*, February 25, 2023.

Ehresman, Chris. "A Legacy of Caring." *Half and Half Magazine*, summer 2021. https://halfandhalfmag.com/stories-1/2021/6/22/a-legacy-of-caring.

Fair World Project. "Letter to Paul Rice." Fair World Project, September 17, 2020. https://fairworldproject.org/wp-content/uploads/2021 /05/FTUSA-letter-9-17-2020_updated.pdf.

Gold, Amanda, Wenson Fung, Susan Gabbard, and Daniel Carroll. "Findings from the National Agricultural Workers Survey (NAWS) 2019–2020: A Demographic and Employment Profile of United States Farmworkers." *JBS International*, January 2022. https://www.dol.gov/sites/dolgov /files/ETA/naws/pdfs/NAWS%20Research%20Report%2016.pdf.

Heeb, Gina. "As Small U.S. Farms Face Crisis, Trump's Trade Aid Flowed to Corporations." CNBC News, September 2, 2020. https://www .cnbc.com/2020/09/02/as-small-us-farms-face-crisis-trumps-trade -aid-flowed-to-corporations.html.

Lee, Curtis, and Liliana Michelena. "Can the United Farmworkers Rise Again?" *New York Times*, March 11, 2021. https://www.nytimes .com/2023/03/11/business/economy/farmworkers-ufw-california.html.

Packer, Peggy. "Wholesum Reflects on 10 Years of Fair Trade Certification." AndNowUKnow, August 18, 2022. https://m.andnowuknow.com /buyside-news/wholesum-reflects-10-years-fair-trade-certification-ricardo -crisantes/peggy-packer/79977.

Pompliano, Polina. "The Profile Dossier: Hamdi Ulukaya, the Shepherd-Turned-Billionaire CEO." *The Profile*, July 22, 2020.

Romeo, Nick. "Not Just for Foreign Foods: Fair-Trade Label Comes to U.S. Farms." *The Salt* (NPR), April 19, 2017. https://www.npr.org /sections/thesalt/2017/04/19/524377647/not-just-for-foreign-foods -fair-trade-label-comes-to-u-s-farms.

Sainato, Michael. "'A Lot of Abuse for Little Pay': How US Farming Profits from Exploitation and Brutality." *The Guardian*, December 25, 2021.

Schemmel, Jack. "Salute to Farmers: Si-Ellen Dairy Farm." KMVT, September 16, 2020. https://www.kmvt.com/2020/09/17/salute-to -farmers-si-ellen-dairy-farm.

Trainer, David. "Chobani's Low Growth Business Is Priced for Hyper Growth." *Forbes*, January 4, 2022. https://www.forbes.com/sites/great speculations/2022/01/04/chobanis-low-growth-business-is-priced-for -hyper-growth.

US Department of Agriculture (USDA), Economic Research Service. "2024 Farm Sector Income Forecast." USDA, Economic Research Service, February 7, 2024. https://www.ers.usda.gov/topics/farm-economy /farm-sector-income-finances/farm-sector-income-forecast.

USDA, Economic Research Service. "The Number of U.S. Farms Continues Slow Decline." USDA, Economic Research Service, last updated February 29, 2024. https://www.ers.usda.gov/data-products/chart-gallery/gallery /chart-detail/?chartId=58268.

CHAPTER 7: CREATING VALUE ALONG THE SUPPLY CHAIN

Alves, Rae-Anne, Lauren Rogge, Glenn Steinberg, Sumit Dutta, and Cate Mork. "How Sustainable Supply Chains Are Driving Business Transformation." Ernst & Young, September 20, 2022.

Business Wire. "NatureSweet® Becomes World's Largest Controlled Environment Agriculture (CEA) Company to Achieve B Corp Certification." Business Wire, June 22, 2023. https://www.businesswire.com /news/home/20230622341427/en/NatureSweet®-Becomes-World's-Largest -Controlled-Environment-Agriculture-CEA-Company-to-Achieve-B -Corp-Certification.

Henrich, Jan, Jason Li, and Fernando Perez. "Future-Proofing the Supply Chain." McKinsey and Company, June 14, 2022. https://www.mckinsey .com/capabilities/operations/our-insights/future-proofing-the-supply -chain.

International Fresh Produce Association. "NatureSweet Sustainability Case Study." International Fresh Produce Association, 2023. https:// qa.freshproduce.com/resources/sustainability/case-studies/naturesweet -sustainability-case-study.

Koenig, Pamina, and Sandra Poncet. "The Effects of the Rana Plaza Collapse on the Sourcing Choices of French Importers." *Journal of International Economics* 137, no. 103576 (July 2022).

Packer, The. "Fair Trade Tomatoes Now Sold in Walmart Stores." *The Packer*, 2022. https://digitaledition.qwinc.com/publication/frame.php?i =774635&p=&pn=&ver=html5&view=articleBrowser&article_id =4435972.

Sorvino, Chloe. "How Whole Foods Favorite Vital Farms Made Pasture-Raised Eggs Mainstream." *Forbes*, May 18, 2018.

Sustainable Business. "Is Walmart's Move to Cheap Organic Food a Good Thing?" Sustainable Business.com, April 2014. https://www

.sustainablebusiness.com/2014/04/is-walmart39s-move-to-cheap-organic
-food-a-good-thing-52302.

Vital Farms. "2023 Impact Report." Vital Farms, March 9, 2023. https://
vitalfarms.com/wp-content/uploads/2023/03/0323-VF-ImpactReport
-FINAL.pdf.

Westerman, Ashley. "4 Years After the Rana Plaza Tragedy, What's Changed
for Bangladeshi Garment Workers?" *Parallels* (NPR), April 30, 2017.

Wohl, Jessica. "Walmart Aims to Push Organic Foods into Mainstream."
Chicago Tribune, April 10, 2014. https://www.chicagotribune.com/business
/ct-xpm-2014-04-10-ct-walmart-organic-wildoats-0410-biz-20140410
-story.html.

CHAPTER 8: FOR PEOPLE AND PLANET

American Apparel and Footwear Association. "Product Safety Guidance:
Restricted Substances List (RSL)." American Apparel and Footwear Asso-
ciation, February 2023. https://www.aafaglobal.org/AAFA/Solutions
_Pages/Restricted_Substance_List.aspx.

Behrer, A. Patrick, R. J. Park, G. Wagner, C. M. Golja, and D. W. Keith.
"Heat Has Larger Impacts on Labor in Poorer Areas." *Environmental
Research Communications* 3, no. 9 (September 2021). https://iopscience.iop
.org/article/10.1088/2515-7620/abffa3/meta.

Davenport, Coral. "Heat Is Costing the U.S. Economy Billions in Lost
Productivity." *New York Times*, July 31, 2023. https://www.nytimes
.com/2023/07/31/climate/heat-labor-productivity-climate.html.

Foster, Josh, James Smallcombe, Simon Hodder, Ollie Jay, Andreas D.
Flouris, Lars Nybo, and George Havenith. "An Advanced Empirical Model for Quantifying the Impact of Heat and Climate Change on
Human Physical Work Capacity." *International Journal of Biometeorology* 65 (2021): 1215–1229. https://link.springer.com/article/10.1007
/s00484-021-02105-0.

International Federation of Red Cross and Red Crescent Societies
(IFRC). "Central America: Hurricanes Eta & Iota—6-months Operation Update." IFRC, June 22, 2021. https://reliefweb.int/report
/guatemala/central-america-hurricanes-eta-iota-6-months-operation
-update-mdr43007.

Jha, Shaleen, Christopher M. Bacon, Stacy M. Philpott, V. Ernesto Mendez,
Peter Laderach, and Robert A. Rice. "Shade Coffee: Update on a Disap-
pearing Refuge for Biodiversity." *BioScience* 64, no. 5 (May 2014): 416–428.
https://academic.oup.com/bioscience/article/64/5/416/2754235.

NOAA Office for Coastal Management. "Sea Level Rise Viewer." NOAA
Office for Coastal Management, accessed February 29, 2024. https://coast
.noaa.gov/digitalcoast/tools/slr.html.

Ontl, Todd, and Lisa Schulte. "Soil Carbon Storage." *Nature Education Knowledge* 3, no. 10 (2012): 35. https://www.nature.com/scitable /knowledge/library/soil-carbon-storage-84223790.

Paustian, Keith, Eric Larson, Jeffrey Kent, Ernie Marx, and Amy Swan. "Soil C Sequestration as a Biological Negative Emission Strategy." *Frontiers in Climate* 1 (2019). https://www.frontiersin.org/articles/10.3389 /fclim.2019.00008/full.

Science Based Targets. "SBTi Launches World-First Net-Zero Corporate Standard." Science Based Targets, October 28, 2021. https://sciencebased targets.org/news/sbti-launches-world-first-net-zero-corporate-standard.

Walmart. "Product Supply Chain Sustainability." Walmart, accessed February 29, 2024. https://corporate.walmart.com/purpose/esgreport /environmental/product-supply-chain-sustainability.

Warren, Liz. "Report: Fashion Is Dyeing Africa's Water Blue, Burning Locals' Skin." *Sourcing Journal*, August 19, 2021. https://sourcingjournal .com/denim/denim-mills/africa-water-witness-international-denim-dye -water-pollution-burns-cotton-296600.

CHAPTER 9: WHO PAYS FOR THE COST OF SUSTAINABILITY?

Calabria, Rebeca. "The Poison Comes from the Sky." Dan Watch, December 14, 2017.

Dorfner, Micah. "Go Bananas for . . . Bananas." Mayo Clinic, April 4, 2017. https://newsnetwork.mayoclinic.org/discussion/go-bananas-forbananas.

Edmonds, Kevin. "Going for Broke: The Corporate Players Behind the Demise of the Caribbean Banana Trade (Part 2)." *NACLA Report on the Americas*, May 31, 2012.

Fairtrade International. "The External Costs of Banana Production: A Global Study." Fairtrade International, 2018.

Fassler, Joe. "Bananas Are Getting Cheaper. That Low Cost Comes with a Hidden Price." *The Counter*, May 20, 2019.

First Insight. "The Sustainability Disconnect Between Consumers and Retail Executives." First Insight, 2021.

Frey, Sherry, Jordan Bar Am, Vinit Doshi, Anandi Malik, and Steve Noble. "Consumers Care About Sustainability—and Back It Up with Their Wallets." McKinsey & Company, February 6, 2023. https://www .mckinsey.com/industries/consumer-packaged-goods/our-insights /consumers-care-about-sustainability-and-back-it-up-with-their-wallets.

GreenPrint. "Business of Sustainability Index." GreenPrint, March 2021. https://greenprint.eco/wp-content/uploads/2021/03/GreenPrint-Business -of-Sustainability-Index_3.2021.pdf.

Hainmueller, Jens, Michael J. Hiscox, and Sandra Sequeira. "Consumer Demand for Fair Trade: Evidence from a Multistore Field Experiment."

Review of Economics and Statistics, 2015. https://web.stanford.edu/~jhain
/Paper/REST2015.pdf.

Koeppel, Dan. *Banana: The Fate of the Fruit That Changed the World*. New
York: Plume, 2008.

National Geographic. "The Surprising Science Behind the World's Most Popular Fruit." *National Geographic*, October 24, 2017.

Organic Trade Association. "Organic Food Sales Break Through $60 Billion
in 2022." Organic Trade Association, May 10, 2023.

Piper Sandler. "Taking Stock with Teens: 22+ Years of Researching U.S.
Teens GenZ Insights." Piper Sandler, spring 2023.

CONCLUSION: WILL CAPITALISM BEND
TOWARD SUSTAINABILITY?

European Commission. "Regulation on Deforestation-Free Products." European Commission, 2023. https://environment.ec.europa.eu/topics/forests
/deforestation/regulation-deforestation-free-products_en.

McMillon, Doug. "Regeneration Speech." Walmart, accessed February 29,
2024. https://corporate.walmart.com/content/dam/corporate/documents
/policies/rtp-2020-regeneration-speech-dm-milestone-summit-transcript-1.pdf.

INDEX

PAUL RICE IS AN AWARD-winning social entrepreneur and the founder and visionary behind Fair Trade USA, the leading certifier of Fair Trade products in North America.

Rice launched Fair Trade USA (formerly known as TransFair USA) in 1998 in a one-room warehouse in downtown Oakland, California. Under Rice's leadership, Fair Trade has become one of the fastest-growing segments of the US food and apparel industries by enlisting the support of over 1,700 major brands and retailers, including Whole Foods, Costco, Walmart, Kroger, Target, and Albertsons. Fair Trade USA now certifies coffee, tea, cocoa, fresh produce, dairy, fish, apparel, home goods, and many more products. In 2024, consumer recognition of the Fair Trade Certified label hit 65 percent. And by 2024, the organization and its industry partners had generated over $1.2 billion in cumulative financial impact for over 1 million farmers, workers, and their families in seventy countries worldwide.

Rice is a pioneering figure in the conscious capitalism movement. Prior to Fair Trade USA, he worked with farmers for eleven years in the highlands of Nicaragua, where he founded and led the country's first Fair Trade coffee export cooperative. This firsthand experience with Fair Trade in the field was profound and transformative for him, ultimately inspiring him to return to the United States with the dream of building the Fair Trade movement in this country. Rice's rich experience over the last forty years in the fields of sustainable agriculture, grassroots economic development, global supply chain transparency, responsible business, and consumer activation is unique in the certification world. He is now a leading advocate of ethical sourcing as a powerful strategy for poverty alleviation, environmental stewardship, and sustainable business.

Rice has been named Ethical Corporation's 2019 Business Leader of the Year and has been recognized four times as Social Capitalist of the Year by *Fast Company* magazine. Rice is also a recipient of the prestigious Skoll Award for Social Entrepreneurship, the World Economic Forum's Social Entrepreneur of the Year, and the Ashoka Fellowship. He has spoken at the World Economic Forum, Clinton Global Initiative, Skoll World Forum, Conscious Capitalism CEO Summit, TEDx, and numerous universities and conferences around the world.

You can learn more about Paul Rice at www.fairtradecertified .org/about-us/our-history.

PublicAffairs is a publishing house founded in 1997. It is a tribute to the standards, values, and flair of three persons who have served as mentors to countless reporters, writers, editors, and book people of all kinds, including me.

I. F. STONE, proprietor of *I. F. Stone's Weekly*, combined a commitment to the First Amendment with entrepreneurial zeal and reporting skill and became one of the great independent journalists in American history. At the age of eighty, Izzy published *The Trial of Socrates*, which was a national bestseller. He wrote the book after he taught himself ancient Greek.

BENJAMIN C. BRADLEE was for nearly thirty years the charismatic editorial leader of *The Washington Post*. It was Ben who gave the *Post* the range and courage to pursue such historic issues as Watergate. He supported his reporters with a tenacity that made them fearless and it is no accident that so many became authors of influential, best-selling books.

ROBERT L. BERNSTEIN, the chief executive of Random House for more than a quarter century, guided one of the nation's premier publishing houses. Bob was personally responsible for many books of political dissent and argument that challenged tyranny around the globe. He is also the founder and longtime chair of Human Rights Watch, one of the most respected human rights organizations in the world.

· · ·

For fifty years, the banner of Public Affairs Press was carried by its owner Morris B. Schnapper, who published Gandhi, Nasser, Toynbee, Truman, and about 1,500 other authors. In 1983, Schnapper was described by *The Washington Post* as "a redoubtable gadfly." His legacy will endure in the books to come.

Peter Osnos, *Founder*